**MARY AND JOHN GRAY LIBRARY
LAMAR UNIVERSITY**

In Memory of

Thelma Long McCoy

Mrs. Dorothy Yezak
donor

DISCARDED

WOMEN AND THE ECONOMY

WOMEN AND THE ECONOMY

A Comparative Study of Britain and the USA

A. T. Mallier
and
M. J. Rosser

Foreword by Baroness Seear

St. Martin's Press   New York

Text © A. T. Mallier and M. J. Rosser, 1987
Foreword © The Macmillan Press Ltd., 1987

All rights reserved. For information, write:
Scholarly & Reference Division,
St. Martin's Press, Inc., 175 Fifth Avenue, New York, NY 10010

First published in the United States of America in 1987

Printed in Hong Kong

ISBN 0-312-88732-9

Library of Congress Cataloging-in-Publication Data
Mallier, A. T. 1931-
Women and the economy.
Bibliography: p.
Includes index.
1. Women—Employment—Great Britain.   2. Women—
Employment—United States.   3. Women—Great Britain—
Economic conditions.   4. Women—United States—Economic
conditions.   I. Rosser, M. J., 1949-   .   II. Title.
HD6135.M35   1987   331.4'0941   86-4011
ISBN 0-312-88732-9

Contents

List of Tables	vii
List of Figures	x
Acknowledgements	xii
Foreword by Baroness Seear	xiv

1	INTRODUCTION	1
2	THE DEMOGRAPHIC AND ECONOMIC PERSPECTIVE	9
	The Sources of Demographic Data	10
	The Demographic Background	12
	The Changing Age Distribution of the Female Population	13
	Twentieth-Century Changes in the Marital Status of Women	16
	Employment Trends	19
	The Female Economic Activity Rate	21
	Conclusions	29
3	EMPLOYMENT TRENDS IN THE TWENTIETH CENTURY	30
	Industrial Distribution of Female Employment	32
	Change within the Productive Industry Sector	35
	The Development of Service Industry Employment	40
	Change in the Relative Female Contribution to Industry	43
	Occupational Distribution of Female Employment	45
	The Relative Female Contribution to the Occupational Classes	52
4	THE SUPPLY OF FEMALE LABOUR	59
	Economic Methodology	64
	Theories of Labour Supply	65
	Methods of Testing	68
	Data Bases and Overview of Cross-Section Studies	70
	Factors Affecting the MFAR	71
	Cyclical Fluctuations	79
	Long-Term Trends	80

Contents

5	**THE DEMAND FOR FEMALE LABOUR**	89
	Why is there a Demand for Labour?	89
	The Level of Labour Demand in Britain and the USA	93
	Why the Demand for Female Labour Grew	106
	Conclusion	112
6	**EQUAL OPPORTUNITY AND PAY**	114
	The Evidence of Inequality	114
	Explanations of the Observed Inequalities	120
	Theories of Discrimination	125
	Conclusions	130
7	**ISSUES OF THE 1980s: PART-TIME EMPLOYMENT, UNEMPLOYMENT AND THE NEW TECHNOLOGY**	133
	Part-Time Employment	133
	Unemployment	145
	The Effects of the New Technology on Female Employment	157
8	**INTERNATIONAL COMPARISONS**	166
	Female Employment in Free Market Industrialised Economies	166
	Women in the Soviet Union	180
9	**A MARXIAN PERSPECTIVE**	190
	The Role of Domestic Labour	193
	Women and the Reserve Army of Labour	195
	Conclusion	199

References and Selected Bibliography	200
Author Index	212
Subject Index	216

List of Tables

2.1	Population of Great Britain, total and female, 1901-81	12
2.2	Population of the United States, total and female, 1900-80	12
2.3	Percentage distribution of the age structure of the British female population, 1901-81	14
2.4	Percentage distribution of the age structure of the US female population, 1900-80	14
2.5	Married female population, Great Britain, aged 15-64 years, 1901-81	17
2.6	Married female population, USA, aged 15-64 years, 1900-80	17
2.7	Median age of marriage by spinsters in the USA and England and Wales, 1900-80	18
2.8	Total and female labour force, Great Britain, 1901-81	20
2.9	Total and female labour force, United States, 1900-80	20
2.10	Female labour force activity rates, Great Britain, 1901-81	23
2.11	Female labour force activity rates, United States, 1900-80	23
2.12	Female labour force activity rates, for Great Britain by marital status, 1900-81	28
2.13	Female labour force activity rates for United States by marital status, 1900-80	28
3.1	Sectoral changes in total employment, Britain 1901-81 and the United States 1900-80	31
3.2	Industrial distribution of gainfully occupied female population in Britain, selected years	36
3.3	Industrial distribution of gainfully occupied female population in USA, selected years	37
3.4	Industrial sectors of gainfully occupied British female population as percentage of total in each industrial sector of gainfully occupied population, selected years	44
3.5	Industrial sectors of gainfully occupied US female population as percentage of total in each industrial sector of gainfully occupied population, selected years	44

List of Tables

3.6	Occupational class of gainfully occupied female population in Britain, selected years	47
3.7	Occupational class of gainfully occupied female population in USA, selected years	48
3.8	Occupational class of gainfully occupied British female population as percentage of total in each occupational class of gainfully occupied population, selected years	53
3.9	Occupational class of gainfully occupied US female population as percentage of total in each occupational class of gainfully occupied population, selected years	54
3.10	Occupational segregation, 1971 and 1981, England and Wales	56
3.11	Changes in occupational segregation, 1971-81, England and Wales	57
4.1	Changes in female labour supply, Great Britain, 1951-81	60
5.1	Principal trends in British employment, 1955-80	98
5.2	Principal trends in US employment, 1955-80	104
6.1	Deployment of male and female employees by key industrial sector, 1980-1	115
6.2	Deployment of male and female employees in selected occupations, 1980-1	116
6.3	Dispersion of full-time adults' total earnings, 1983	118
6.4	Length of employment with current employer, 1979	124
6.5	Selected subjects successfully attempted at summer examinations, 1982	124
7.1	Part-time employment in Great Britain, 1971-83	136
7.2	Part-time employment in the USA, 1965-82	137
7.3	Part-time employment in Great Britain, 1981	138
7.4	Age distribution of female part-time workers	139
7.5	Unemployment by sex and reason, USA, 1970 and 1982	155
7.6	Unemployment by sex and age group, Great Britain, 1971 and 1981	156
7.7	Females in selected occupations, Great Britain, 1981	160
7.8	Females in selected occupations, USA, 1982	161
8.1	Females as a percentage of total civilians in employment	167
8.2	Female activity rates	167

8.3	Females in civilian employment by industrial sector, 1980	169
8.4	Total civilian employment by industrial sector	170
8.5	Employment of married women	171
8.6	Part-time working in the EEC, 1979	179
8.7	Ratio of female to male earnings (annual), selected years	180
8.8	Female proportion of occupation grous, 1982	181
8.9	Economic activity in the USSR	182

List of Figures

2.1	Female economic activity rates by age, Great Britain, 1901, 1951, 1981	25
2.2	Female economic activity rates by age, United States, 1900, 1950, 1980	26
2.3	Married female economic activity rates by age, Great Britain, 1901, 1951, 1981	27
3.1	Percentage of female labour force employed in the service sector, 1900-81	34
3.2	Female employment in selected manufacturing industries, Great Britain, 1901-81	38
3.3	Female employment in selected manufacturing industries, United States, 1900-80	39
3.4	Female employment in selected service industries, Great Britain, 1901-81	41
3.5	Female employment in selected service industries, United States, 1900-80	42
4.1	Female economic activity rates by age and marital status, Great Britain, 1981	62
4.2	Female economic activity rates by age and marital status, United States, 1982	63
5.1	Trends in British employment, 1955-80	95
5.2	Trends in United States employment, 1955-80	96
5.3	Percentage of labour force in productive industry and service industry, Great Britain and USA	108
6.1	Profile of full-time adult gross weekly earnings by age, sex and status, 1983	117

List of Figures

6.2	Percentage distribution of female schoolteachers by level of post, 1982	119
6.3	Male and female economic activity rate by age, Britain and the United States, 1980-1	123
7.1	Unemployment in Great Britain, 1950-83	146
7.2	Unemployment in the USA, 1950-83	147
7.3	Female labour supply in Great Britain, 1971-83	152
7.4	Female labour supply in the United States, 1962-82	154
8.1	Female labour force participation by five-year age groups: Australia	171
8.2	Belgium	172
8.3	Denmark	172
8.4	Finland	173
8.5	France	173
8.6	West Germany	174
8.7	Japan	174
8.8	Ireland	175
8.9	Italy	175
8.10	Netherlands	176
8.11	New Zealand	176
8.12	Sweden	177
8.13	United Kingdom	177
8.14	United States	178

Acknowledgements

The authors wish to express their thanks to the Controller of HM Stationery Office for permission to

(a) allow the reproduction of the *Reports of the Census of Population for Great Britain*, or parts thereof:
(b) quote from *Equal Pay: a Guide to the Equal Pay Act 1970* and *Sex Discrimination: a Guide to the Sex Discrimination Act 1975*;
(c) use data from the *Employment Gazette*, OPCS demographic data, and data from the *New Earnings Survey*.

We wish to thank the following institutions, individuals and publishers for permission to use copyright material:

OECD, Paris
International Labour Office, Geneva
Department of Education and Science, London
S. J. Lord, formerly of Keele University
Alastair McAuley, University of Essex
Allen & Unwin, for material from I. Brown, *Economics and Demography*
Cambridge University Press, for material from (a) J. R. Maroney, *Economic Journal*, volume 89, 1979; and (b) C. H. Lee, *Regional Employment Statistics 1841-1971*
Macmillan, for material from Guy Routh, *Occupation and Pay in Great Britain, 1906-79*
The *Manchester School*, for material from E. James, 1962.
The authors also wish to acknowledge the use of US government statistics which are in the public domain, and data from the *EEC Labour Force Sample Survey*.

We would also like to thank Mrs M. W. Fyvie and Mrs M. Lloyd for their invaluable assistance in typing the tables and diagrams.

Finally, we would like to acknowledge the contribution that our students over the years have made to the way that this book has developed.

A. T. MALLIER
M. J. ROSSER

Foreword
By Baroness Seear

Anyone who proposes to give a lecture or write an article on equal opportunity for women should get hold of this book, especially if the author intends, as so many authors do, to make comparisons between the position in the United Kingdom and in the United States of America. The extensive collection of statistics and tables provides answers to many of the questions that discussion on this subject inevitably raise and the impressive bibliography points the way to further study.

It is the work of economists, not of sociologists, and the intention of the authors is to examine the statistical evidence for the many statements made about the causes and extent of inequality and the progress, or lack of it, in the drive towards equality. As such it is a valuable corrective to many less soberly based presentations of the subject.

As a bonus, the book finishes with a Marxian analysis of sex equality.

NANCY SEEAR

1 Introduction

The rapid increase in the size of the female labour force has been one of the most significant features of the economies of Britain and the USA since the Second World War. There have also been substantial changes in the industrial and occupational distribution and in the demographic composition of the female labour force. The female proportion of the total labour force has grown from 29 per cent at the start of the century to 39 per cent in the last few years in Britain, and in the USA it has grown from 18 per cent to 42 per cent over the same period. There was a time-lag before the significance of these trends came to be appreciated, but in recent years there has been a number of studies which have sought to explain this growth and to analyse the impact of the changing structure of the female labour force.

The subject of women and the economy is a wide-ranging one, and in this introduction the method of approach and the scope of this book are explained so that it can be made clear what the book does and does not seek to do. The literature on this topic spans many disciplines, including sociology, politics and demography, as well as economics. Although it is not possible to isolate these disciplines from one another completely, and although there will be some inevitable overlap, the purpose of this book is to consider economic analyses and explanations of the changes in the female labour force. Thus, first the available statistics are analysed to understand exactly what changes have taken place and then economic explanations of why things happened as they did are considered.

This is also a comparative study of Britain and the USA, and as each aspect of the female labour force is examined, statistical evidence and economic explanations from both countries are considered. Although this book is a survey of the different explanations which economists have put forward for the changes that have occurred in the female labour force, research on this subject is continually producing new material, and consequently no one survey can ever be completely comprehensive. Rather, the objective is to summarise the main findings in this area, with emphasis on the most recent research.

At present the published material on the economics of the female labour force tends to fall into one of the three categories:
(1) Descriptive statistical analyses, with relatively little explanation of why the changes identified in the statistics have taken place.
(2) Economic analyses that seek to explain the changes in the female labour force. These, though, are usually inaccessible to the average reader. They are usually published in various academic journals and other publications, and often involve advanced economic and statistical analysis that is unfamiliar to many people with an interest in the question of why the female labour force has altered.
(3) Studies concerned with identifying areas of sex inequality and sex discrimination in the labour market and with policies which are designed to remove these inequalities.

This book attempts to bridge the gap between (1) and (2), and to provide information that will be useful to those interested in (3). It endeavours to bring together in one volume, and place in context, the different pieces of economic research that have been carried out on the subject of women and the economy. It also tries to explain the findings of this research in a manner that those largely unfamiliar with the economist's approach should be able to understand. Although the sex equality issue is considered within the context of the changes in female employment that have taken place this topic is not the main concern of this study.

An economist's explanation of why certain events have taken place is different to the explanation that might be found in some other academic disciplines. Economists will usually only accept those explanations that can be supported by statistical evidence. The fundamental methodology of economics, as with many other disciplines, is initially to construct a theoretical model that is a simplified picture of the real world and which can then be tested against statistical evidence. The economist's approach is not necessarily to seek to gain an understanding of the actual reasons that women had for joining the labour force, or which employers had for employing a higher proportion of women workers, although some knowledge of what these are may be of use in constructing a theoretical model. Only those explanations which can be backed up by statistical testing are accepted. Thus economists may be happy to use a set of unrealistic assumptions in a model if the model proves to be a reasonably accurate explanation of observable data, e.g. economists may try to explain the economic activity of a married woman in terms of her level of education, husband's income, or other observable characteristics, even though the woman herself might give a completely different explanation of her decision to enter the labour force.

The plan of this book and the way that these ideas are developed is as follows.

Chapters 2 and 3 provide an overview of the long-term trends in the female labour force since the start of the century. This allows Chapters 4 to 7, which consider economic explanations of more recent trends, to be placed in their historical context. Thus Chapters 2 and 3 are more descriptive in character than the later chapters, which is inevitable given that most of the recent research on this subject has been based on post-war data. Chapter 8 makes some comparisons with female labour force changes that have taken place in countries other than Britain and the USA, and Chapter 9 provides a Marxian perspective of the changes that have taken place.

The female labour forces of both Britain and the USA have grown both in terms of absolute numbers and relative to the size of the total labour force. The absolute growth in numbers was partly the result of population growth since 1900, and it is the relationship between the growth of the female labour force and population increases, and other demographic changes, that are the subject of Chapter 2. In comparing the demographic changes that have occurred in Britain and the USA some features are common to both nations, such as a reduction in the age of first marriage and a decline in the fertility rate. There are contrasts, though. The major difference has been the fact that the total US population has trebled since the start of the century, with a slightly higher rate of growth in the female population, whereas in Britain the population of both sexes has only grown by about 50 per cent over the same period. Apart from population increase, the other major factor behind the growth in the female labour force in both countries has been the increase in the proportion of the female population of working age who are economically active. In Britain, though, the only significant increase occurred in the post-war period. In both nations it has been the economic activity rate of married females that has experienced the greatest increase.

Chapter 3 forms the second part of the overview of the twentieth century and is concerned with the long-term changes in the industrial and occupational distribution of the female labour force. The industries that have absorbed the growth in the number of working women are predominantly in the service sector. In 1900 in both economies over 50 per cent of employed women worked in the service sector, with a high proportion in domestic service. By 1980 the percentage of working females who were employed in the service sector had risen to 75 per cent, but the significance of domestic service had been replaced by new service industries, including professional services such as education and health care. While in the USA the service sector initially drew labour from the declining farm sector, in Britain this was not the case. Neither did labour come from the manufacturing sector, which grew over the long term but at a slower rate than the service sector. Most of the female workers that entered the expanding service industries were new or re-entrants to the labour force. Although industrial change has altered the demand for labour in those occupations that are associated with particular industries, and technical change has altered the job content of many occupations, the occupational distribution of females has shown a remarkable stability over the long term. Not until around 1970 did any significant changes in the sex distribution of different occupations begin to take place, and these have still been fairly modest inroads into the pattern of occupational segregation by sex that has persisted in both Britain and the USA for some time.

Chapter 4 looks at the factors that affect the supply of female labour. The major part of the post-war growth in the female labour force has come from the increased participation of married women in the labour force. Consequently, most research on the supply of female labour has been concerned with discovering what factors influence the economic activity of married women. Studies tend to fall into two categories. A number of researchers have used cross-section data to try to find out, using statistical analysis, which observable characteristics of a married woman are likely to increase the probability of her being economically active and to increase the number of hours worked if she is employed. Although there are some variations in the results of these studies, in general they agree on most of the factors that are correlated with economic activity. For example, results suggest that the probability of a married woman being economically active will be higher the more education she has received, the higher her potential wage is, and if she lives in a big city; it will be lower the higher is her husband's income, the more children she has, and if local unemployment is high. It is more difficult to explain the long-term growth in the female labour supply. Apart from the absence of consistent data sources over a long period of time there is also the problem that it is difficult to identify which is cause and which is effect over the long term, e.g. did the ownership of household labour saving devices increase because more women decided to go out to work and used the money earned to buy these devices to cut down on time spent on domestic work, or did the appearance of these devices in the shops prompt many women to decide to look for employment when they found that as a result of buying these devices they had more free time? The answer to this and other similar questions is that most likely both of these factors contributed to what happened, but it has proved a problem to test statistically for the relative significance of each. Some economists have attempted to use information on the factors affecting a married woman's economic activity obtained from cross-section studies to explain the long-term trends, but it has been found that only part of the increase can be explained using this method. Attitude changes have been important, but it is difficult to measure changes in attitude. It is also difficult to distinguish between attitude changes which came about through the observation and acceptance of married women who had been brought into the labour force because of changes in wages, job opportunities, or other observable economic factors, and attitude changes which were due to other, non-economic influences.

One of the areas of uncertainty among economists is whether the growth in women's employment has been supply-led, i.e. it took place because more women wished to work, or was it demand-led, i.e. it occurred because employers desired to employ more women. It is known that in the First World War large numbers of women entered the labour force to replace the men who went to war, but afterwards many of these left the labour force. The evidence indicates that a similar pattern occurred at the time of the Second World War, but then in the 1950s women began to re-enter the labour force. The available statistical data show employment levels rising in the 1950s against a background of historically low levels of unemployment. A second change in the post-1945 era was an increase in the size of the service sector, an area traditionally associated with female employment. These two factors together provide the basis for the argument, examined in Chapter 5, that the initial growth in female employment in the 1960s was demand-led. It is, though, more difficult to sustain this argument as an explanation for the continued growth in the female labour force after the mid-1960s when unemployment in both countries was increasing, unless consideration is given to the special characteristics that females bring to the labour market which matched the requirements of employers. It is recognised, though, that the rise in demand for females increasingly began to lag behind the growth in supply.

The question of whether females receive or should receive equal opportunities and rewards in the labour market is one of wide social interest. In Chapter 6 the initial objective is to examine the form discrimination may take and whether it does actually occur. The statistical evidence does show that females receive unequal treatment in employment, but that alone does not prove necessarily that discrimination is present, as there may be economic reasons for the inequality of treatment. These reasons, however, do not entirely explain the position identified, and therefore it has to be assumed that discrimination does take place. Economists have developed a number of theoretical models to explain the existence of discrimination and these are examined prior to a consideration of the legislative measures designed to remove discrimination.

Chapter 7 deals with three issues that are currently having a great impact on the female labour force: part-time employment, unemployment, and the effects of new technology.

A large proportion of the growth that has taken place in the female labour force, particularly in Britain, has come from married women entering part-time employment. Basically there have been two sets of reasons for this growth of part-time employment. Firstly, most of the expansion in the total labour force has been in the service sector industries where part-time employment has always been common. Secondly, part-time employment has become more widespread in nearly all industries as employers see the use of this type of labour as a way of keeping down unit costs. Part-time workers can help provide labour to cope with peaks in demand and it is generally more flexible from an employer's viewpoint. It can also be cheaper to employ part-timers if they do not receive overtime or anti-social premiums on top of their hourly wage and if employers provide less in the way of pension rights, holidays, sick pay, and other non-monetary benefits that are received by full-time employees.

The increases in female unemployment experienced on both sides of the Atlantic are partly a reflection of general economic conditions, and the female unemployment rate generally moves in line with the male rate. However, the fluctuations in female unemployment have usually not been so severe as the fluctuations in male unemployment, because males are usually employed in manufacturing industries and these are much more responsive to changes in the level of aggregate demand in the economy than the service industries where most females are employed. Also, in Britain, a large number of women looking for work have been excluded from the official unemployment figures because of the peculiarities of the British system of counting the unemployed. The proportion of hidden unemployment has fallen over the last decade, though. Many of the married women who have been attracted into the labour force, often into part-time jobs, were previously not included in the official unemployment figures because they were not entitled to claim for any form of state unemployment benefit. Part-time jobs have increased in number while the number of full-time jobs has diminished; this has contributed to the rise in unemployment among younger single females who usually prefer full-time employment and who are entitled to register for some form of benefit, and who thus appear in the published unemployment figures.

Developments in microelectronics, as well as opening up new areas of possible application, have brought down the cost of computer control of production and information processing. Women will be particularly affected by the changes introduced by this new technology. In manufacturing industries women tend to be concentrated in those jobs that involve repetitive work suitable for computer-controlled machinery to take over. Thus, relative to the number employed in manufacturing, women will be affected more severely than men, although the total number affected will be less. However, the main impact of the new technology on female employment is likely to be in clerical work. A large proportion of employed women work in this occupation and developments already underway, particularly in information processing, storing and retrieval, will significantly affect the demand for those trained in clerical skills. Although it is impossible to predict the exact effect on total employment that this new technology will have, it is certain that the demand for labour in those occupations where many women are now employed will fall. Any new demand for labour that may be created will tend to be in those areas where women are currently underrepresented, such as electronic engineering, programming, equipment selling and machine maintenance.

Chapter 8 makes some wider international comparisons of changes in the female labour force. Firstly, the trends in the female labour force in some of the major Western industrialised economies are compared. It appears that a pattern of change similar to that experienced in Britain and the USA has also occurred elsewhere, although there have been variations from this general trend. A major factor that has affected the speed of change has been the general level of economic development of an economy. Female employment growth appears to have been greatest in the more advanced economies where the service sector developed early. In those countries where the move from agriculture to manufacturing was relatively late, female employment growth has been slower.

A more detailed study is made of female employment patterns in the planned economy of the Soviet Union. Although female economic activity is higher than in most Western economies, this is not purely due to differences in the way the economy is run. Other historical factors are also important, in particular the shortage of males brought about by the tremendous loss of life that the Soviet Union suffered as a result of the revolution and the two world wars. Furthermore, although women are spread over a wider range of industries and occupations than in most Western economies, there is still a substantial degree of sex segregation, on a pattern similar to that found elsewhere.

Chapter 9 looks at the Marxian mode of economic analysis, which is often neglected by many economists. A number of contemporary writers have been concerned with the question of whether or not the relatively inferior economic position of women can be explained in terms of Marxian analysis. Some consider that it can, but some feminist writers argue that aside from the workings of the economic system there is a system of patriarchal exploitation which is the fundamental cause. The question of whether the recent growth in the female labour force can be interpreted as the use of women as part of a reserve army of labour has also been the subject of much of the work in this area.

2 The Demographic and Economic Perspective

The recognition of a relationship between the size of a nation's population and its potential labour force has long been accepted by economists. When Adam Smith (1970, p. 62) expressed the view that the prosperity of a country was dependent upon the increase in the number of its inhabitants, he was acknowledging the relationship between economic change and demographic change. Therefore in examining the changing significance of the female component of the labour force during the twentieth century, in either Britain or the USA, demographic changes need to be considered.

While over a prolonged period it can be anticipated that there are changes in both demographic and economic conditions, the relationship between economic and demographic change is not always clear. That a relationship exists is acknowledged by economists and demographers, but views differ over its nature, there being two opposing hypotheses. Certain economists and demographers suggest that a change in demographic conditions will either increase or slow down the pace of economic change. The alternative view is that a major factor in bringing about demographic change is the change in the economic conditions within an economy.

Although it is possible to agree with Brown (1976, p. 130) that 'population growth, size and distribution cannot be discussed rationally except in the contexts of economic growth and change', it would be equally possible to claim that economic growth and change cannot be discussed rationally except in the context of population growth, size and distribution. It is therefore necessary to determine to what extent changing demographic factors have influenced the economic position of women, and to what extent the changing economic position of women has influenced demographic change.

An illustration of this relationship arises when comparing contemporary Britain with the Britain of the beginning of the century. There have been demographic changes, e.g. family size in Britain is now, on average, smaller than at the beginning of this century, and there have been economic changes, e.g. a higher percentage of married women take paid employment. Census data provide evidence that these changes have occurred. However, it has not been established that because married women have smaller families they now have time to spend on other activities, including paid employment, or that because married women desire to experience and benefit from paid employment they limit their families in order to be able to do so.

Sweezy (1971) has observed with respect to the USA, and the same may well be true for Britain, that female fertility appears to follow a cyclical trend often unrelated to economic phenomena. Consequently different generations of married women may have potentially a greater or lesser opportunity to participate in the labour force. If correct, such observations would imply that exogenous factors, i.e. demographic considerations, directly influence the potential economic activity of females. A contrary view is held by Butz and Ward (1979), who suggest that endogenous factors may be the decisive influence, i.e. economic considerations may influence demographic patterns. In a series of detailed area studies of Britain, James (1962, p. 285) found that:

> Certain sectors of the working class were precocious in their family limitation habits, notably textile workers. This is associated with greater opportunities for married women's employment, so perhaps in a sense demand for female labour created its own supply. Mineworkers were behind in family limitation . . . however, opportunities for female work were usually scarce in mining areas.

Although the exact nature of the cause and effect relationship between economic activity and demographic change in general is disputed, it is recognised that the economic activity of females over their life cycle is much more responsive than males to changes in demographic factors, such as marriage and family formation.

THE SOURCES OF DEMOGRAPHIC DATA

In both Britain and the USA the practice is to undertake a full population census once every ten years; it is from these decennial censuses that the data discussed below are drawn. The censuses are not undertaken in the same year, the latest census in the USA being in 1980, while in Britain the most recent was in 1981. However, the closeness is such that comparisons of changes over each decade can still be made with reasonable accuracy.

There are difficulties in relying on a decennial census to provide data over an extended period because the circumstances in which the censuses are held and the questions posed have changed. However, census information is used here to provide only an indication of the long-term general trends which may have influenced the economic role of women. The desire is to obtain an overview, and the census data are the only source of comprehensive data over the last eighty years. Over this prolonged period exact comparability is not always possible, and the census data provide only a framework within which to work.

Territorial changes can affect the comparability of data over time. When Alaska and Hawaii became part of the USA in 1959 this made a difference of the order of only one per cent to the population figures. Most of British data presented here are for Great Britain rather than for the United Kingdom, which includes Northern Ireland, because this is the area for which comparable statistics are available. Until 1923 the Irish Republic was a part of the United Kingdom and thus comparisons of the UK data before and after that date would not be meaningful.

There have also been subtle changes in the character of the employment data which sometimes go unnoticed. With respect to the USA, Galenson and Smith (1978, p. 11) have drawn attention to a major change in the nature of the employment data. Between 1900 and 1930 the labour force was defined as those who were gainfully occupied, but the 1940 census introduced the concept of labour force, and this replaced the gainful worker definition. Hence from 1940 potential workers who lacked experience but were looking for their first job were included in the totals (previously they had been excluded), while experienced workers not seeking work for seasonal considerations were excluded (whereas they had previously been included). Galenson and Smith considered that the changes tended to have offsetting effects and that long-run comparisons were still valid.

Until 1951 the British census identified individuals who were 'occupied', whereas from 1961 they recorded those who were regarded 'economically active', a definition that was designed to include those seeking work. Gales and Marks (1974) considered that it was not possible to quantify the effect of the change in definition when making inter-censal comparisons. A more serious limitation of the US data when used for studying trends in female employment is that it was not until the census of 1940 that the position of married women within the female labour force was clearly identified. This was the first US census to relate female employment status to both age and marital status and to analyse female employment by industry as well as occupation.

THE DEMOGRAPHIC BACKGROUND

In Britain and the USA in the second half of the twentieth century women have constituted just over half the total population (see Tables 2.1 and 2.2).

TABLE 2.1 *Population of Great Britain, total and female, 1901-81*

	Total population (000's)	Female population (000's)	Females as % of total
1901	36 999	19 098	51.6
1911	40 831	21 077	51.6
1921	42 769	22 346	52.2
1931	44 796	23 337	52.1
1941*	—	—	—
1951	48 854	25 403	52.0
1961	51 285	26 498	51.7
1971	53 979	27 781	51.5
1981	54 285	27 946	51.5

*No census was taken in 1941.
SOURCE   *Census of Population*, various years.

TABLE 2.2 *Population of the United States, total and female, 1900-80*

	Total population (000's)	Female population (000's)	Females as % of total
1900	75 995	37 178	48.9
1910	91 972	44 640	48.5
1920	105 711	51 810	49.0
1930	122 755	60 638	49.4
1940	131 669	65 608	49.8
1950	150 697	75 864	50.3
1960*	179 323	90 992	50.7
1970*	203 211	104 300	51.3
1980*	226 546	116 493	51.4

*Figures for these years include Alaska and Hawaii.
SOURCE   *US Census of Population*, various years.

In Britain the proportion of women in the population has remained remarkably stable at around 51.5 per cent, with slight increases after the two major wars which can be accounted for by the relatively greater loss of male lives. The USA situation has been rather different: not until the 1940s did the number of females equal the number of males. Since then the proportion of females in the USA population has gradually converged with the British figure. Thus during the present century the relative significance of females within the USA population has grown.

In both nations the growth in the total population has bought a simultaneous increase in the number of females, but with respect to overall population growth the experience of the two nations has been different. In 1981 the total population of Britain was approaching 50 per cent above the 1901 figure, with the female population increasing by a similar percentage. This population growth can be attributed almost entirely to natural growth, i.e. an excess of births over deaths. Migration to Britain has taken place, but the number of immigrants arriving has, in most years, been exceeded by the number of emigrants leaving.

In only one decade in this century, the first, did the total population in Britain increase by more than 10 per cent. The reverse has been the case in the USA, and in only one decade, 1930-1940, did the total population grow by less than 10 per cent. Throughout its history the USA has attracted large numbers of migrants to its shores and this, together with natural growth, led to the trebling of the US population over the period 1900-1980, with a marginally higher increase for the female population. Thus the absolute contribution of females, both as producers and as consumers, to the economies of Britain and the USA will have increased because of the overall growth in numbers. However, in both nations there have simultaneously occurred changes in the age structure of the female population which have had further important implications for the size of the potential female labour force.

THE CHANGING AGE DISTRIBUTION OF THE FEMALE POPULATION

For the first few decades of the century in Britain and the USA the proportion of females aged 15 to 64 years, the age group most likely to enter employment, increased. By 1940 this age group represented almost 70 per cent of the total female population of Britain, while in the USA the figure was only marginally lower. From then onwards, however, the proportion in this age group began to fall, with the decline being rather slower in Britain than in the USA. Furthermore, as Tables 2.3 and 2.4 show, although the decline was of a greater magnitude in the USA until 1960, the trend then reversed. In the USA the proportion of females aged 15-64 years then began to rise again while in Britain it continued to decline. Thus by the early 1970s, for the first time, there was a higher proportion of the US female population in the 15-64 year age group than there was in Britain.

TABLE 2.3 *Percentage distribution of the age structure of British female population, 1901-81*

	15-64	Age group under 15	65 and over
1901	63.3	31.5	5.2
1911	64.4	29.8	5.8
1921	66.8	26.5	6.6
1931	68.9	23.0	8.1
1941*	—	—	—
1951	66.5	21.1	12.4
1961	64.0	22.0	14.1
1971	61.5	22.7	15.9
1981	61.9	20.8	17.3

*No census was taken in 1941.
SOURCE *Census of Population*, various years.

TABLE 2.4 *Percentage distribution of the age structure of USA female population, 1900-80*

	15-64	Age group under 15	65 and over
1900	61.2	34.8	4.1
1910	62.9	32.7	4.4
1920	63.2	32.1	4.7
1930	65.2	29.4	5.5
1940	68.2	24.8	7.0
1950	65.3	26.2	8.5
1960*	59.9	30.1	10.0
1970*	61.6	27.2	11.2
1980*	65.4	21.6	13.0

*Figures for these years include Alaska and Hawaii.
SOURCE *US Census of Population*, various years.

During the present century the general trend has been for the proportion of the total female population who are under fifteen years of age to decline. This trend, though, has not been a monotonic one and after the Second World War the decline was reversed for a few decades. While the drop in the female population who were under fifteen years was greater in the USA, down from 34.8 per cent to 21.6 per cent, than in Britain, where the drop was from 31.5 per cent to 21.0 per cent, the implications for Britain are of greater significance. In Britain the absolute number of females under the age of fifteen years has fallen, whereas in the USA it has continued to rise, reflecting the faster rate of increase in the total population. The long-term implication of the continuing decline in the proportion of the female population who are under fifteen years of age is that the proportion of females of working age will begin to decline in the 1990s.

The factors that have contributed to the relative decline in the proportion of the female population who are under fifteen are numerous. One obvious explanation is that it is a consequence of females living longer. Thus the relative proportion of the old has risen, with a relative decline in the proportion who are young. There are also other demographic changes that are relevant to the growth in the numbers of females entering the labour market. During the course of this century the level of female fertility has fallen. In Britain at the beginning of the century, the General Fertility Rate, i.e. all births per 1000 women aged 15-44 years, was 113.0, while in recent years it has averaged 62.1. The explanations for this decline vary. Schultz (1978) regards it as a consequence of a secular decline in fertility but a decline which did simultaneously permit an increase in female participation in labour market activities. Other observers have held to the view that the decline in the level of female fertility reflects a change in the role of females in society, a change which has led to less time being devoted to bearing and bringing children up and rather more time being devoted to a wider economic role which includes paid employment outside the home.

In both Britain and the USA the relative size of the 65+ age group in relation to the total female population has trebled. The number of females in this age group in Britain grew from one to five million, while in the USA, in part due to the larger population increase, there was a tenfold rise to fifteen million. The increased numbers in the over-65 age group can have a distorting effect on estimates of the female economic activity rate.

These age distribution patterns also have implications for some of the analyses of female employment patterns discussed in subsequent chapters. Heer (1968) is one of numerous observers who have drawn attention to their consequences in a wider employment context. A young labour force is a more flexible one able to adapt more quickly to new technologies, while an older labour force has the benefits that arise from experience, even if it is often more conservative in its response to change.

A second consequence for employment arising from the ageing of the population flows from the differing demands for goods and services which the different age groups have. The presence of children within a family does not lead to an increase in the demand for goods and services, although the actual nature of the demand will vary from that of families with no children. However, those beyond the age of sixty-five often remain active consumers in their own right, and as the size of this age group has grown there has been a corresponding increase in the demand for leisure facilities, medical care and social services. These sectors of the economy are all heavily dependent upon female labour. Thus the relative decline in the proportion of the population who are young has permitted a growing proportion of females in the 15-64 age group to enter paid employment. The increase in the proportion of the population who are sixty-five and over has created a demand for female employees in certain sectors of the economy.

TWENTIETH-CENTURY CHANGES IN THE MARITAL STATUS OF WOMEN

A further demographic feature that has affected female employment patterns has been the increase in the relative size of the married female population in the 15-64 age group. On the basis of the census data, shown in Tables 2.5 and 2.6, it is possible to identify similarities in the broad trends in the USA and Britain, but at the same time certain dissimilarities are also observable.

At the beginning of the present century barely half of the women in Britain who were in the 15-64 age group were married. The proportion was rather higher, at 58 per cent, in the USA. For the first half of the century in the USA the percentage of this age group who were married continually rose until a peak was reached in the 1960s at 70 per cent. In Britain the percentage continued to rise until a peak of nearly 72 per cent was reached in the early 1970s. In the period 1960-1980 in the USA the percentage of females in the 15-64 age group who were married fell back relatively quickly to 60 per cent, a percentage comparable to that existing in 1910. While this was a higher percentage than at the very beginning of the century it did represent a reversal of the upward trend over the previous half century.

The Demographic and Economic Perspective

TABLE 2.5 *Married female population, Great Britain, aged 15-64 years, 1901-81*

	Female population (000's)	Married female population (000's)	Married % of total
1901	12 094	6 113	50.5
1911	13 572	7 019	51.7
1921	14 937	7 961	53.3
1931	16 086	8 856	55.0
1941*	—	—	—
1951	16 900	11 138	65.9
1961	16 955	11 808	69.6
1971	17 083	12 191	71.4
1981	17 307	11 510	66.5

*No census was taken in 1941.
SOURCE *Census of Population*, various years.

TABLE 2.6 *Married female population, USA, aged 15-64 years, 1900-80*

	Female population (000's)	Married female population (000's)	Married % of total
1900	22 724	13 260	58.3
1910	28 083	16 976	60.5
1920	32 727	20 465	62.5
1930	39 528	25 009	63.3
1940	44 748	28 503	63.7
1950	49 520	35 243	71.2
1960*	54 508	39 560	72.6
1970*	64 254	43 393	67.5
1980*	73 856	44 544	60.3

*Figures for these years include Alaska and Hawaii.
SOURCE *US Census of Population*, various years.

In Britain the rise in the proportion of females who were married continued a decade longer than in the USA, but since the 1971 peak there has been a decline, although a more modest one than that occurring in the USA. Thus by 1980 the percentage of females in the 15-64 age group who were married in the USA was 2 per cent above the 1900 level. In contrast, in Britain the increase was of the order of 16 per cent, so that by 1981 a third more British women in this age group were married than was the case in 1901. In both countries the increase in the percentage of the age group who were married partly reflects the decline in the median age of marriage by spinsters.

TABLE 2.7 *Median age of marriage by spinsters in the USA and England and Wales, 1900-80*

	United States median age	England and Wales median age
1900	21.9	24.9
1910	21.6	24.5
1920	21.2	24.3
1930	21.3	24.3
1940	21.5	22.7
1950	20.3	22.4
1960	20.3	21.4
1970	20.8	21.3
1980	21.8	21.8

SOURCES *US Census of Population*, various years; *England and Wales, Marriage and Divorce Statistics Series*, FM2, No. 7, OPCS, 1983.

At the turn of the century the median age of marriage by spinsters in the USA was three years below the comparable figure for England and Wales. The median age of first marriage in the USA then fell to just over twenty years of age by the mid-1950s, but in the last quarter of a century it has risen again and by 1980 it was about the same as it had been in 1900. In England and Wales the fall in the median age was of a greater magnitude and occurred over a longer period than was the experience in the USA, the lowest point being reached in 1971, since when the age has risen again. The median age of marriage by British spinsters was, until the late 1970s, always higher than in the USA.

Thus in the USA between 1900 and 1980 there was a rise of 2 per cent in the number of females who were married in the 15-64 age group and the median age of marriage by spinsters remained almost unchanged. Over the same period in Britain there was a rise in the percentage of this age group who were married from 51 per cent to 68 per cent, and a reduction in the age of first marriage.

While the trends in Britain and the USA over this century have been of a similar nature, by the end of the period the situation in Britain, while similar to the USA, had changed significantly from the position that had existed in 1900. Britain not only caught up with the USA but from the 1960s onwards had a higher percentage of females aged 15-64 who were married. The implication of this change, as Stewart (1961) has shown, is that there has occurred a sharp decline in the total number of females in Britain who have remained unmarried. This change has been identified as a unique feature in British demographic history. Williams (1978, p. 85) expressed the view, on the basis of available English vital statistics, that there had never before been such a high proportion of married women in the population under the age of forty. Precisely what induced this change in marital habits in Britain is not known. It would be dangerous to attribute the change entirely to economic factors, but the willingness of employers in the second half of the century to employ females who were married may have influenced to some degree both the age of first marriage and the willingness to marry. The implications of the change in marital patterns for the labour force are clear. As the twentieth century has evolved, the female labour force could only maintain its size, or expand, by accepting a larger proportion of married women to compensate for the relative decline in the number of females who had never married.

The demographic changes discussed above suggest that one reason why there has been an increase in the number of females in employment is that there are now absolutely, and in the USA relatively, more females of working age. One reason for the growth in the numbers of married women in paid employment in both nations is that a higher percentage of the female population aged 15-64 is now married and levels of fertility are lower than in the past. In Britain the total number of females of working age, defined as 15-64 years, rose between 1901 and 1981 by 41 per cent, while the number of married females in that age range rose by 90 per cent. In the USA the corresponding figures for the period 1900-1980 were 215 per cent and 235 per cent respectively.

EMPLOYMENT TRENDS

In Britain since the start of the century the total labour force, both male and female, has risen by 55 per cent, this being marginally above the percentage population increase. This aggregate figure hides the fact that the size of the male labour force increased by one-third, although the male population increased by 50 per cent, while the female labour force doubled in size, which is an increase greatly in excess of the female population growth. Until 1951 the male and female labour forces grew at approximately the same rate and the female proportion of the labour force remained close to 30 per cent, although the situation did differ during the war periods. In the second half of the century a new pattern has emerged. The female proportion of the labour force has grown to 40 per cent, and out of the 3.2 million increase since 1951 in the number of people in the total labour force, three million have been women.

TABLE 2.8   *Total and female labour force,* * *Great Britain, 1901-81*

	Total labour force (000's)	Female labour force (000's)	Female % of total
1901	16 312	4 763	29.2
1911	18 351	5 424	29.6
1921	19 357	5 701	29.5
1931	21 055	6 265	29.8
1941**	–	–	–
1951	22 610	6 961	30.8
1961	23 810	7 740	32.5
1971	25 103	9 186	36.6
1981	25 377	9 878	38.9

*1901-51 'occupied'; 1961-81 'economically active'.
**No census was taken in 1941.
SOURCE   *Census of Population*, various years.

TABLE 2.9   *Total and female labour force,* * *United States, 1900-80*

	Total labour force (000's)	Female labour force (000's)	Female % of total
1900	29 073	5 319	18.3
1910	38 167	8 076	21.2
1920	41 614	8 550	20.6
1930	48 830	10 752	22.0
1940	53 011	12 887	24.3
1950	59 643	16 552	27.8
1960**	69 877	22 410	32.1
1970**	82 049	30 547	37.2
1980**	109 042	45 646	41.9

*1900-1930 'gainfully occupied'; 1940-80 'labour force'.
**Figures for these years include Alaska and Hawaii.
SOURCE   *US Census of Population*, various years.

The growth in the size of the US labour force has been of an entirely different order of magnitude. From 1900 to 1980 the total USA labour force increased in size by 275 per cent, while the female labour force rose by 750 per cent. This increase in the female labour force occurred against a background of a 300 per cent increase in the female population of working age. The rise in the female labour force in the first half century was of the order of 200 per cent, from 5.3 million to 16.5 million. From 1950 to 1980 the rise was 275 per cent, from 16.5 million to 45.6 million.

The fact that the female labour force grew relatively more than the total labour force meant that there was an increase in the relative contribution of females to the total labour force. In 1900 under 20 per cent of the US labour force were female, a percentage significantly below the figure of 30 per cent for Britain at that time. Unlike the British experience, though, the percentage of the US labour force who were women rose virtually continuously until 1980. Until 1940 the trend upwards was relatively slow, but after 1950 the percentage contribution of females increased at an unprecedented rate, and by 1960 it was for the first time on a par with the British figure. Since the Second World War the relative contribution of females to the US labour force has continued to increase at a rate faster than that experienced in Britain.

Thus although the trends in both nations have been in the same direction the rates of change have been quite different. As a proportion of the total labour force the contribution by females in Britain has grown by one-third and in the USA it has doubled, although in the latter case the starting base was lower.

The experience with respect to the trends in female employment in both the USA and Britain in the period after the Second World War have been radically different from the experiences of the first half of the century. Over the last three decades the relative contribution of women to the British labour force has increased by one-third and in the USA by 50 per cent, and in both nations females now constitute over 40 per cent of the national labour force.

THE FEMALE ECONOMIC ACTIVITY RATE

The total female population and the female labour force have so far been examined in isolation. In order to allow for the effect of population growth in explaining labour force changes it is necessary to consider whether the ratio of the female labour force to the size of the female population of working age has altered. This ratio is known as the Female

Activity Rate in Britain, but in the USA it is also known as the Female Participation Rate. To be more precise the Female Activity Rate is the proportion of a specified section of the population who are economically active in the labour force. For the purpose of the British Census in 1981 activity rates were calculated as follows:

ACTIVITY RATE = [LABOUR FORCE x 100] divided by [POPULATION AT RISK]

where the **LABOUR FORCE** is defined as those gainfully employed, including those working on their own account, as well as employers, plus those who are unable to seek work through sickness and those seeking, but unable through unemployment to take employment, and where the **POPULATION AT RISK** is defined as all those within the specific population being examined.

The precise definitions of the activity rate have been subject to change over time. Here, and in subsequent chapters, two specific populations will usually be considered: the total female population, excluding those under fifteen years, and the married female population. Where appropriate, reference will be made to the Female Activity Rate (FAR) and the Married Female Activity Rate (MFAR). The decision to exclude those under the age of fifteen reflects the recognition that during the course of this century in both Britain and the USA the trend has been to extend schooling to a higher age. At the beginning of the century it was not unusual in both countries for young females of twelve years of age to be engaged in paid employment. During the course of this century there has been a trend to raise the minimum age below which children are not able to leave school. In addition, within the USA there has been a lengthening of the school year and this too has reduced the possibility of the relatively young formally participating in the labour market.

Some broad trends with respect to the FAR are identifiable from Tables 2.10 and 2.11. Throughout the first half of this century the FAR for Britain remained remarkably stable at around the 38 per cent mark. In the USA the situation was quite different and over the same period there was a rise from a FAR of 20 per cent in 1900 to one of 30 per cent half a century later, although there were fluctuations around this rising trend. For a rise of this magnitude to have taken place against the background of an expanding population necessitated a trebling in the number of females in the US labour force to just over fifteen million, this rate of increase being more rapid than the rate at which the total population was

TABLE 2.10 *Female labour force activity rates, Great Britain, 1901-81*

	All women 15-64 years
1901	38.3
1911	38.9
1921	37.2
1931	38.0
1941*	–
1951	40.2
1961	44.2
1971	52.1
1981**	57.5**

*No census was taken in 1941.
**All women aged 16-64 years.
SOURCE *Census of Population*, various years.

TABLE 2.11 *Female labour force activity rates, United States, 1900-80*

	All women 15-64 years
1900	20.6
1910	25.4
1920	23.7
1930	24.8
1940	25.8
1950	29.0
1960*	34.5
1970*	41.6**
1980*	51.1**

*Figures for these years include Alaska and Hawaii.
**All women aged 16-64 years.
SOURCE *US Census of Population*, various years.

growing. Thus, unlike Britain where the proportion of females in the labour force was constant for half a century, in the USA the proportion rose steadily.

In the second half of the century there has been a greater degree of similarity between the two countries. The FAR in Britain increased from

38 per cent in 1951 to 46 per cent in 1981. Some observers believe it may have been even higher in the late 1970s prior to the onset of the latest economic recession. During the same period in the USA the FAR continued to rise, but at an accelerated rate, and during the 1970s for the first time the FAR for the USA moved above that of Britain. Thus throughout the twentieth century the trend has been for the gap between the FAR of the two nations to close, until by 1980 the figures were almost the same.

The pattern of the FAR by age group, which is given for selected years, provides more detailed information on the character of the trends noted above (see Figures 2.1 and 2.2). In Britain at the beginning of the century the pattern is one of the level of FAR declining with age, the main fall occurring between the ages of 20 and 30, reflecting both marriage and family formation. After the age of 30 the FAR trend continues downwards but not so steeply. By mid-century, however, a new pattern may be seen as emerging, with a rise in FAR for those over 35 years. The curve for 1981 indicates that a bi-modal pattern has become a significant feature of the FAR in Britain. After declining the FAR rises for women aged between 30 and 50, prior to a second decline for those of 55 and over. In 1981 the level of the FAR for females aged 40–49 was treble the 1901 value.

The overall direction of the FAR curves for USA females follows a broadly similar pattern to that identified for Britain. The USA FAR curve for 1900 has a similar sharp decline until the mid-30s age group and thereafter a more gentle decline. By mid-century it is possible to identify the emerging bi-modal pattern of the FAR in the USA which was to develop later in Britain. Similarly, in 1980 the curve representing the FAR in the USA has the main characteristics identified in the British curve. After an initial rise for the below-20 age group there is a clear decline in the level of FAR through to the age of 30, and thereafter a rise prior to the second fall for the 50 and over age group. As in Britain, the FAR for those in the 40–49 age group was three times that which had existed in 1900.

When the age-specific FARs of the two countries are compared for both the beginning and end of the period being considered it may be noted that the peaks in the age-specific FAR curves are lower on both occasions in the USA than in Britain.

These age-specific FAR patterns are also to be found, but in a more exaggerated form, when the Married Female Activity Rate for Britain is examined. The highest level of the MFAR in 1901 was for the 15–24 age group. In 1981 the highest MFAR was for the 45–54 age group, which was six times its 1901 value. It is thus clear that the earlier possible explanation that there were more married females at work because there were now proportionately more married females in the female population is only a

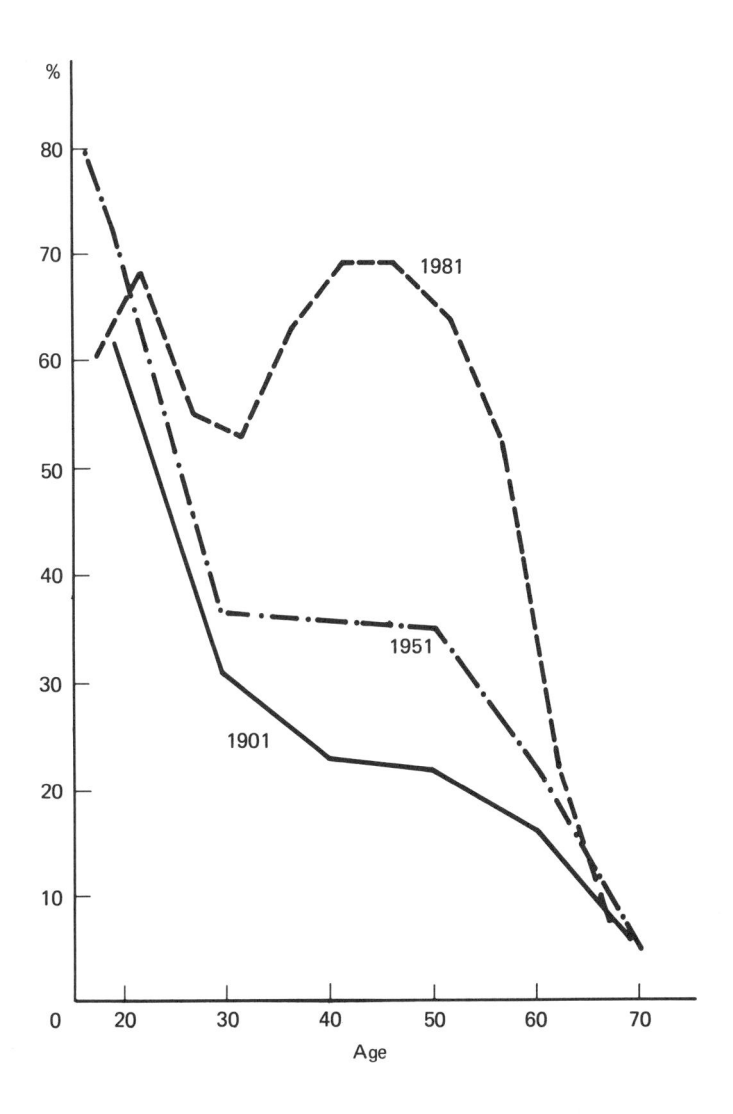

FIGURE 2.1 *Female economic activity rates by age, Great Britain, 1901, 1951, 1981*
SOURCE *Census of Population*, 1901, 1951, 1981.

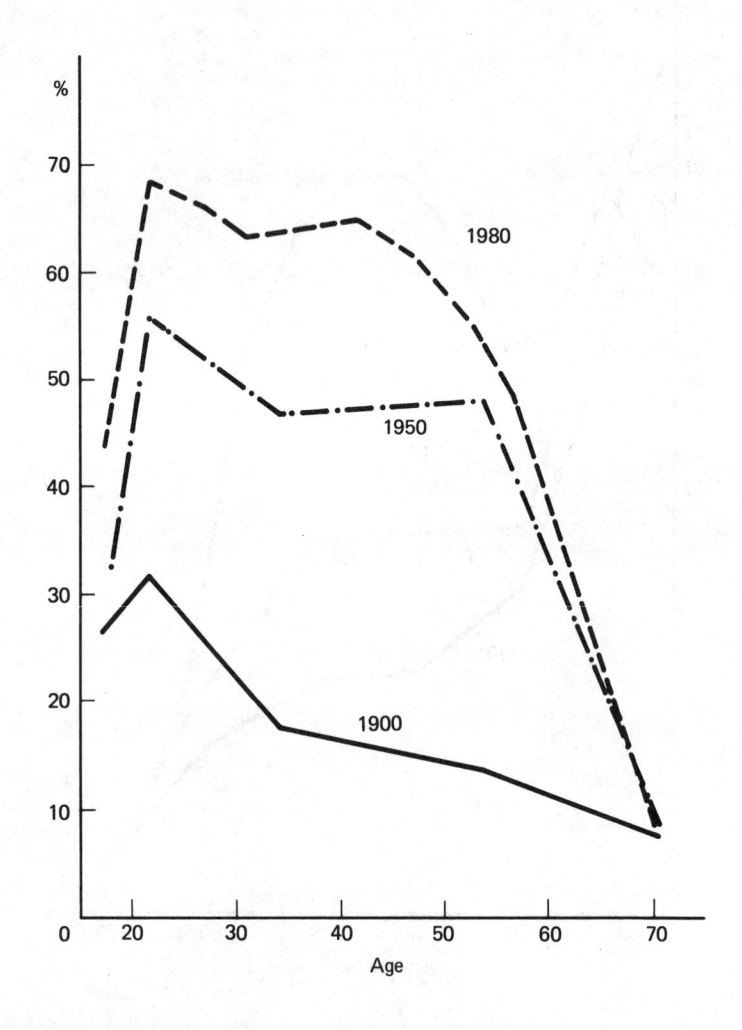

FIGURE 2.2 *Female economic activity rates by age, United States, 1900, 1950, 1980*
SOURCE *US Census of Population*, 1900, 1950, 1980.

part of the explanation. The detailed age-specific MFAR data plotted in Figure 2.3 reveal that an increasing proportion of married women now actively participate in the labour market, and this is especially true of women over 35 years of age. Similar detailed data concerning labour market participation by married females in the USA is not available prior to 1940. However, given the rise in both the number of married females in the USA prior to 1940 and the coincidental growth in the female labour

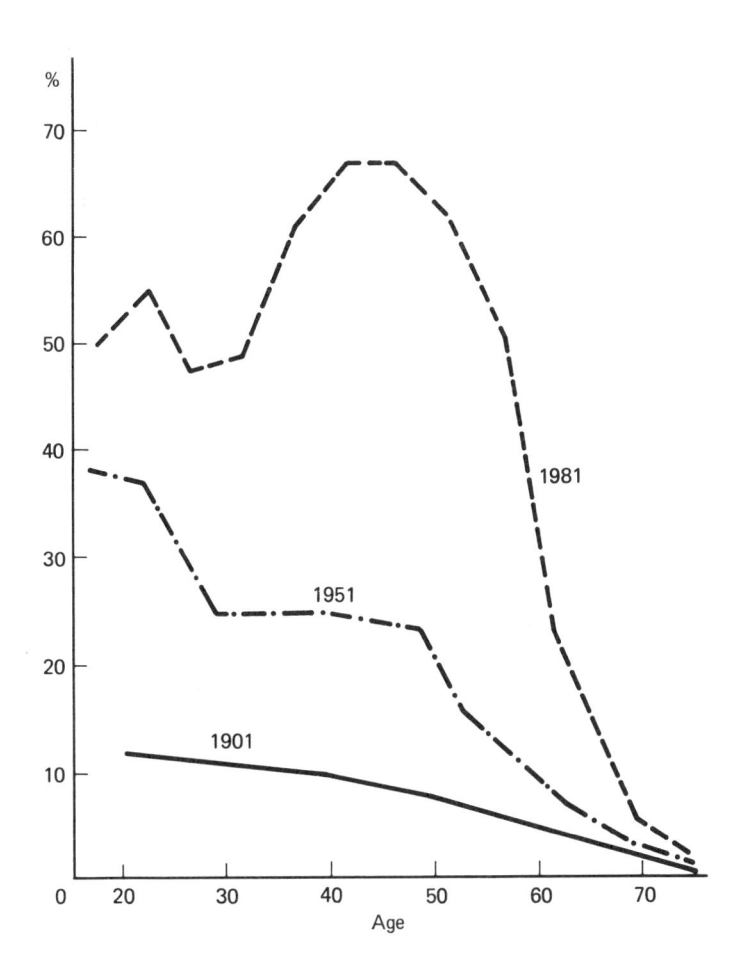

FIGURE 2.3 *Married female economic activity rates by age, Great Britain, 1901, 1951, 1981*
SOURCE *Census of Population*, 1901, 1951, 1981.

force, together with the similarity in the patterns in the two countries post-1940, it is not unrealistic to suggest that the US trend has been similar to the British one.

In 1901, the MFAR in Britain was of the order of 10 per cent. Over the next fifty years it was to double to 21.5 per cent. From 1951 to 1981 it more than doubled again, with the fastest increases occurring in the 1960s. At the beginning of the century the MFAR in the USA was 5.6 per cent, just above half the British figure. The increase over the period to 1950 was more rapid in the USA and the MFAR quadrupled in these fifty years, double the rate of increase experienced in Britain, with the consequence that by 1950 the MFARs were similar in both nations. Since 1950 there has been a further rapid growth of the MFAR in the USA, just as in Britain.

Between 1950 and 1980, the direction of change in the FAR for single females in the two countries was different. In Britain there was a fall from 73 per cent to 61 per cent in the single female group participating in the

TABLE 2.12 *Female labour force activity rates for Great Britain by marital status, 1951-81*

	Single	Widowed and divorced	Married
1951	72.9	20.9	21.5
1961	69.6	22.9	29.4
1971	59.7	23.1	42.0
1981	60.8	22.9	47.2

SOURCE *Census of Population*, economic activity tables, various years.

TABLE 2.13 *Female labour force activity rates for United States by marital status, 1950-80*

	Single	Widowed and divorced	Married
1950	50.5	36.0	24.8
1960	44.1	37.1	31.7
1970	53.0	36.2	41.4
1980	61.5	41.0	50.7

SOURCE *US Current Population Survey*, various years.

labour force. This fall occurred mainly in the 1960s and coincided with the expansion of educational provision. In the USA the reverse process can be seen to have taken place, the percentage of single females in the labour force rising from 50 per cent to 61 per cent. Hamermesh and Rees (1984, p. 17) paradoxically attribute this also to an expansion of educational take-up, but because the cost of education in the USA has risen more rapidly than the rate of inflation, increasing numbers of female students join the labour force on a part-time basis.

CONCLUSIONS

In the early part of this century, on both sides of the Atlantic, the women who were in the labour force were predominately young and single. Upon marriage the practice was for a high proportion to withdraw permanently from paid employment. Three-quarters of the females who were in the labour force at the start of the century, in Britain and in the USA, were under 35 years of age, and only 13 per cent and 8 per cent respectively of those in the labour force were married. In Britain only one woman in ten was both married and in paid employment, and in the USA the figure was one in eighteen. It is difficult to conceive of a greater contrast with the situation eighty years later. By 1980-1 less than 45 per cent of the females in the labour force in both countries were under the age of thirty-five years, while 60 per cent of the females who were then economically active were married, every other married woman aged 15-64 being in the labour force.

While the character of the female labour force has changed it is important to note that the female activity rates for *all* age groups in both Britain and the USA have risen during the present century. These changes in activity rates for all age groups cannot be attributed to a single demographic factor. Indeed the demographic experience of Britain and the USA has differed in a number of ways, while the rise in activity rates has been a common experience. The implication of this is that possible explanations for the changes in the female contribution to the labour force are also to be found in non-demographic factors, including economic considerations, which simultaneously influenced females of differing marital status in all age groups on both sides of the Atlantic.

3 Employment Trends in the Twentieth Century

Britain and the USA were two of a group of only half a dozen nations which by 1900 could be regarded as being 'mature economies'. They had technically advanced manufacturing industries and were in the process of evolution towards the next identified stage of economic development, mass consumption. This chapter explains how, as this economic development was taking place, changes in the structure of industry had an important influence on the pattern of female employment. In both nations the agricultural sector has contracted as an employer of labour while simultaneously a growth in service sector employment has taken place. In the productive sector, which includes manufacturing, mining and construction, the pattern has differed. Until the 1960s the relative importance of this sector increased on both sides of the Atlantic, but since then its relative significance has declined (see Table 3.1).

These shifts in the structure of industry, together with new technological and organisational developments within industries, have significantly altered the numbers employed in different occupations. It is, though, not only the case that the numbers in different occupations have changed, but also many occupations which existed in 1900 have disappeared and have been replaced by entirely new occupations. In certain instances where statistics suggest that an occupation has been in existence continuously, the content of the occupation has changed radically.

Britain and the USA have both experienced a decline in the significance of the occupations which were directly related to agriculture, the extractive, and the basic manufacturing industries. Occupations within these industrial sectors were often reliant on physical strength and over time had become largely closed to females, a situation reinforced in certain instances by legislation. The occupations that have evolved in the growing industrial sectors have often required different characteristics, e.g. a high degree of

TABLE 3.1 *Sectoral changes in total employment, Britain 1901–81 and the United States 1900–80*

	Total in Employment (000's)		Change (%)
Britain	*1901*	*1981*	
Agriculture*	1 371	516	−62
Productive industry**	8 485	8 509	0
Service sector†	6 425	13 892	+116
Total	16 281	22 917	+41
United States	*1900*	*1980*	
Agriculture*	10 438	3 117	−70
Productive industry**	10 220	32 719	+220
Service sector†	8 629	68 222	+691
Total	29 287	104 058	+255

*Agriculture includes forestry and fishing.
**Productive industry includes all manufacturing, mining, construction and public utilities.
†Service sector includes transport and communications.
SOURCE *Census of Population*, 1901 and 1981; *US Census of Population*, 1900 and 1980.

manual dexterity, or non-manual skills, and are therefore not always regarded as solely male preserves.

The changes in female employment that have taken place as a result of economic development are the consequence of two processes which Hunter and Mulvey (1981, p. 106), refer to as an 'industrial effect' and an 'occupational effect'. The industrial effect is the shift in the distribution of employment between industries. This shift between industries is the consequence of a series of factors which may or may not take place simultaneously. When consumer demand changes, certain industries grow to provide the increasing demand but other industries, whose products were previously demanded, decline. Over time the availability of raw materials changes, and this too will induce a shift in employment opportunities between industries. During this century technology has developed, resulting in the creation of new industries or modifying the employment opportunities in existing ones. The occupational effect refers to the changing character and significance of the different occupations in an economy. There are few occupations in either Britain or the USA that have not been affected by the process of technical change in the twentieth century. Technical change has in certain instances made some occupations redundant while simultaneously creating new ones. Technical change within industries has changed the relative significance of certain occupations and altered the content of the job. When the demand for goods changes this also affects occupational structure, as the occupational mix within industries differs. The growth in demand for one commodity and the decline in demand for another will cause employment in some occupations to increase and in others to decrease. In seeking to identify trends in the nature and character of female employment, an examination of how the industrial effect and the occupation effect have developed over time will be necessary.

Apart from the long-term trends in the industrial and occupational structure of industry, two special periods have had considerable influence on employment patterns. During the two world wars women were required to enter the labour force as direct substitutes for male workers in unprecedented numbers and to undertake tasks previously thought unsuitable for females, because of the physical conditions of work, the required skill levels or simply because women were not accepted in those jobs. What available evidence there is suggests this 'war effect' was of greater significance in Britain than in the USA, where entry to both wars was later and the degree of mobilisation for the war effort did not reach the level achieved in Britain. Nevertheless, the real significance of the war periods was that they widened the potential work opportunities for females then and in later years. It is not really possible to say to what extent this was a consequence of females becoming more aware of their own potential or to what extent it was due to employers gaining a greater appreciation of the contribution that women could make.

INDUSTRIAL DISTRIBUTION OF FEMALE EMPLOYMENT

In 1900 the agricultural sector accounted for 38 per cent of US employment, but by 1980 this figure had fallen to 3.6 per cent, even though the USA remained the world's most important food producer. While total female employment has grown over the twentieth century, by 1980 this sector employed only a third of the number of females it employed in 1900. The employment decline of the US agricultural sector did, however, have a greater impact on female employment than these figures suggest, for the process of agricultural decline increased the proportion of women living in urban areas where employment prospects tended to be more plentiful.

In Britain, at the turn of the century, agriculture as a source of female employment was less significant than in the USA, providing 2 per cent of total female employment compared with nearly 20 per cent in the USA. By the final quarter of this century the agricultural sector had shrunk to marginally above 1 per cent of total female employment in both nations. In 1900 the US agricultural sector employed more people than either the productive industry sector or the service sector. In Britain, though, the productive industries were already the key employment sector in terms of employment. However, the major British industries at the beginning of the century, e.g mining, shipbuilding and textiles, have declined in significance, while new industries, e.g. vehicles, electronics, banking and insurance, have grown to a size which in 1901 would have appeared unthinkable. It is these same industrial sectors that have also grown rapidly within the US economy. Inevitably female employment has been affected by these changes. There have been too many industrial and occupational changes over the last eighty years to allow a detailed examination of how employment in each industry and occupation has altered. In a comparative study such as this one, there is also the problem that different industrial and occupational classification systems make detailed comparisons impossible. For these reasons only the broad trends are analysed here.

Industries can be categorised into four broad groupings: productive industry, which includes all manufacturing, mining and construction; the service sector industry, which includes paid private domestic service; the agricultural sector; and a grouping of transport, communications and the public utilities. By adopting this approach it becomes clear for both Britain and the USA that the developing service sector provides the key to female employment growth (see Figure 3.1). Throughout this century at least 50 per cent of total female employment has been in this sector. Indeed by 1980 three out of four employed women worked in the service sector. Thus female employment has increasingly become concentrated in the industrial sector that has grown most rapidly over the twentieth century.

Agriculture and productive industry have in the past been important employers of female labour and even in the 1980s one working woman in five is employed in the latter sector. It is, though, the service sector that has been and is now the major source of female employment on both sides of the Atlantic. However, important differences in female employment patterns between Britain and the USA have existed. In the USA, productive industry as a source of female employment has never had the significance it has had in Britain, reflecting the greater importance of agriculture in the US economy.

In Britain between 1901 and 1951 the proportions of the female labour force in the productive industry sector and the service industry sector were

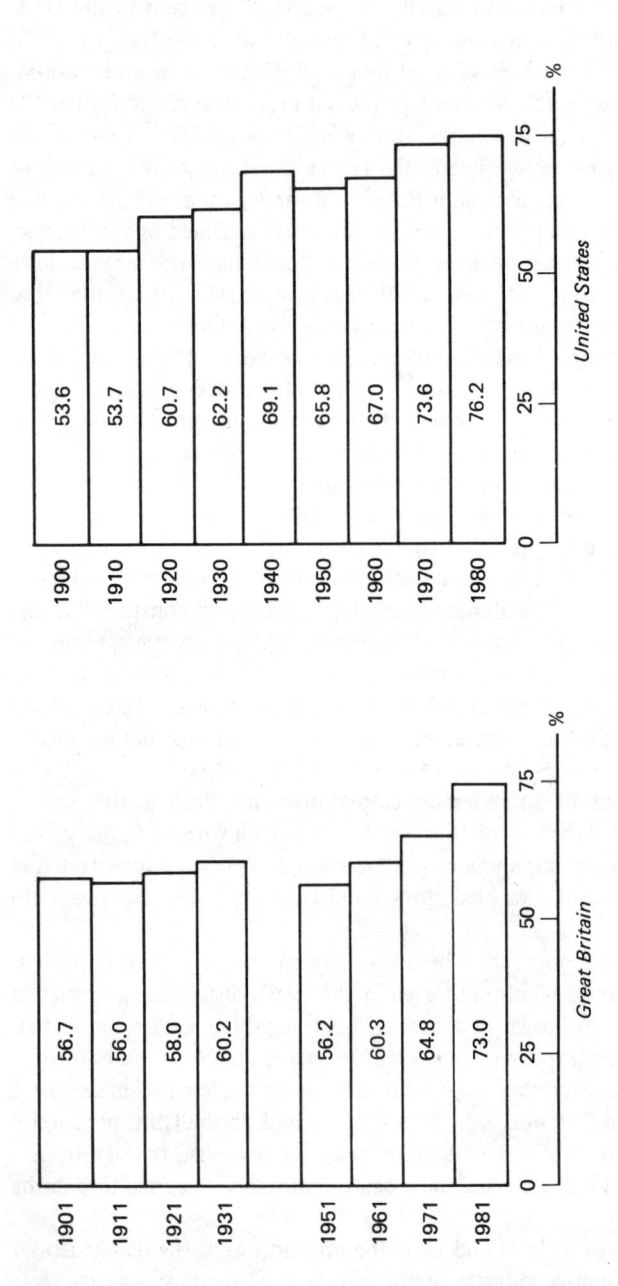

FIGURE 3.1 *Percentage of female labour force employed in the service sector, 1900–81*
SOURCE *Census of Population* 1901–81; *US Census of Population* 1900–80.

fairly constant, at 39 per cent and 56 per cent respectively (see Table 3.2). Since 1951 these relative shares have been modified, and by 1981 the percentage of working women in productive industries had fallen to 21 per cent, while the proportion in the service sector had risen to 75 per cent. Given that since 1951 married female employment has increased most rapidly, it would appear that the service sector has grown mainly by attracting women entering or re-entering the labour force rather than at the expense of the productive industry sector. In absolute figures the productive industry labour force declined by 750,000 over the period 1951-81, while at the same time in the service industry sector female employment increased by three million.

The US experience has differed from the British one in two significant ways. Firstly, the agricultural sector was in the early part of the century more important in the USA than in Britain, and the relative decline in agricultural employment for females was compensated by growth in the employment of females in the service industry sector (see Table 3.3). Total female employment in the service industry sector grew by 1100 per cent between 1900 and 1980, while the percentage of female labour employed in this sector rose from 54 per cent in 1900 to 76 per cent by 1980. In the same period agriculture's relative significance as a source of female employment fell from 18.4 per cent to 1.2 per cent. While the relative significance of agriculture as a source of female employment declined, the service industry sector grew. The long-term trend, shown in Table 3.3, confirms the view of Urquhart (1984) that 'prior to 1967 the employment shift to the services sector was primarily the result of the relative decline of agriculture'.

The second way in which the US experience differed from that of Britain was in the relative significance of productive industry as a source of female employment. During the first half of the century US productive industry provided a quarter or less of total female employment compared with the British figure, which approached 40 per cent. In the second half of the century the difference between the relative significance of the productive industry sector in the two countries has closed, but this owes more to the declining significance of this sector as a source of female employment in Britain than a growth in its significance in the USA.

CHANGES WITHIN THE PRODUCTIVE INDUSTRY SECTOR

Within the productive industry sector, which grew in absolute employment terms until the 1960s in Britain and continued to grow in the USA up to

TABLE 3.2 *Industrial distribution of gainfully occupied female population in Britain, selected years*

Industrial sector	1901 Employment (000's)	%	1921 Employment (000's)	%	1951 Employment (000's)	%	1971 Employment (000's)	%	1981† Employment (000's)	%
Agriculture, forestry, fishing	99.5	2.1	112.0	2.0	115.0	1.7	110.0	1.3	89.7	1.0
Productive industry,* including	1848.0	38.8	2200.4	39.0	2621.8	38.4	2529.1	29.1	1945.6	21.3
Food, drink and tobacco	69.8	1.5	233.3	4.1	275.6	4.0	290.1	3.3	172.9	3.0
Engineering	74.6	1.6	248.0	4.4	650.1	9.5	839.9	9.7	599.9	6.6
Textiles	715.7	15.0	764.0	13.6	548.2	8.0	275.1	3.2	141.1	1.5
Clothing and footwear	765.1	16.1	537.0	9.5	476.3	7.0	344.5	4.0	244.3	2.7
Transport, communications and public utilities	26.9	0.6	51.9	0.9	246.4	3.6	327.1	3.8	359.8	3.9
Service sector, consisting of	2701.4	56.7	3271.7	58.0	3836.6	56.2	5641.6	64.8	6678.4	73.0
Distribution	342.0	7.2	778.1	13.8	1152.2	16.9	1562.1	18.0	1605.9	17.6
Insurance, banking etc.	3.2	0.1	85.7	1.5	150.0	2.2	477.4	5.5	835.0	9.1
Professional and scientific	315.9	6.6	274.8	4.9	893.3	13.1	1859.2	21.4	1943.1	21.2
Miscellaneous	2011.4	42.2	1732.1	30.7	1369.5	20.1	1290.3	14.8	1675.8	18.3
Public admin. and defence	28.8	0.6	401.0	7.1	271.1	4.0	452.5	5.2	618.1	6.8
Totals**	4763.4	100.0	5637.0	100.0	6825.7	100.0	8701.0	100.0	9151.5	100.0

*Productive industry consists of all manufacturing plus mining and construction.
**Totals shown include female employees who were not classified by industry.
†1981 census introduced new industrial classifications, therefore the figures are not strictly comparable.

SOURCE Lee, C. H. *British Regional Employment Statistics 1841–1971*, Cambridge University Press, Cambridge, 1979; *Census of Population*, 1981.

TABLE 3.3 Industrial distribution of gainfully occupied female population in USA, selected years

Industrial sector*	1900 Employment (000's)	%	1920 Employment (000's)	%	1940 Employment (000's)	%	1970 Employment (000's)	%	1980 Employment (000's)	%
Agriculture, forestry and fishing	980	18.4	1084	12.7	487.1	4.4	355.3	1.2	522.0	1.3
Productive industry** including	1375	25.8	2033	23.8	2377.4	21.3	6467.3	21.2	7599.7	18.3
Food, drink and tobacco	25	0.5	100	1.2	199.1	1.8	412.1	1.4	467.8	1.1
Engineering	21	0.4	120	1.4	223.1	2.0	1472.0	4.8	2294.8	5.5
Textiles	295	5.5	480	5.6	477.7	4.3	473.3	1.6	449.7	1.1
Apparel and kindred trades	710	13.3	622	7.3	515.3	4.6	1022.2	3.3	1017.6	2.4
Transport, communications and public utilities	116	2.2	241	2.8	345.1	3.1	1155.2	3.7	1753.0	4.2
Service sector, consisting of	2858	53.6	5190	60.7	7700.2	69.1	22471.8	73.6	31760.1	76.2
Wholesale and retail trade	241	4.5	768	9.0	2029.5	18.2	6712.2	22.0	9138.2	21.9
Finance and insurance	75	1.4	487	5.7	454.3	4.1	1973.2	6.5	3421.7	8.2
Professional and related	423	8.1	1016	11.9	1845.1	16.6	8779.3	28.8	13144.8	31.6
Miscellaneous services	2099	39.4	2186	25.6	3031.9	27.2	3670.7	12.0	3952.8	9.5
Public administration	28	0.4	733	8.6	339.4	3.0	1336.4	4.4	2102.6	5.0
Totals	5329	100.0	8550	100.0	11138.2	100.0	30534.7	100.0	41635.0	100.0

*Over time new industries are born; where this has occurred they are incorporated into the relevant industrial class.
**Productive industry consists of all manufacturing plus mining and construction.
SOURCES 1900 estimated from *Twelfth Census of the US, Special Report – Occupations*, pp. 7–9.
1920 estimated from *Fourteenth Census of the US Population*, Volume IV, 1920; 'Occupations', pp. 35–43.
1940 *Sixteenth Census of the US Population*, Volume 3, 1940; pp. 180–3 (detailed industries).
1970 *Nineteenth Census of the US, Subject Report PC(2)-7B*; 'Industrial Characteristics', pp. 1–4.
1980 *Census of Population 1980*, Volume 1, 'Characteristics of the Population', Chapter D, US Summary, PC80-1-D1-A p. 1/362–1/365.

the 1970s, there were quite different trends in the disaggregated industrial sectors. Four of these sectors have been chosen for detailed examination. In 1900 two industrial sectors, textiles and the clothing and footwear industries (known as apparel and kindred trades in the USA), were responsible for providing 70 per cent of female employment in the productive industry sector. In Britain these two industries provided employment for a third of females in paid work in 1901. In the USA these two industries, in 1900, provided more paid female employment than agriculture. In contrast, employment for females in the engineering industries of the two nations at the beginning of the century was more limited.

By mid-century the significance of the textiles and clothing and footwear industries had declined in both nations to 40 per cent of female employment in the productive industry sector. While these industries fell in both countries in their relative importance as sources of female employment, the USA and British experiences differed. In Britain total employment in these industries fell by one third, but in the USA the numbers of females employed rose by 50 per cent. As these industries declined new industries grew in importance. In 1951, 10 per cent of females employed in Britain were in the engineering industry, a proportion which continued until the 1970s, whereas in 1901 this industry had provided only 2 per cent of all female jobs. However, in the USA the engineering sector was always of less significance than in Britain, providing in 1970 less than 5 per cent of total female employment. (See Figures 3.2 and 3.3.)

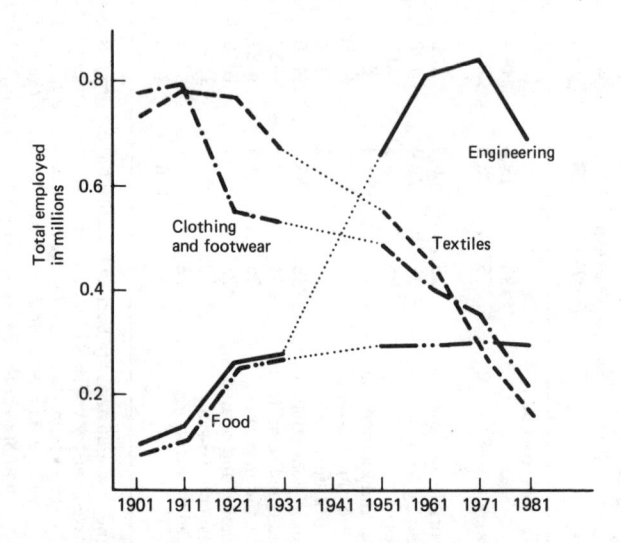

FIGURE 3.2 *Female employment in selected manufacturing industries, Great Britain, 1901-81*
SOURCE   As for Table 3.2.

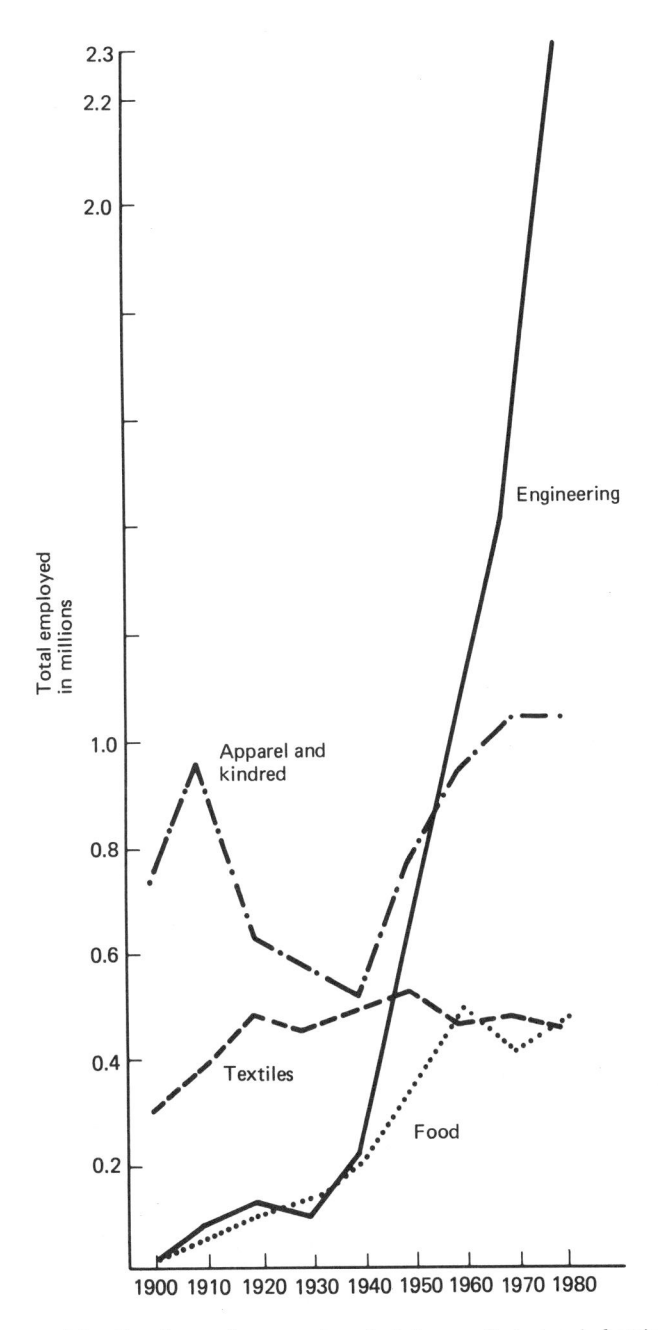

FIGURE 3.3 *Female employment in selected manufacturing industries, United States, 1900-80*

SOURCE   As for Table 3.3.

In the analysis of demographic trends in Chapter 2 the increase in the number of married females who were entering employment was noted. It might be thought that one consequence of this trend would be that wives would have, on average, less time for household chores, e.g. food preparation. Owing to the different definitions of the food manufacturing industry used, it is not possible to make a direct comparison between the USA and Britain. Two trends are identifiable, though. One is that the number of females employed in this sector has grown during this century, although this sector as a source of female employment has always been of little significance. Secondly, the trend in both nations during the first half of the century was for the relative significance of the food manufacturing industry to grow, but after the Second World War when married female employment grew rapidly, its relative significance declined.

THE DEVELOPMENT OF SERVICE INDUSTRY EMPLOYMENT

All the industries that comprise the service industry sector, with the exception of miscellaneous services, have increased their importance, both absolutely and relatively, as areas of female employment during this century. While changes in defining industries cause some distortions over the long term, the magnitude of the changes in this sector are such that the trends are not in dispute. The number of females employed in distribution (i.e. wholesale and retail trade) has increased greatly. In Britain between 1901 and 1971 female employment rose by 340 per cent, although subsequently a modest reduction in its absolute size has occurred. Over the same period in the USA the increase was 2700 per cent. Distribution, until 1971, was the fastest growing sector in both nations for female employment. It was followed in magnitude of growth in both countries by the banking, finance and insurance sector and the professional and scientific sector, which includes teaching and nursing, both of which are major employers of female labour. (See Figures 3.4 and 3.5.)

The exception in the service sector to the upward female employment trends has been miscellaneous services, which in 1900 was the source of 40 per cent of all female employment in Britain, being marginally more important than the entire productive industry sector. Forty per cent of employed US females, in 1900, also found work in the miscellaneous services, double the number engaged in the agricultural sector. Between 1901 and 1951 the numbers employed in this sector in Britain declined by a third, but because total female employment rose throughout the period

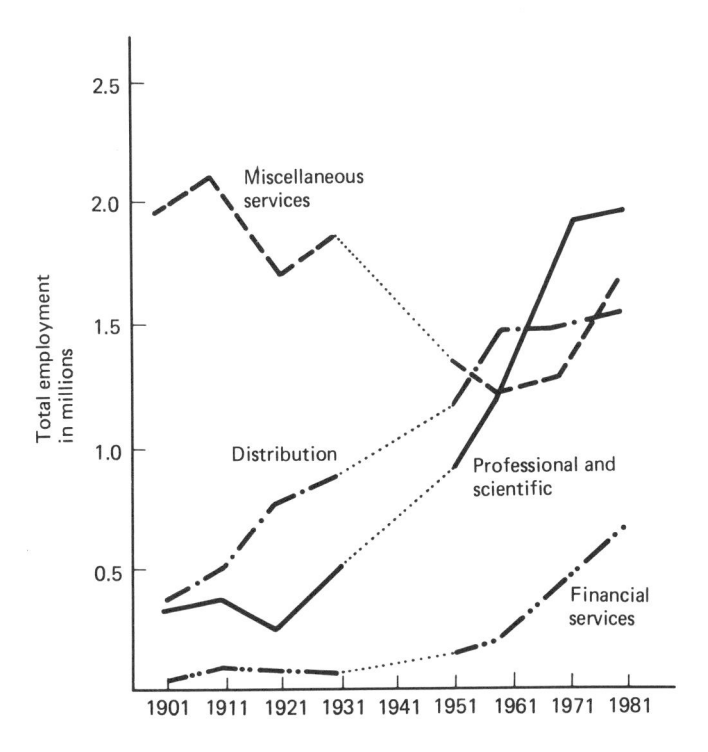

FIGURE 3.4 *Female employment in selected service industries, Great Britain, 1901-81*

SOURCE   As for Table 3.2.

the relative significance of this sector was halved. In the USA total employment in miscellaneous services continued to increase over the same period, in contrast to the British experience. However, the absolute rate of growth of US female employment in this sector was slower than in other sectors and thus its relative significance as an employment source declined by the same order of magnitude as occurred in Britain. In both nations since 1950 total employment in this sector has grown, but the fast increase in female employment elsewhere has meant the relative importance of the miscellaneous services has continued to decline.

Why did miscellaneous services perform differently to the other parts of the service industry sector? The explanation is in the activities that are included in the miscellaneous services sector and in particular with the fortunes of one group of activities, private domestic service. In Britain in

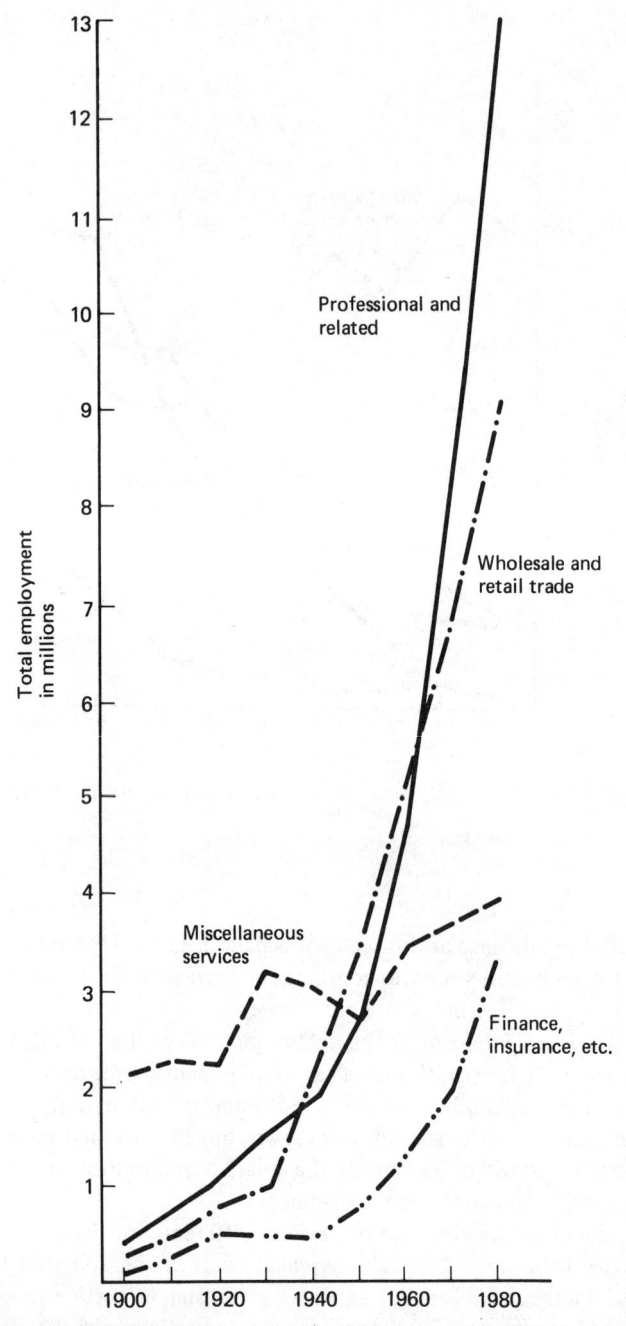

FIGURE 3.5 *Female employment in selected service industries, United States, 1900-80*

SOURCE As for Table 3.3.

Employment Trends in the Twentieth Century   43

1901 private domestic service provided more employment for females than the productive industry sector activities of textiles and clothing and footwear combined. In the USA, private domestic service (i.e. personal services/ private households) employed in 1900 more female labour than the entire productive industry sector. By 1981 female employment in private domestic service in Britain was only 5 per cent of the 1901 figure. In the USA the absolute decline was not as great, but the relative significance of this source of employment for females fell from 16 per cent in 1900 to 2.5 per cent of total USA female employment in 1980. The untypical trends in the miscellaneous services employment pattern owes much to the decline of private domestic service.

CHANGES IN THE RELATIVE FEMALE CONTRIBUTION TO INDUSTRY

The industrial deployment of females has been continuously changing throughout the present century, these changes occurring against a background of economic development and increasing numbers of females entering paid employment.

In 1901, 29 per cent of the total occupied labour force in Britain were female, although this was an aggregage percentage and there were variations between sectors. One can, therefore, define an industry as being one in which females are 'overrepresented', or 'underrepresented', if the female percentage of the workforce in the industry is greater, or less, than the female percentage of the total labour force in the economy.

In the productive industry sector in both countries females have been underrepresented, and the relative contribution of females to the productive industry sector has not increased as rapidly as the female contribution to the total labour force. In productive industries, despite the shift towards lighter industry and the development of new technology, females have become proportionately less significant since the start of the century.

Within the British productive industry sector females have on average provided a quarter of the total labour force. In the USA the female contribution was generally less, and a 25 per cent contribution level was not achieved until the late 1960s. However, Tables 3.4 and 3.5 show that in certain industries there were exceptions; females have always been overrepresented in the textiles and clothing and footwear industries. In the service industry sector the reverse situation has held. Females have been overrepresented relative to their contribution to the labour force and over time the degree of overrepresentation has increased. In Britain females

TABLE 3.4 *Industrial sectors of gainfully occupied British female population as percentage of total in each industrial sector of gainfully occupied population, selected years*

Industrial sector	1901	1951	1971	1981
Productive sector, including	25.4	25.6	24.8	23.5
Food, drink and tobacco	24.1	37.1	39.3	39.8
Engineering	6.0	20.9	22.9	21.1
Textiles	61.2	59.3	46.5	49.2
Clothing and footwear	67.2	70.5	73.5	71.2
Service sector, consisting of	52.9	44.2	52.2	54.7
Distribution	26.2	43.1	51.8	51.1
Insurance and banking	1.9	34.5	50.1	46.5
Professional and scientific	50.2	58.6	64.1	69.7
Miscellaneous	77.5	58.5	54.7	58.8
Public administration	7.0	15.9	28.8	38.6
All employment	29.2	30.8	36.7	42.6

SOURCE   as for Table 3.2.

TABLE 3.5 *Industrial sectors of gainfully occupied US female population as percentage of total in each industrial sector of gainfully occupied population, selected years*

Industrial sector	1900	1950	1970	1980
Agriculture, forestry and fishing	9.4	8.6	11.9	17.9
Productive sector, including	18.5	20.0	24.4	26.5
Food and kindred trades	7.8	23.0	27.9	30.5
Engineering	4.0	17.8	23.0	26.0
Textile mill products	51.3	42.5	46.9	47.5
Apparel and kindred trades	80.9	71.0	78.2	78.3
Service sector	30.1	41.7	49.8	53.9
Wholesale and retail trade	12.8	33.9	41.8	45.8
Finance, insurance, etc.	13.3	41.1	67.2	58.1
Professional and related	36.0	58.8	63.5	66.4
Miscellaneous	36.9	49.2	52.7	48.4
Public administration	9.0	26.2	30.8	40.8
All employment	18.2	28.2	38.1	42.6

SOURCE   as for Table 3.3.

have come to constitute over half the service industry labour force, and a similar position has developed in the USA since 1970. In each of the industries which contribute to the British service industry sector there has been a growth in the female contribution relative to the total numbers employed, with the one exception of miscellaneous services, but even this one exception did not occur in the USA.

In the twentieth century the industrial distribution of female employment on occasions differed between Britain and the USA. In Britain, until the 1960s, productive industry employment grew in parallel with service industry employment, but in the USA this was not so. While total female employment in the productive industry sector grew in parallel with male employment in this sector, its significance declined relative to the service industries, which grew more rapidly. Within the general trends there were contrary movements. The textile and clothing and footwear industries, while of great significance for female employment in 1900, became less important over time. Simultaneously new knowledge-based industries grew as areas of female employment. A similar process occurred in the service industries. Private domestic service, where in the early years of the century a high percentage of females were employed, has declined in significance as a source of employment. It has been overtaken in importance by a range of other service industry activities that have developed in response to economic change.

OCCUPATIONAL DISTRIBUTION OF FEMALE EMPLOYMENT

With the evolution of the economy there are simultaneously modifications in the skill content of occupations. Certain occupations will sub-divide, others will merge, and some will disappear altogether. Those responsible for conducting censuses regularly define and redefine the content of occupations. The census results are the only source of continuous information on occupational distribution over a long period, but however informative the results may be for one census year, the changes in occupational definition make comparable analysis over the twentieth century extremely difficult.

One approach that helps to overcome the problem of comparability is to aggregate occupations with identifiable characteristics into a limited number of broad 'occupational classes'. This approach provides the possibility of identifying general trends but at a possible cost of losing insights into variations about the trend within specific occupations. In the British censuses this century the number of occupations identified, together with their content, has varied. Routh (1980), however, used an approach which grouped the occupations identified in the censuses between 1911 and 1971 into nine broad 'occupational classes'. This approach is adopted here to explain the occupational distribution of British female employment, with Routh's results updated to 1981. A comparable exercise has also been undertaken using USA census data from 1910 to 1980. While such an approach will not give complete accuracy, it provides a data base for an examination of the long-term trends.

In Table 3.6 the 'professional class' has been relatively unimportant as a source of female employment, although the significance of this class has clearly grown. In 1911 only 7 per cent of employed females were in this class but by 1981 the proportion was 16 per cent. When the professional class is sub-divided into higher professions and lower professions an uneven distribution between the two categories becomes clear. Some 95 per cent of females in the professional class are employed in the lower professions, and within this group four out of five have always been employed in the two occupations of nursing and teaching.

While strict comparability of British and US occupational data is not possible, the summary of the US census material in Table 3.7 reveals a similar pattern to the British one. It should be noted, though, that the US situation has changed between 1970 and 1980. In 1910-11 there was a remarkable similarity in the US and British situations with respect to the percentage of females employed in the professional occupations of nursing and teaching, in Britain 78 per cent and in the USA 79 per cent. Sixty years on, in Britain 75 per cent of the females employed in professional work were still in these two occupations, and the 3 per cent shift may owe more to changes in definition than to the widening of female opportunities into other forms of professional employment. The US data suggest that professional employment widened more rapidly and significantly than in Britain. Employment in the two occupations identified above provided, in 1970, 60 per cent of the number of jobs for females in the professions. This widening of professional occupations continued in the USA between 1970 and 1980, by which time nursing and teaching represented only 50 per cent of all female professional employment, while in Britain the figure was 65 per cent.

On either side of the Atlantic female employment in the professions has risen continuously, and these occupations have become increasingly significant as a source of female employment. Only in the USA have females made serious inroads into a wider range of professional occupations than was the case in 1900, and this has only occurred over the last generation.

TABLE 3.6 Occupational class of gainfully occupied female population in Britain, selected years

Occupational class*	1911 Number (000's)	%	1931 Number (000's)	%	1951 Number (000's)	%	1971 Number (000's)	%	1981** Number (000's)	%
Professional										
Higher	11	0.2	18	0.3	36	0.5	50	0.5	125	1.4
Lower	352	6.5	428	6.8	567	8.2	1000	11.0	1322	14.5
Employers and proprietors	232	4.3	278	4.4	223	3.2	251	2.8	292	3.2
Managers and administrators	125	2.3	100	1.6	189	2.7	321	3.5	458	5.0
Clerical workers	179	3.3	648	10.3	1414	20.4	2466	27.0	2643	28.9
Foremen, inspectors and supervisors	10	0.2	28	0.5	79	1.1	168	1.8	184	2.0
Skilled manual	1344	24.8	1196	19.1	884	12.8	775	8.5	560	6.1
Semi-skilled manual	2898	53.4	3101	49.5	2988	43.1	3005	32.9	2747	30.0
Unskilled manual	275	5.0	467	7.5	550	8.0	1098	12.0	820	9.0
Totals	5425	100.0	6264	100.0	6930	100.0	9138	100.0	9151	100.0

*Occupation class as defined by Routh (1980), Appendix A, pp. 221-5.
**1981 figures and percentages estimated by applying criteria determined by Routh (1980).
SOURCE 1901-71 Routh, G., *Occupation and Pay in Great Britain 1906-1979*, Macmillan, London, 1980, pp. 6-7.
          1981 Census of Population.

TABLE 3.7 Occupational class of gainfully occupied female population in USA, selected years

Occupation class*	1910 Number (000's)	1910 %	1930 Number (000's)	1930 %	1950 Number (000's)	1950 %	1970 Number (000's)	1970 %	1980 Number (000's)	1980 %
Professional, excluding nurses and non-college teachers	180	2.2	437	4.1	641	4.1	1975	5.9	3417	8.3
Nurses and non-college teachers	555	6.9	1089	10.1	1306	8.3	2880	9.4	3500	8.5
Proprietors, managers and administrators, including farm	484	6.0	586	5.4	791	5.0	1156	3.8	3007	7.3
Clerical and kindred	589	7.3	1987	18.5	4273	27.2	10515	34.4	14502	35.2
Sales workers	461	5.7	907	8.4	1324	8.4	2249	7.4	2796	6.8
Craft and kindred	611	7.6	245	2.3	237	1.5	548	1.8	752	1.8
Operatives	1229	15.2	1774	16.5	3068	19.5	4570	15.0	4426	10.7
Labourers	1449	18.6	700	6.5	586	3.7	489	1.6	846	2.1
Service										
Household	1310	16.3	1635	15.2	1359	8.6	1186	3.9	1015	2.5
Non-household	1158	14.3	1425	13.3	1918	12.2	5061	16.6	7019	17.0
Totals	8076	100.0	10752	100.0	15736	100.0	30535	100.0	41243	100.0

*Figures for 1910 and 1930 are based on the same occupational classification system. There have been subsequent changes in the occupational classification system.

SOURCES 1910 and 1930 *Fifteenth Census of the US, Population Volume V*, 1930; 'Occupations', pp. 40–9.
1950: *Seventeenth Census of the US, Special Report PE No. 1B*: 'Occupational Characteristics', 1B/15-1B/22.
1970: *Nineteenth Census of the US, Subject Report PC(2)7A*; Occupational Characteristics p. 1–11.
1980: *Census of Population 1980, Volume 1, Characteristics of the Population*, Chapter D, US Summary PC80-1-D1-A p. 1/166–1/175.

Employment Trends in the Twentieth Century

Within the second broad class of occupations, 'employers, managers and administrators', only a marginal change in their significance as an employment source for females in Britain has taken place, although the magnitude of the change suggests it may be the consequence of modified definitions in the census. In the USA, a similar pattern is identifiable until 1970. As in Britain, the number of females in this occupational class increased, but more slowly than the aggregate growth in female employment, and hence its relative significance as a source of female employment declined. However, after 1970 there was a considerable increase in the USA in the number of females employed, and its significance as an employment source began to increase, reversing the previous long-term trend. Unlike Britain, where information is available, it is not possible over the long term to identify, or quantify, employment trends in the lower levels of management from US data. For Britain the data indicate a growing relative significance of the foremen and supervisory occupations, but it also indicates that few females have been employed in such occupations.

While some trends relating to the above occupational classes are identifiable, these occupations are of relatively little importance to the occupational distribution of female labour in either Britain or the USA. The occupations associated with clerical or manual work are the crucial ones, these occupations together being the source of over 80 per cent of female employment in Britain until the 1970s. In the USA an almost identical situation existed, the 1970 census recording 81 per cent of employed females as being in the clerical and manual occupations. Although a movement towards the higher occupational classes has occurred in both nations over the last decade, by 1981 75 per cent of females employed in Britain were still in the clerical and manual occupations, but in the USA the figure had fallen by a quarter to 62 per cent.

Clerical work in Britain provided employment for 180,000 females in 1911, i.e. 3 per cent of total female employment. Numbers grew rapidly, and by 1971 the number of females employed in this occupation class had increased by 1300 per cent to nearly two and a half million, and during the decade to 1981 a further increase in female employment took place. By 1981 nearly one in three of employed British females followed clerical occupations. By 1910 the clerical occupations were already significant as a source of female employment in the USA, with 7.4 per cent of the total female labour force being engaged in them. Over the following seventy years the number of females in these occupations increased by 2,350 per cent, and by 1980 over one in three USA females were employed in clerical occupations. The growth in the numbers of females and the relative significance of clerical occupations occurred partially because the number of clerical workers increased. In Britain the numbers quadrupled between 1911 and 1971. However, the main reason is that there has been an increase in the female percentage of the total workforce employed in these occupations. In 1911 one in five of the British clerical workforce was female, and in the USA it was one in three in 1910. By 1980 four out of five clerical workers on both sides of the Atlantic were female. A change of this magnitude reflects not only the acceptance of females in the office environment but also changes in the content of the work clerical workers are expected to undertake. Clerical work was possibly the area of least resistance to the introduction of females during the two war periods, especially the 1914–18 war. However, overemphasis on the effect of the war periods on the growth of the female contribution to the clerical occupations would be wrong. Gross (1968) has suggested that the process really began as early as 1880 in the USA.

One in four British employed females in 1911 was classified as a skilled manual worker. In the USA the figure was one in forty, although this substantial difference was partly due to differences in methods of classifying occupations, illustrating the problem of making comparisons of occupational distributions between different countries. By 1981 only one in twenty-five British females in employment qualified for classification as a skilled manual worker, the number of skilled manual females falling by over two-thirds. The main reason for this contraction in numbers of females classified in skilled manual occupations is related to the changes in industrial sector employment. In 1911 over 80 per cent of the females in skilled manual occupations were in either the textile or the clothing and footwear industries. The decline of these industries and the technical changes which were designed to deskill the tasks undertaken by females in skilled occupations combined together to bring about a reduction of 80 per cent of these two industries' skilled female labour forces, down from 1.1 million in 1911 to under 200,000 in 1981. When allowance for the changes in these two industries is made, the number of females in other skilled occupations doubled, and the significance of skilled manual occupations other than those associated with textiles and clothing and footwear as a source of employment rose.

The number of females in Britain identified as pursuing semi-skilled manual occupations remained at approximately three million between 1911 and 1971, but in the following ten years there was a 25 per cent decline. Over the same period female employment rose and thus the semi-skilled manual occupations declined in their relative importance for female employment. Every other female in paid employment in 1911 was in a semi-skilled occupation, and by 1981 one in four were so classified. Major changes in the composition of the semi-skilled occupations have occurred, in particular the demise of the household domestic service employees, who for the purpose of the British statistics were regarded collectively as semi-skilled. Thus while the semi-skilled employment figure in 1971 is similar to the 1911 figure, there has been a replacement of the 1.25 million jobs which disappeared with the decline of paid domestic service. However, many of the new semi-skilled jobs for females that have emerged in Britain are often identical in job content to those previously undertaken by females in paid domestic service but are now located in hotels, restaurants and catering (see Routh, 1980). Finally, the significance of the unskilled female occupations in Britain exhibited an upward trend until 1971, the number employed quadrupling, and the percentage of the female labour force following these occupations more than doubling. Since 1971 the numbers employed in unskilled occupations and their significance as an employment source have fallen. The unskilled female occupations were in both the productive industry and service industry sectors and many of these occupations contained work tasks similar to work undertaken by females in the home. For example, in 1971, 40 per cent of the females engaged in unskilled occupations were charwomen and office cleaners.

US census data permit a similar examination of the female contribution to manual employment. However, unlike the categorisation of skilled workers' occupations adopted by Routh, the US data identify a more restricted class, 'craft and kindred trades'. This occupational class contained only 2.5 per cent of US female employees in 1910, and while the numbers employed in this class had quadrupled by 1980, its relative significance as a female employment source had fallen below 2 per cent.

While US data include an operative class, this is not comparable with the British semi-skilled worker group. Firstly, US census data classify household domestic staff separately, and, secondly, textile workers who in Britain are classified as skilled workers are classified in US statistics as operatives. The relative significance of the operative class in the USA halved between 1900 and 1980, a reflection of the decline of the textiles and the apparel and kindred trades industries as a source of female employment.

The difference in definition between the British 'unskilled' and the US 'labourers' are not as significant as in the two previous examples, but there is another difference which makes comparisons unrealistic. In the early part of the twentieth century a high proportion of US females counted in this category worked in agriculture, a sector which has subsequently reduced its employment levels. If allowance is made for the farm sector, then the numbers and significance of the non-farm labourers increased, but not to the level found in Britain.

Detailed information on other occupational classes is available from the US data. At the beginning of the century the foremost occupational group was personal services/private households. In this occupational group the number of females employed increased between 1910 and 1950, but since then numbers have declined by 25 per cent. The changes in the numbers employed in personal service/private households occurred against a background of increasing female employment, and the relative significance of this occupational group has fallen. In the USA in 1910, one woman in six was employed in this occupational class, but by 1980 this had become one in forty. Other female service workers, i.e. those not directly employed in households, have, as in Britain, risen in number continuously. The growth was faster than the increase in the size of the total female labour force, resulting in these occupations becoming relatively more significant. The same has been true of female sales workers. However, although the number of females employed in this occupation has continued to grow since the 1950s, the rate of growth has been less than that of the female labour force. For the non-household service occupational group this did not occur, and its significance as an employment source has continued to grow.

When the occupational classes in both countries are divided into the two groups 'clerical and manual' and 'all others', i.e. professional, managerial, etc., then the trend has been for the latter group to grow in relative significance. The relative rates of change, however, varied in size and timing, reflecting the different pace of economic development in the two countries. In the USA the relative contribution of the higher professional occupations began an upward trend in the 1950s, but it is only since 1970 that the increase has been rapid, and nothing of that character appears to have occurred in Britain. One commentator on the British 1981 census, Beacham (1984), suggests that the number of women working rose in the traditional areas of 'women's work', i.e. cleaners, cooks, waitresses, clerks and typists.

THE RELATIVE FEMALE CONTRIBUTION TO THE OCCUPATIONAL CLASSES

The female contribution to total employment in the USA rose from 21 per cent to 42 per cent, and in Britain from 30 per cent to 43 per cent, between 1910-11 and 1980-1, but over the same period the female contribution to specific occupational classes varied.

Employment Trends in the Twentieth Century

In 1911 30 per cent of the British labour force were female, but when the occupational groups identified above are examined individually, wide variations are found in the level of female representation. For example, in the higher professional class only 6 per cent of the labour force were female. In contrast, in the lower professional class females constituted 63 per cent of the labour force (see Table 3.8).

TABLE 3.8 *Occupational class of gainfully occupied British female population as percentage of total in each occupational class of gainfully occupied population, selected years*

Occupational class	1911	1931	1951	1971	1981
Professional					
Higher	6.0	7.5	8.3	6.1	11.1
Lower	62.9	58.8	53.5	51.4	56.4
Employers and proprietors	18.8	19.8	19.9	23.8	21.5
Managers and administrators	19.9	13.0	15.2	15.6	18.7
Clerical workers	20.2	44.2	58.8	70.9	71.0
Foremen, inspectors and supervisors	4.2	8.7	13.4	17.4	20.4
Skilled manual	24.0	21.3	15.8	14.4	14.5
Semi-skilled manual	40.0	42.1	40.7	47.6	44.8
Unskilled manual	15.5	15.0	20.3	36.8	42.0
All occupations	29.6	29.8	30.8	36.5	39.9

SOURCE as for Table 3.6.

In Britain females were only overrepresented in two of the occupational classes in 1911. One, the lower professionals, reflected the numbers of females in the nursing and teaching professions. The other was the semi-skilled occupations, which incorporated those employed in the household domestic service occupations. In the USA female overrepresentation is identifiable in the corresponding occupational classes (see Table 3.9). Where the USA differed from Britain is that by 1910 there was already female overrepresentation in the clerical occupational category. By the 1980s females continued to be overrepresented in the occupational classes identified above. In Britain the level of overrepresentation fell in these two occupational classes, but the outstanding change was with respect to clerical staff. By 1921 over 40 per cent of those employed in this occupational class were female, at a time when only 30 per cent of the total workforce were female. The level of female overrepresentation in the clerical occupational class continued to grow. By 1980 over 70 per cent of

TABLE 3.9 *Occupational class of gainfully occupied US female population as percentage of total in each occupational class of gainfully occupied population, selected years*

Occupational class	1910	1930	1950	1970	1980
Professional, excluding nurses and non-college teachers	17.5	23.0	19.7	22.7	30.7
Nurses and non-college teachers	81.4	80.3	81.5	76.7	78.3
Proprietors, managers and administrators, including farm	6.7	7.6	8.6	14.6	24.2
Clerical and kindred	34.3	49.4	62.2	73.8	80.1
Sales workers	14.5	18.3	34.0	40.1	45.3
Craft and kindred	11.5	3.6	3.1	4.9	6.0
Operatives	22.5	23.2	24.0	31.8	32.0
Labourers	17.9	11.5	10.1	10.2	14.2
Services					
Household	83.3	81.8	94.9	96.9	97.5
Non-household	46.8	50.8	44.9	55.8	58.9
All occupations	21.2	22.0	27.8	37.2	41.9

SOURCE as for Table 3.7.

employed females in Britain were in three occupational classes, lower professional, clerical and semi-skilled, although these occupations employed only 30 per cent of males. In the unskilled occupational class an increase in the level of female representation also took place. In 1911 females were underrepresented in this occupation, but by 1971 female representation equalled their contribution to the total labour force. Since then, however, their percentage representation has fallen.

US identifiable patterns of representation in occupational classes are similar. Females' overrepresentation continued in nursing and non-college teaching and among the semi-skilled occupations, while the female proportion of those employed in clerical occupations has followed the same path as in Britain. In the more narrowly defined US labourers class the level of underrepresentation has, in contrast to Britain, increased. While female employment has grown during this century, and females have become a more significant part of a larger labour force, their distribution over identified occupational classes continues to reflect past patterns. This led Waldman and McEaddy (1974) to remark that contemporary figures on US female employment bore a striking resemblance to those of yester-year. At that time, i.e. the 1970s, females on both sides of the Atlantic were

Employment Trends in the Twentieth Century 55

overrepresented in a small number of occupations, and their contribution to the labour force was concentrated in only a small number of jobs; by 1980-1 females continued to be overrepresented in the same broad occupational groups.

Against the background of increasing female participation in the labour forces of both Britain and the USA this chapter has sought to identify the distribution of female employees over major industrial sectors and occupational classes, and the changes that have taken place in these distributions during this century. It has also been possible to relate the female contribution to the total employment in these sub-groups and thus to identify where the female contribution has been higher or lower than anticipated. The study of the female contribution to specific occupations is one that has attracted the attention of other commentators on female employment, e.g. Oppenheimer (1976) and Hakim (1979). The approach adopted in these studies is one of examining the 'occupational segregation' that may arise given the sex of individuals in the labour force. The observations in this chapter provide evidence that men and women often do different types of work, that certain industries have an above-average proportion of males or females in their labour force, and that certain occupations are predominantly male or female. It is difficult to find out to what extent occupational segregation has changed due to legislative changes which have been introduced over the last twenty years, and to what extent other factors have caused it to alter. In the period between the last two British censuses, 1971 and 1981, female employment has increased both in number and relative to males, and in this period equal pay and equal opportunities legislation has come into effect.

The 1981 census in Britain adopted a new approach to the classification of occupations which complicates the analysis of the changing occupational structure of the female labour force between 1971 and 1981. However, although there are no comparable figures for the detailed occupational divisions used in the 1981 census, there are provided comparable figures for 1971 and 1981, broken down into 162 broader occupational groups. There has been some evening out of the sex distribution of employment, but as Tables 3.10 and 3.11 show, the overall effect has been marginal.

Women have entered occupations that are male-dominated at quite a fast rate, but since still only a small proportion of the female labour force are employed in these occupations the overall occupational segregation pattern is more influenced by what happens to the much larger number of females employed in certain female-dominated occupations. For example, the number of females in the legal profession grew by 417 per cent between

TABLE 3.10 Occupational segregation, 1971 and 1981, England and Wales

% of employed females in occupations where % of females was	1971	1981	% of employed males in occupations where % of males was	1971	1981
90%+	24.3	25.1	90%+	54.9	44.1
80%+	38.7	38.8	80%+	70.3	75.5
70%+	47.9	46.1	70%+	77.4	80.2
60%+	73.4	72.8	60%+	81.8	84.9
50%+	80.0	80.3	50%+	83.9	83.3

SOURCE *1981 Census of Population*, Economic Activity Table A.

1971 and 1981, and the proportion of females in this occupational group in 1981 was nearly four times its 1971 value. However, the total number of females employed in this occupational group was still only 0.01 per cent of the total number of women in employment, and the female percentage of this occupation group only rose from 3.8 per cent to 14.5 per cent. On the other hand, the number of females employed as clerks only grew by 13 per cent, and the female proportion of this occupational group increased from 61.5 per cent to 69.7 per cent, but as 17.5 per cent of all employed women work in this group the total effect on the occupational structure of the female labour force was quite significant.

The figures in Tables 3.10 and 3.11 suggest that females are making some inroads into male-dominated occupations, but males are not entering female-dominated occupations in any number. The pattern does alter depending upon the level of segregation that is considered. For example, female employment growth was higher in the occupations that were more than 70 per cent male in 1971 than in those which were more than 50 per cent male, and there was less growth in the number of females in those occupations that were more than 70 per cent female in 1971 than in those that were more than 50 per cent female. However, the overall progress towards sex equality in the occupational distribution of the labour force has been slow.

Studies into the degree and change in occupational segregation in the USA can be divided into two categories. A number of researchers have sought to examine the long term, while more recent research has been concerned with the more recent past. In the first category the pioneering work was undertaken by Gross (1968), who based his study on the detailed occupations in the censuses of 1900 to 1960. Gross reached an initial con-

TABLE 3.11 Changes in occupational segregation, 1971–81, England and Wales

Employment in occupations which in 1971 were:	1971 Male	1971 Female	1981 Male	1981 Female	Change 1971–81 Male	Change 1971–81 Female
More than 70% female:	543 190	3 756 180	518 730	3 814 070	−24 460	57 890
(% of total)	(12.6)	(87.4)	(12.0)	(88.0)	(−4.5)	(+1.5)
More than 70% male	10 052 380	933 920	9 663 690	1 124 550	−854 390	190 630
(% of total)	(91.8)	(8.2)	(89.6)	(10.4)	(−8.2)	(+20.4)
More than 50% female:	2 184 810	6 278 790	1 953 640	6 518 940	−231 117	240 150
(% of total)	(25.8)	(74.2)	(23.1)	(76.9)	(−10.6)	(+3.8)
More than 50% male:	11 407 650	1 494 540	10 466 980	1 680 780	−940 670	186 240
	(88.4)	(11.6)	(86.2)	(13.8)	(−8.2)	(+12.5)

SOURCE *1981 Census of Population*, Economic Activity Table A.

clusion that the degree of sexual segregation remained largely unchanged, but his statistical analysis did indicate that male occupations in 1900 had, by 1960, become more segregated, while female occupations were less so. These conclusions were challenged by Williams (1976, 1979), who incorporated data from the 1970 census. Williams's results identified a modest decline in occupational segregation and drew attention to the fact that the rate of decline varied between decades. The work undertaken more recently permits consideration of the effect of legislation in the 1960s, the Civil Rights Act 1964 and the amendment to the Fair Labor Standards Act 1963. Using data from the 1979 Current Population Survey, and paying special attention to the young, Meyer and Maes (1983) concluded that the previously existing patterns of occupational segregation persisted in the new generation of women workers who were entering the labour market. Rytina and Bianchi (1984) drew upon the 1970 and 1980 censuses. They concluded that there had been a decline in occupational segregation over the decade, but their conclusion should be treated with caution, for what appears to have taken place was a growth in sex-neutral occupations, while sex-differentiated occupations had either remained constant or declined in size. Where occupational segregation previously existed it remained, where it had not existed it had not been introduced. There was only one unexplained exception: large increases in the female share of certain professional and managerial occupations took place.

Over the last decade, then, one can conclude that in both Britain and the USA there has been an evening out of the sex distribution of occupations, but overall progress has been slow. Although female entry into some occupations, such as the professions, has been quite rapid, the overall employment distribution has been only marginally affected by these changes. Most women work in occupations that have been traditionally female-dominated, and as relatively few men have entered these occupations sex inequalities in occupational distribution remain substantial.

4 The Supply of Female Labour

During the course of the twentieth century the supply of female labour for paid employment has increased substantially. The supply of female labour has not simply adjusted automatically to meet the increased demand generated by the expansion of the predominantly female employing industries and occupations. Although demand changes have had an important influence, the female labour supply is also influenced by a number of other factors, the relative contribution of which economists have attempted to identify and to estimate.

The term 'female labour supply' is usually assumed to mean the total number of women in the labour force. For example, it might be said that according to the Great Britain 1981 census of population the total female labour supply was 9 878 218, i.e. the number of economically active females. However, out of this total only 57 per cent worked full-time (defined as over thirty hours a week), while 36 per cent worked part-time and 7 per cent did not work at all, being either unemployed or sick. Thus this simple definition can give a misleading picture of the true quantity of female labour supplied. In the context of economic theory the 'female labour supply' describes the relationship between the number of units of labour that females would be willing to supply in a specified time period at a given wage rate, e.g. X hours per week at dollars Y per hour. The actual size of the female labour force at any one time can then be described as the 'quantity of labour supplied at the current wage'. However, labour markets rarely adjust to a perfect equilibrium in response to wage changes, as supply and demand theory suggests, and excess demand (i.e. unfilled vacancies) and excess supply (i.e. unemployment) often exist simultaneously. In this chapter the term 'female labour supply' is used in the usual looser sense to mean the number of females in the labour force, except in some instances, where the question of the number of hours supplied is also considered. The spread of part-time employment has attracted more attention to the variations in hours of work supplied by females, and recent research in this area has been helped by the publication of more statistics on hours of work and by the development of statistical techniques that allow empirical testing of the hours of work relationship.

Research into the changes in the female labour supply has centred almost exclusively on seeking to explain the factors influencing the Married Female Economic Activity Rate (MFAR). Although the dramatic increase in the MFAR has perhaps been the most important single factor affecting the size of the female labour force in the past few decades, it must be remembered that the supply of female labour also depends on the size of the married female population, and the size and economic activity rate of the non-married female population of working age, and the hours of work of both.

In Table 4.1 changes in the population and economic activity are shown for females aged 15-64 in Great Britain according to marital status. It can be seen that the overall growth of 2.9 million in the number of economi-

TABLE 4.1 *Changes in female labour supply, Great Britain, 1951-81 (aged 15-64 years, thousands except percentages)*

Females	1951	1961	1971	1981	1951-81 Actual change	% change
Total population	16 912	17 187	17 031	17 311	+ 399	+ 2.4
Total economically active	6 806	7 579	8 882	9 702	+2 896	+ 42.6
Total activity rate (%)	40.2	44.1	52.1	56.0	+ 15.8	+ 39.3
Married population	11 163	12 031	12 168	11 528	+ 365	+ 3.3
Married economically active	2 608	3 866	5 664	6 211	+3 603	+138.2
Married activity rate (%)	23.4	32.1	46.5	53.9	+ 20.5	+130.3
Single population	4 579	4 062	3 688	4 272	− 307	− 6.7
Single economically active	3 654	3 158	2 540	2 660	− 994	− 27.2
Single activity rate (%)	79.8	77.7	68.9	62.3	− 17.5	− 21.5
Widowed and divorced population	1 169	1 094	1 175	1 510	+ 341	+ 29.2
Widowed and divorced economically active	489	555	658	830	+ 341	+ 69.7
Widowed and divorced activity rate (%)	41.8	50.7	56.0	55.0	+ 13.2	+ 31.6

SOURCE *Censuses of Population*, Great Britain, Economic Activity Tables.

cally active females between 1951 and 1981 was the net result of a 3.6 million increase in the number of married women economically active, plus approximately a third of a million widowed and divorced women, less a decrease of one million in the number of economically active single females. The growth in the number of economically active married women was the compounded result of a 3.3 per cent growth in population plus a 130 per cent increase in the MFAR. For widowed and divorced women the population grew by 29.2 per cent and the activity rate by 31.6 per cent, and for single females both population and the activity rate fell, by 6.7 per cent and 21.5 per cent of their original values respectively. Thus the rise in the MFAR would in fact have increased the size of the British female labour force by more than the amount of the actual increase that did take place, had it not been modified by a drop in the single female labour force. In the USA the female population of all marital status groups increased and there are not such striking differences between them as in the British case. Although the largest growth in the US female labour force, in terms both of numbers and growth in the activity rate, has come from married females, the population and activity rate of single females have also both risen. The fastest growing group has been divorced women, who also have a very high economic activity rate, being around 75 per cent, but they still only made up just under 10 per cent of the total US female labour force in 1980.

There has been relatively little work undertaken on the determinants of the activity rates of non-married females. Although it is true that the proportion of non-married females in the British female labour force aged 15 to 64 declined from 61 per cent in 1951 to 36 per cent in 1981, this still remains a significant contribution which perhaps deserves more attention. The drop in the activity rate for single females in Britain has been due primarily to the growth in the number of females in full-time education. It should be noted in comparing the years that the figures in Table 4.1 are not adjusted to allow for the raising of the minimum school leaving age to 16 in 1973. If one did make this adjustment then the single female activity rate for this more restricted age group would only have dropped to 69.4 per cent by 1981. The rise in the single female activity rate identified in some published US statistics is in the same way exaggerated between 1960 and 1970 by the switch to the use of data on females over 16 instead of those over 14. Age profiles of the female activity rate by marital status are shown in Figures 4.1 and 4.2. In both Britain and the USA the rise in the activity rate for widowed and divorced females taken together has been rather less than that experienced by

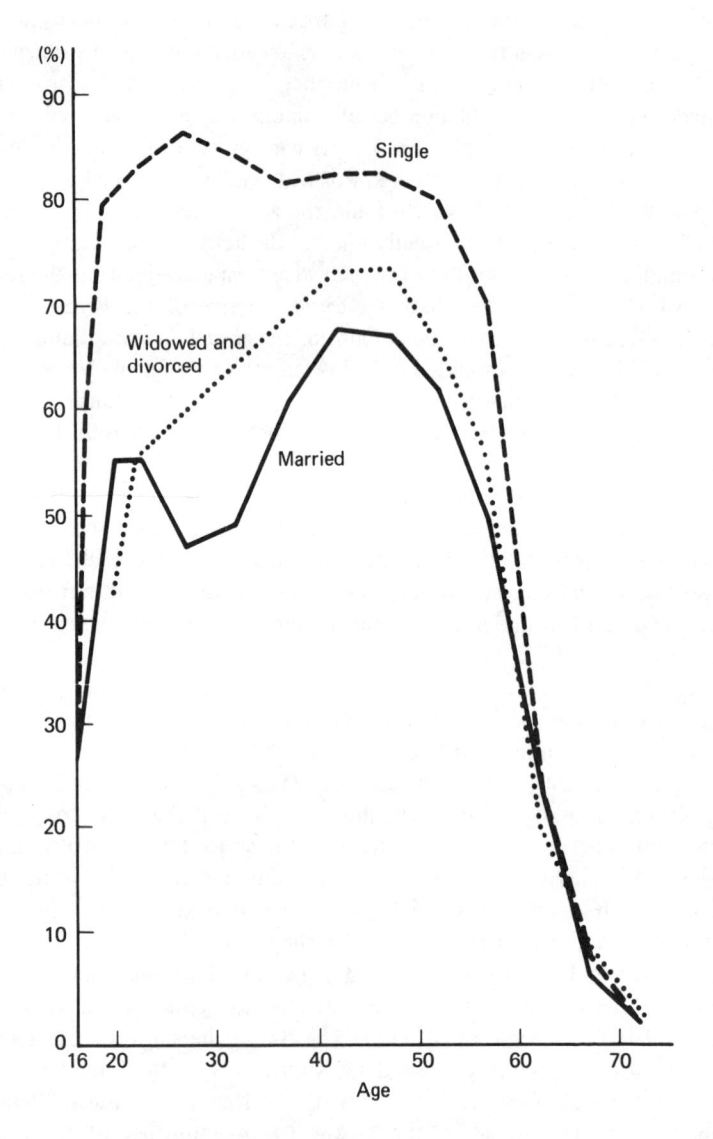

FIGURE 4.1 *Female economic activity rates by age and marital status, Great Britain, 1981*
SOURCE *1981 Census of Population*, Economic Activity Table 4B.

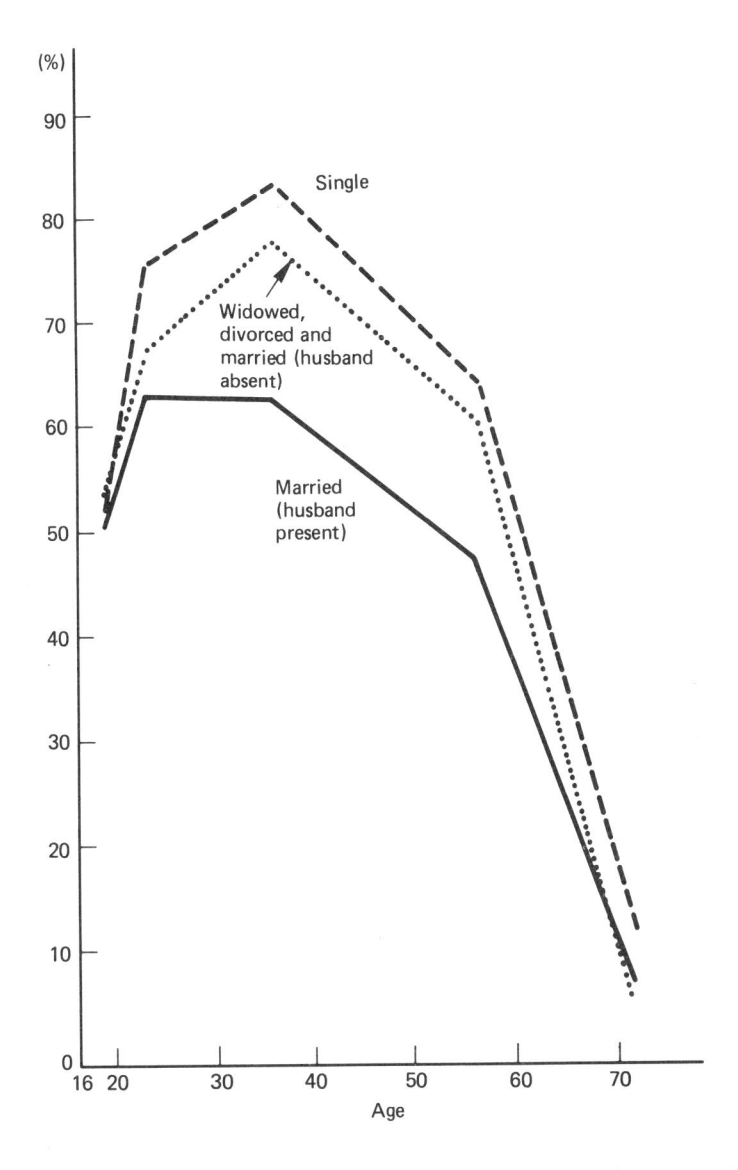

FIGURE 4.2 *Female economic activity rates by age and marital status, United States, 1982*
SOURCE *Statistical Abstract of the US, 1984*, Table 682.
NOTE Activity rate = per cent of civilian non-institutional population of each group in civilian labour force.

married women, but the figure was relatively higher to start with in both countries in the 1950s.

Having put the contribution of the changes in the MFAR to the growth in the total supply of female labour into perspective, the extensive body of literature that exists on the MFAR can now be examined. Studies usually fall into two categories:

1. *Cross-section studies.* These seek to identify the factors that affect the MFAR, and to estimate the relative strengths of these different influences by statistical analysis of cross-section data.
2. *Time trend studies.* These usually investigate how the factors which have been identified in cross-section studies as influencing the MFAR have changed over time and consequently caused the MFAR to alter.

Although the long-term rise in the married female labour force is perhaps the most interesting phenomenon that researchers have sought to explain, there are other reasons for studying the determinants of the MFAR. One needs to know what affects the MFAR to be able to make forecasts about future labour force trends, and the government is interested in the effect that policy measures such as changes in income tax rates, social security payments or child care provision might have on the female labour force. At a microeconomic level, Mallier and Rosser (1980d) have shown how information on the factors influencing the MFAR can help explain local labour market conditions, which might be useful to government agencies in tackling problems such as high localised female unemployment.

ECONOMIC METHODOLOGY

In economic studies of the MFAR it is usual to go straight to the analysis of an 'economic model' of the labour supply decision process of a married woman without any explanation of the methodology on which this whole approach is based. The few lines below are designed to clear up any misunderstandings about the economist's rather unrealistic picture of the labour supply decision process that may arise for those who are not completely familiar with this methodology.

When economists say that they are trying to 'explain' the factors influencing a married woman's decision to participate in the labour force, they do not mean that they are trying to discover the reasons that the woman herself would say had influenced her decision. What economists mean is that they are attempting to identify those observable characteristics, such as education level or income of husband, that are statistically correlated with economic activity. Unrealistic assumptions about the behaviour of individuals can be justified if the model that is developed upon these assumptions provides reasonably accurate predictions. For this reason economists do not place a great reliance on 'attitude-to-work' questionnaire surveys. A married woman's decision to seek employment is usually the result of a multitude of different factors, and it is unlikely that an attitudinal questionnaire would identify them all; such a survey would certainly not be able to discover the extent to which each different factor contributed to the decision.

There is general agreement in empirical studies on those factors that significantly affect the MFAR, although there remain a few areas of dispute. There is, however, a wide variation between the estimated magnitudes of the effects that these different factors have on the MFAR, and in some cases there is disagreement with respect to the direction of the effect. These variations in results can be due to differences in:
1. the economic theory that a study is based on;
2. the methods of testing the theoretical model statistically;
3. the data set that the model is tested on.

Because of the considerable number of studies on the MFAR that have been published, particularly in the last decade, it is not feasible to examine all three aspects of each study in turn. Instead, the main trends in the development of the theory and testing methods are surveyed and the different empirical results are then summarised. Not all studies necessarily set out an economic model as a basis for their empirical work, though; for example, Wabe (1969) proceeds straight to the testing of a statistical model without any preliminary discussion of the theory.

THEORIES OF LABOUR SUPPLY

There are two main approaches to the theory of the labour supply decision of a married woman, the single-period decision model and the life-cycle model. Not all authors, however, make it clear exactly which one they are testing. The main developments that have taken place in the theory, practically all of which have come from the USA, are summarised below. For a more in-depth survey of these theories see Heckman (1978), Lloyd, Andrews and Gilroy (1979), or Smith (1980).

The single-period decision model

This is in essence an extension of the basic neoclassical theory of an individual's labour supply as set out in most microeconomics textbooks, e.g. Laidler (1981). This assumes that individuals derive utility from both leisure and income, and have a preference ordering which allows them to rank in order of preference different combinations of the two. An individual is assumed to choose that combination of hours of leisure and hours of work (which will earn income) that will yield the maximum level of satisfaction possible subject to the exogenously set constraints of the hourly wage rate and the total available time that can be split between leisure and work.

This model by itself does not yield many predictions about the expected direction of the effects of changes in factors affecting the labour supply decision. An increase in the hourly wage rate could lead to an increase or a decrease in the number of hours supplied, because the income and substitution effects of a wage increase work in opposite directions. A higher hourly wage allows an individual to take some more leisure time, i.e. work less, but still receive more income, while on the other hand the opportunity cost of taking an extra hour of leisure becomes more expensive and so there is an incentive to take less leisure. It is usually assumed that as the wage rate rises the number of hours supplied will first increase, and then start to decrease at higher wage rates. One can predict, though, that an increase in income from other sources will mean fewer hours worked. All other factors, such as the presence of children, are assumed to affect 'tastes', i.e. the nature of the leisure-income preference ordering, and their effects can only be discovered by empirical testing.

This basic model has been extended by Becker (1965) and others, who recognise that time not spent in paid employment is not all leisure time, and it is divided into domestic work and leisure. Home production of goods and services is sometimes regarded as a substitute for goods and services which are bought with income from employment, and it is assumed that an individual derives satisfaction from a combination of home production, income and leisure. The assumption is also made that an individual will seek to achieve the maximum possible level of satisfaction subject to exogenous constraints which will also include the 'productivity' of work in the home. In the case of married couples there will be a joint decision on the division of time between these three activities reflecting the preferences, market wage and 'home productivity' of both partners. Once again, one can only discover the direction of the effect that different factors have by empirical testing, although some assumptions have to be made about the likely influencing factors to know what to include in an empirical test. Gronau (1973) and Ben-Porath (1973) suggest some possible formulations; Gronau (1977) estimated that an increase in the market wage rate would reduce work in the home, although the effect on work in the market and leisure was indeterminate in this study based on US data. Why it should usually be the wife that specialises in home production is seldom considered, it being assumed that there are non-economic factors that will affect the way that a household makes its decisions which are not the responsibility of economists to explain. Indeed, having stated that the theory of a joint household decision on labour supply is the basis for their model, many researchers then proceed to construct a model that assumes husband's income, or state of employment, to be exogenously determined. Only a few, such as Greenhalgh (1980), do at least acknowledge that evidence, such as Greenhalgh (1979), suggests that male labour supply is not very responsive to many of the variables that are considered to affect female labour supply, and so this sort of assumption is not unreasonable. Knieser (1976) and Theeuwes (1981) do actually produce some estimates of the joint responses of both husband and wife to different factors. Developing further the theory of family labour supply, Graham and Green (1984) suggest that time spent in home production can also sometimes serve as leisure. One could also say that market work can give satisfaction and is not always done purely for the income it brings, although the standard theory of individual labour supply assumes that this will affect the form of the leisure-income preference function rather than assuming leisure to be incorporated in some of the work hours.

Life-cycle models

Mincer (1962a) was one of the first to consider the female labour supply decision in a lifetime context. Taking into account factors such as the number of children, husband's income and opportunities for employment, a married woman is assumed to decide how much time to spend over her lifetime to paid employment. Those who support the approach based on Friedman's (1957) permanent income hypothesis consider that transitory changes in such factors will not alter the lifetime decision, but others argue that the timing of labour supply is influenced by transitory factors. Because of the difficulties involved in properly testing this type of model relatively few empirical studies, e.g. J. P. Smith (1977), Heckman and MaCurdy (1980) and Moffitt (1984), have incorporated it.

The study of work history patterns is another approach to the analysis of long-term labour supply decisions. Stewart and Greenhalgh (1984), using British data, found that although most married women experienced at least one interruption to their period of attachment to the labour force, periods of absence were generally short compared to periods spent in the labour force. Work history patterns were related to age, school-leaving age, marital status and first occupation, and frequent interruptions tended to have a detrimental effect on later labour force position. For the USA, Mincer and Polachek (1974) agree that work history patterns affect wage differences among women as well as average wage differences between men and women. However, Corcoran (1979) found that although most working women had discontinuous work history patterns, these discontinuities did not significantly affect wage differentials.

METHODS OF TESTING

Only the basic methods and problems involved in testing models of female labour supply are explained here. For a fuller exposition of these methods see any textbook on econometrics, the study of how theoretical models can be tested with empirical data, e.g. Theil (1971). The usual approach in empirically testing an economic relationship is first to specify the relationship in a mathematical form. For example, one of the simplest models of a married woman's labour supply that has been used takes the form of a linear equation:

$$MFLS = a + bA + cI + dC + eE$$

where $MFLS$ = hours of labour supplied by a married woman, A = age, I = other household income, C = number of children, and E = years of education, and where a, b, c, d, and e are parameters that take values that are estimated to make the equation the best explanation of the pattern of observations contained in the data. More complex models can be used, for example, to incorporate two-way relationships.

When testing theories of female labour supply the first question to ask is what it is that the models are trying to explain. The single-period decision model explains hours supplied per time period, and the life-cycle model the fraction of a married woman's life that she spends in employment. However, in practice researchers have often modified the theory according to the data that is available. Hanoch (1980) carefully explains the time dimension of the theory of labour supply.

The Supply of Female Labour

One common approach, particularly in British studies, is to test for the effect of a series of variables on the average MFAR of different localities. This entails a cross-section study using data on the MFAR, and such variables as average male wage, average family size, and the local unemployment rate for each local government area. The simplest method of estimation is to use a linear single equation model for the relationship and to test it using ordinary least squares regression analysis. Greenhalgh (1980) spells out that the MFAR in this type of model can be interpreted as the average participation per year, assuming all married women are in the labour force, but others are rather vague as to how the MFAR relates to labour supply theory. An alternative approach, adopted by Spencer (1973), where actual hours of work are not known but where one has data on individuals, is to use dummy variables. A dummy variable is just a variable used to represent a non-numerical characteristic, and it is assigned a certain numerical value if a particular factor applies to an individual, e.g. 0 = not in labour force, 1 = in labour force, so that its statistical significance can be tested for. However, average participation probabilities predicted by this method using a linear single equation model can be misleading. Heckman and Willis (1977) estimated that the distribution of participation possibilities was 'U'-shaped and most women had a participation probability close to either unity or zero, with relatively few being close to their data sample mean value of 0.4. More recent British studies, e.g. Greenhalgh (1980), Layard, Barton and Zabalza (1980), and Zabalza (1983) try to explain the hours of work of married women as opposed to an average MFAR. These studies also recognise that the relationship between hours of work and the influencing factors is not a continuous mathematical function. Some married women do not work at all, and it is only when the factors influencing labour supply reach a certain value that work begins. This discontinuity in the function cannot be dealt with by the ordinary least squares regression analysis used in the earlier studies, and it is necessary to use more sophisticated econometric methods such as probit analysis, explained by Tobin (1958).

The statistical problems involved in seeking to estimate empirically the parameters of a life-cycle labour supply model are too complex to explain properly here, although obtaining data on life-cycle patterns of work, and other relevant variables present obvious problems. Suffice it to say that even in one of the more advanced studies of this type, Heckman and Macurdy (1980), the authors later concluded that their assumptions were incorrect and published a corrigendum (Heckman and MaCurdy, 1982) with a modified set of results.

An alternative approach to the identification of the factors that influence the amount of labour supplied is to estimate the reservation wage. This is the estimated minimum wage that a married woman would be prepared to work at, given her own particular characteristics, such as education level, number of children, etc. Nearly all the studies using this approach are American, and Schultz (1980) and Cogan (1980) survey the different results that have been obtained.

DATA BASES AND OVERVIEW OF CROSS-SECTION STUDIES

In the USA, studies have utilised data from a wide variety of sources, ranging from census material for the whole population to localised panel data. In particular, many authors have made use of National Longitudinal Survey data. In Britain there have been no comprehensive studies that match the pioneering American works of Mincer (1962a), Cain (1966) and Bowen and Finnegan (1969), and a much narrower range of data has been used. With a few exceptions, such as Wabe (1969), who used data from the 1951 and 1961 census of population, there was little published work on cross-section statistical tests of the labour supply relationship for married women until a number of studies appeared in the late 1970s which drew upon activity rate and other information in the 1971 census of population, together with other data from different sources. These include Greenhalgh (1977), McNabb (1977), and Lightman and O'Cleireacain (1978). A 'second generation' of British studies appeared a few years later that incorporated hours of work data from the General Household Survey and included Greenhalgh (1980), Layard et al. (1980) and Zabalza (1983).

In the last decade there has also been a number of studies using data from other countries. In Canada, following earlier work such as Spencer (1973), research has progressed quite rapidly. Gunderson (1977), Carliner, Robinson and Tomes (1980), Nakamura, Nakamura and Cullen (1979) and others have been able to apply many of the recent US developments in the study of the labour supply of females to Canadian data. As well as panel survey data, the Public User Tapes that Statistics Canada makes available containing data on annual official surveys have been used. In Australia, however, apart from Fuller (1979), who considered all females, and Miller and Volker (1983), who only considered married females, there has been relatively little published work on cross-section studies of the labour supply of married women. Hill (1983) investigated the labour supply decision of women in Japan, and looked at whether the decision to work in the informal sector, family businesses being much more common

The Supply of Female Labour

in Japan than in Europe or North America, differed from the decision to work in formal employment. In Chapter 8 some studies of the female labour supply in the Soviet Union are examined. Perhaps the most wide-ranging data set used has been the cross-section study by Winegarden (1984), which incorporated data on a number of different variables from ten different countries. There have, of course, been many other studies, and this summary of the more recent work is only designed to provide an overview of the progress made.

FACTORS AFFECTING THE MFAR

As already explained, there are too many sets of results to present them all individually. In most cases they agree qualitatively, if not quantitatively, so it is possible to summarise the general findings. Nakamura and Nakamura (1983) in fact have specifically tried to find out if changes in the data set can significantly affect the estimated parameters by arbitrarily splitting in two some sample groups of US and Canadian working wives. In their model explaining hours of work, they found some parameter instability between the two data sets, but not enough to change the sign of the coefficients. It must be borne in mind that, first, some studies estimate the effects of different variables on the probability of participation in the labour force, while others estimate the effects on hours worked; and second, of course, that the estimated effects of the different variables discussed below are *ceteris paribus*, i.e. assuming all other factors to be held constant.

Own wage

Although the neoclassical theory of individual labour supply predicts that hours of work supplied will rise with the hourly wage until a certain wage rate above which less hours will be supplied, once the wage has risen high enough to induce someone into the labour force there is no higher wage at which they will be induced to leave; that is, although the predicted response of hours worked to a rise in the hourly wage is ambiguous, the effect on average participation rates is always expected to be positive. Results confirm that the higher the wage that a married woman can expect to earn, the greater is her probability of participation and there is also a positive correlation with hours worked. Most recent British estimates of the elasticity of participation with respect to own wage suggest that it is around 1.0. The elasticity of participation with respect to the wage rate is defined as the ratio of the percentage increase in the MFAR to the percentage increase in the wage. The hours elasticity is the ratio of the percentage increase in hours of labour supplied to the percentage increase in the wage. Thus if participation elasticity was 1.0, then a 1 per cent rise in female wages would cause a 1 per cent increase in the MFAR. Greenhalgh (1980) and Zabalza (1983), who estimate separately hours and participation components, say that the hours elasticity is larger than the participation elasticity. Greenhalgh puts the hours and participation elasticities at around 0.68 and 0.36 respectively, and estimates that although the hours supply function may become backward-bending at higher wages, the level at which it does so is very much higher than the mean wage of the sample of working wives that she studies. Zabalza agrees on the participation elasticity, but estimated the hours elasticity to be somewhat larger, well over unity and in line with US estimates, which have varied from just over 1.0 to over 4.0.

There are problems involved in using wages in a labour supply cross-section study. If one is looking at the MFAR in different localities, it can be argued that the average female wage, which is the variable used in this type of study, is not really exogenous. Wage rates in a free market are determined by supply and demand, and so the female wage rate will be affected by the supply of and demand for female labour; in addition there will be a causal relationship in the other direction. However, local wage levels are not always responsive to local market conditions, and are influenced by the national economic climate, collective agreements, and standardised payment systems in multi-establishment companies, and so not too much may be lost by assuming this to be exogenous. McNabb (1977) incorporated this two-way relationship in a simultaneous equation model but found that the results did not differ substantially from those he obtained from a simpler single equation model.

When data on individual married women is used, there is the problem that one does not have a wage for those women not actually working. One approach is to estimate the wage that a married woman could expect to obtain given her other characteristics. Another method is to use a woman's level of education as a proxy variable for wage, since higher qualifications on average enable a woman to earn a higher wage, and similar results to those using actual wage have been obtained (see the section below on education, though).

One exception to the usual pattern of results was the Canadian study by Nakamura, Nakamura and Cullen (1979), which found that hours of work fell when the hourly wage was increased. It could be that Canadian working wives are closer to the point where the labour supply schedule bends backwards than elsewhere, although the authors considered that the functional form they used could also account for this. Moffitt (1984) provides evidence that a married woman's lifetime employment profile is associated with her lifetime wage profile.

Other income

Other income can be treated as one variable or split into different components, i.e. husband's wage, investment income, etc., but whichever measure is used, the theoretical prediction that an increase in other income will decrease the amount of labour supplied by married women is supported by empirical evidence. Recent results suggest that the elasticity of married women's labour supply with respect to their husband's wage rate is around three-quarters of the value of the elasticity measure with respect to their own wages, but with a negative sign. This is important when it comes to the explanation of long-run changes in the female labour supply in the next section. These elasticity estimates predict that if both male and female wage rates rose by the same amount, the net effect of the two forces working in opposite directions would be an increase in the female labour supply, e.g. if wage rates rose by 100 per cent, then the net result would be:

+100% − 75% = +25%

Blau (1984) investigates the hypothesis that the labour supply of married women has an equalising effect on the distribution of family wage rates and earnings. Evidence from some sample cohorts of white women in the USA confirms this and suggests that although the equalisation effect on wage rates declines over a couple's lifetime, the effect on family earnings does not.

Children

The presence of children has been found to be one of the most significant factors affecting the probability of participation for married women and the hours of work for those in employment. This variable usually has a relatively large negative coefficient, as one would expect given that women still usually perform most of the work involved in child-rearing, despite the moves that have been made towards equality in recent years. The ages of the children are also important. It has been shown that when very young children, below school age, are present the negative effect is stronger. When a variable is included to represent the presence of older teenage children the effect is not so significant, and in some studies its coefficient has actually had a positive sign, i.e. the extra expense of keeping teenage children has outweighed the extra work that they cause in the home, and the incentive to seek employment is increased.

Although the variable representing children usually has a relatively large coefficient, in most cross-section studies this only shows the short-run effect. The total percentage lifetime reduction in hours of labour supplied will be much smaller because the presence of young children is only a temporary phase in a married woman's working life. Greenhalgh (1980) estimated that although the immediate effect of an extra child would be to reduce participation by 35 per cent and annual hours by 40 per cent, because this negative effect would only operate while the child was cared for by its parents, assumed to be until the age of sixteen, and would be weaker in the later childhood years, total lifetime hours supplied would only be reduced by 12.5 per cent.

Stolzenberg and Waite (1984) estimated that the local availability and cost of child-care facilities were significant factors influencing the relationship between children and the probability of a married woman working. They did this by first using US 1970 census data on individual married women to estimate separately for 409 different local areas the relationship between labour force participation and a set of explanatory variables. They then tried to explain the variation between areas in the estimated values of the coefficients for the variables representing the presence of children by estimating the relationship between these coefficients and local child-care facility availability and cost, and found a significant correlation.

A few studies include a variable to represent the presence of other dependent persons in the household, e.g. an elderly relative. This usually has a negative coefficient, confirming that women tend to shoulder most of the additional responsibility caring for other dependents as well as children, and consequently have less time available to work in paid employment.

It can be argued that the decision to have children depends on how one weighs the benefits against the possible drop in earnings that might result. Results from Cramer (1980) suggest that although in the long run the decision to have children is endogenous and depends on future employment and earnings prospects, in the short run the number of children can be considered to be exogenously determined. This backs up the assumption made in most cross-section studies that the presence of children is an exogenous factor, but there are still problems in trying to fit children into a life-cycle model. Robinson and Tomes (1982) tried to incorporate into their model the complex relationship between schooling, fertility and the lifetime profiles of a married woman's economic activity and her husband's wage. Using Canadian data, they found that when their sample was split into those married women who had never worked in their lifetime and those who had (as opposed to the usual division according to current employment status), there was no evidence that children were time intensive.

Unemployment

Unemployment can have two opposing effects on a married woman's labour supply. These are
1. *The discouraged worker effect.* If unemployment is high then the poor chances of finding a job and the extra search costs involved will discourage some women from entering or re-entering the labour market. Another possible disincentive is that in some cases social security payments to an unemployed husband may be cut if his wife works.
2. *The encouraged, or added, worker effect.* If their husbands are unemployed some married women may be encouraged to seek employment to make up family income.

Most cross-section studies suggest that the discouraged effect dominates, but evidence is not conclusive. Kraft (1973), for example, found that the added worker effect dominated. It is important to note that in (1) it is the unemployment rate in the area that a married woman lives that causes this effect, whereas in (2) it is just the unemployment of her own husband. Some studies have included both of these as separate variables and have found that although high local unemployment has a negative effect on the probability of a married woman's participation in the labour force, the unemployment of her husband has a positive effect.

Education

The higher a married woman's level of education the higher the wage that she can usually expect to earn and also the more pleasant and interesting her job is likely to be. Thus one would expect the probability of participation in the labour force to be higher, although, as with an increase in the hourly wage, the effect on hours supplied could be in either direction. In those studies that included both education and wage as separate variables, instead of using education to represent both, it was found that education had a zero or even a negative effect. Why, when the higher wage element is separated out, education should diminish participation has not been fully explained. In some cases higher qualifications might enable women to choose a job with hours to their liking instead of having to work a standard working week, but better qualified women are also more likely to hold primary labour market 'career' jobs where full-time work is expected rather than poorly paid secondary labour market part-time jobs. Standing (1976) explains that highly educated women are likely to marry educated men, who tend to be in relatively well paid jobs. This could cause their wives' labour supply to decrease, but this effect should be picked up separately by the husband's income variable included in most studies.

The magnitude of the effect of the education variable varies according to the different ways in which it is represented. Most frequently education is measured in terms of years of schooling, or level of qualification attained. This is not necessarily the best measure, though. Six years of study for a PhD in Classics may yield a lower chance of employment than half that time studying a more vocational subject. When a finer breakdown of post-school education has been made, e.g. Spencer (1973), results show that women with vocational and technical qualifications are more likely to work than those with more academic qualifications. On the other hand, Elias and Main (1982) found that for a large number of working women their employment did not actually require them to use their vocational qualifications, or if it did the skills learned were often only called upon for a small proportion of the work involved in their jobs.

Age

In Chapter 2 it was shown that economic participation alters with age. This age profile for economic activity is affected by variables other than age itself, e.g. the presence of children. In cross-section studies where the effects of these other factors are separately accounted for, age itself has been found to be significant, with younger married women being more likely to be economically active than older ones.

In life-cycle models, e.g. J. P. Smith (1977), that try to explain the timing of a married woman's labour supply over her lifetime, linking it with her lifetime profile of other variables such as her own and her husband's wage, this correlation with age itself is not so obvious.

Residence

Several studies have found that participation is lower in rural areas and higher in large cities. Several possible explanations have been put forward for this. There are often fewer opportunities for work in rural areas, particularly in the service sector. Travel-to-work distances are often longer than in urban areas for the jobs that are available and, even when the actual distance is not that far, public transport can be inadequate. Because many women prefer to work part-time, the cost and time of this extra travel in relation to the reward from their employment is high. Public transport is important because when a family has only one car it is usually the husband who will use it for travelling to work. Andrews (1978) showed that economic activity was sensitive to actual journey-to-work time, and Simpson (1982) found that economic activity was also affected by the employment structure within a big city. Another possible explanation is that recorded statistics may exaggerate the lower economic activity in rural areas as unpaid work on family farms may not be recorded in official employment surveys.

Ethnic origin

Studies in both the USA and Britain have found that black women have a higher than average female economic activity rate. This could be tied to the encouraged worker effect resulting from the high male unemployment and low incomes for black families, but most studies have included variables that measure these effects separately. Hoffman (1982), however, found that by separately testing a labour supply model for two US samples, one of black married women and one of white married women, the relationship between the explanatory variables and economic participation was itself somewhat different. In particular there was less reliance on husband's income for black married women.

The same results do not apply for all other ethnic groups, though. Monck and Lomas (1975), in their study of four British cities with large ethnic minority populations, found that although women of Caribbean origin had a high economic activity rate, the figure was relatively lower for those whose origin was the Indian sub-continent. The British Community Relations Commission (1975) produced figures showing that within this latter group women of usual child-bearing age (15-45) of Indian origin had a much higher economic activity rate (40 per cent) than those whose origin was Pakistan (16 per cent). Monck and Lomas also found that women of both West Indian and Asian origin who did work were much more likely to work full-time than white females in the same age group.

Socio-economic status of husband

A few British studies have looked at the relationship between the socio-economic status of a married woman's husband and the probability of her being economically active. The MFAR tends to be relatively high for the wives of skilled manual workers and personal service workers and relatively low for the wives of farmers, self-employed professional workers and employers and managers of large establishments. To some extent this pattern could reflect income differentials, but if this is allowed for separately there would still remain some 'attitude' factor due to socio-economic status. There is also the possibility that the wives of farmers and self-employed professionals contribute unrecorded labour to their husband's businesses.

Demand for female labour

According to the economic theory of supply and demand, a change in demand only causes a movement along a supply function as opposed to a shift in the whole schedule. It is not unreasonable, though, to assume that the availability of employment opportunities will influence the proportion of married women who decide to enter the labour force. Some studies have used a variable that attempts to represent the level of demand for female labour in a locality, e.g. the proportion of industries that are predominantly female-employing. It could be argued that this is not an entirely exogenous variable, but most industries in Britain and the USA are located in specific areas because of their proximity to input sources or market outlets rather than the availability of a large number of females who wish to work. Results have shown the MFAR to be positively correlated to variables measuring the demand for female labour.

Region

Some researchers have tried to relate economic activity to the region in which a married woman lives. This might reflect differences in attitudes to work, or employment opportunities, or other factors which might vary between regions. Studies including areas, such as the Canadian provinces and the thirteen standard British regions, have yielded a mixed set of results. Earlier British work found some correlation between region and the MFAR, which may have been partly due to the concentration of particular industries, and the lack of others, in certain regions. However, more recent studies, such as Molho and Elias (1984) have found region to be less significant. This may partly be due to the evening out of the MFAR over the British regions as the regionally concentrated manufacturing industries declined and the more widespread service sector expanded.

When migration takes place to areas of better employment opportunity it is nearly always the husband's job that has the better prospects. Frank (1978) and Le Louarn and DeCotiis (1983) found that movement was more likely for single career families than dual career families.

Other variables

Several other variables have been included by different economists, but not all have been found to affect the MFAR significantly. Even when they have been found to be significant they have not always yielded information that would be useful for policy purposes, but, of course, if they make the model a better explanation of the data they should be included. For example, Greenhalgh (1980) found, not unsurprisingly, that ill health lowered a married woman's labour supply.

CYCLICAL FLUCTUATIONS

Although based on time series data, several studies have investigated the short-run effects of changes in the level of economic activity. It has been suggested that the encouraged and discouraged worker effects, described above, have caused short-term fluctuations in the long-term upward trend in the female labour force. Corry and Roberts (1970, 1974), using British data from the 1950s and 1960s, tested this hypothesis and found that in general the discouraged worker effect dominated.

Wachter (1972, 1974) considered the possible effects of cyclical fluctuations that are suggested by the permanent and relative income hypotheses. The permanent income hypothesis suggests that married women will be encouraged to work when current wages exceed the expected permanent wage. The relative income hypothesis suggests that they will try to maintain previous standards, and if current wages exceed the expected wage they will take more leisure and work less. Wachter also included a measure of price inflation, the rationale being that wage inflation equal to, or above, this rate will induce money illusion and may encourage increased economic activity. Using US data from 1948 to 1968, he found evidence to support the relative income hypothesis, which strengthens the case for the encouraged worker hypothesis. Using later data, Heckman and MaCurdy (1982) also found some evidence to support the added worker effect.

Fleisher and Rhodes (1976) suggested that the mixed set of results on the effect of unemployment that others had obtained were due to misspecification of the model representing the labour supply decision of a married woman. They offered as an alternative a simultaneous equation model that tried to separate the effects of aggregate demand and unemployment. Kuch and Sharir (1978) estimated that the Canadian female labour force was not as responsive to fluctuations in the rate of unemployment as was the US female workforce. In Australia Haig and Wood (1976) found that the additional worker and discouraged worker effects tended to cancel out over a cycle, although a net positive effect was suggested by their results.

LONG-TERM TRENDS

The long-term trends in the female labour force have been influenced by both supply and demand factors. Also, some of the factors which have been assumed to be exogenous influences on supply in cross-section studies are not necessarily exogenous in the long run. For example, the number of females with higher education qualifications may increase if more females perceive that the possible opportunities for employment have increased. On the other hand, not all of the growth in the number of females attaining higher education qualifications has been demand-induced, and some has been the result of greater provision of educational facilities, but it is difficult to separate out the two contributory factors. Apart from this 'cause and effect' problem there are other difficulties involved in trying to use the results of cross-section studies to explain long-term trends. If the relationship between economic activity and the set of explanatory variables did not change over time, then it might be possible to observe how these explanatory variables altered and then calculate to what extent each played a part in the long-term trend, using the respective coefficients from cross-section studies. However, results show that this relationship itself does appear to change and so this method can only be used with partial success. It is also difficult to test statistically the long-run relationship between the MFAR and the other variables due to data limitations. For regression analysis results to have any meaning the number of data observations must be sufficiently larger than the number of variables in the model, but consistent data on many variables is not usually available over a long time period. In Britain, for example, accurate measures of the MFAR are only available every ten years in the census of population.

For these reasons there are relatively few quantitative estimates of the long-term effects of different factors on the MFAR. In many cases the best that can be done is to observe how the influencing factors have changed over time and comment on the expected direction of the effect on the MFAR. There are, however, a few studies that attempt some quantitative explanation of the effect of changes in various factors on the female labour supply. The simplest method is to take the results from one cross-section study and multiply the elasticities with respect to the different explanatory variables by the amount that these variables have changed over time. Most of the studies that do this concentrate on the wife's wage and husband's income variables. As explained earlier, given that the positive effect of an increase in the wife's wage has generally been found to be around one and a third times the magnitude of the negative effect of an increase in husband's income, the parallel upward trend in both male and female wages that has been experienced on both sides of the Atlantic predicts a rise in female participation. However, this approach usually underestimates the actual rise in the MFAR that has been experienced. The unexplained portion of the rise could then be attributed to changes in other factors or a change in the whole relationship, but one cannot say how much to each. An extension of this method is to test the same model using cross-section data from both the beginning and the end of the period studied, so that any change in the relationship can be identified. Another approach to the problem is to obtain sufficient data, such as the quarterly figures used by Molho and Elias (1984), to run a time series regression.

For the USA Cain (1966) explained over half of the growth in the MFAR between 1939 and 1959 using his basic model that the MFAR depended on the wife's wage and husband's income by multiplying the changes in these variables by their respective regression coefficients. Fleisher and Knieser (1980, p. 128) performed a similar exercise using 1970 data and compared their results with Cain's. However, they found that the model underestimated the rise in the MFAR that actually occurred when the regression coefficients estimated using 1970 data were applied to the changes in their respective variables. The regression coefficients obtained in the latter study differed substantially from those in the earlier study. Although it appears that the relationship between the

MFAR and these factors did alter, it is a problem to establish to what extent this is due to the model not being a true representation of the relationship in the first place. Bowen and Finnegan (1969) tested a similar single equation model using data from 1940, 1950 and 1960. This was updated by Fields (1976), who tested the same model using 1970 data and found some changes in the relationship. With the exception of unemployment, which had a stronger effect, the strength and significance of the explanatory variables were weaker.

More recently, Shapiro and Shaw (1983) have looked at the changing relationship between economic activity and hours of work, and a set of other variables for samples of white married women aged 30 to 34 in both 1967 and 1978. They estimated that half of the observed growth in labour force attachment could be explained by changes in the set of explanatory variables, which included most of the 'standard' factors described in the previous section. However, when a variable that represented changes in attitudes, obtained from questionnaire surveys, was added to the model, the percentage of increased labour force participation that could be accounted for rose to around 90 per cent, and the increase in hours that could be explained rose to 80 per cent.

There have been relatively few British studies that have used cross-section results to make quantitative estimates of the effects of specific variables on long-term trends. Layard, Barton and Zabalza (1980) estimated that the doubling of real wages between 1951 and 1973, for both males and females, could account for about one-third of the increase in the MFAR between these dates. Molho (1983) and Molho and Elias (1984) found that trends in real earnings, family formation and unemployment all contributed to the growth in the MFAR between 1968 and 1977, with earnings having the largest effect. The latter study estimated separately these effects for the thirteen UK regions and found that there was a substantial variation in the amount of the growth in the MFAR that was explained, although they concluded that the convergence of the regional distribution of earnings had caused regional MFAR figures to converge on the national average. The earnings of married men were closely correlated with the earnings of their wives and were therefore omitted from the model. One suspects that this may have left the wives' earnings variable to pick up the effect of other factors rising over time and its significance to be overestimated. The earlier work by Corry and Roberts (1970, 1974) found that a time trend, i.e. a variable given the values 1, 2, 3, etc. for each successive observation, was one of the most significant variables in their time series study. It picked up not only the effect of changes in earnings, but also changes in attitudes and other factors that gradually increased over time and were not included elsewhere in the model. This highlights yet another problem involved in long-run studies. If several variables change together over time, then if just one is included in the model it can pick up the effect of all the others and its coefficient may not be correctly estimated. Fair (1971), using quarterly US data in a time series study, did not find that a time trend was consistently significant, but several other variables used, such as the ratio of total employment to population, may have picked up the time series effect. Although the quantitative estimates of the reasons behind the long-term rise in the MFAR are useful, they usually only compare two points in time, and it is interesting to look at the trends in the explanatory variables more fully even if one does not have precise estimates of the effect on the MFAR. These are considered below where trends in some factors that have not been included in quantitative studies are also looked at.

Children

In Britain the birth rate rose after the Second World War, fell back in the 1950s, rose to a new higher peak in the early 1960s and then steadily fell until 1979, when a modest upturn began again. This would suggest a falling back of the MFAR in the 1960s, which in fact did not occur. This could, of course, be attributed to changes in other variables. However, an examination of the age distribution of the female labour force shows that the main growth in the 1960s was among middle-aged married women, whose children would probably have left school. In the 1970s, when the birth rate was dropping, there was more growth over time in the economic activity rate for younger married women in the child-bearing age group. Legislation obliging firms to re-employ women who had taken maternity leave may have been one factor contributing to this change. Increased provision for child care may also have modified the negative effect of the rise in the birth rate. In the USA the birth rate rose steadily to a peak in the early 1960s, after which a decline set in. As in Britain, this birth-rate pattern does not fit in with changes in the female labour force, and one must look to other factors to explain these changes. Another possible contributory factor might be that the relationship between children and economic activity has changed. Wabe (1967), in his study of working women in London noted that the effect of young children on the female participation rate was much lower in 1961 than in 1951. This and other results, such as Fields (1976) in the USA, confirm that the effect of children as a deterrent to married women working has lessened.

Education

In both the USA and Britain the number of females in full-time education beyond the minimum school-leaving age has increased over the last few decades. One would expect this to increase the MFAR in the long run as more women reaped the higher rewards from employment that result from better qualifications. This growth in the number of full-time students was not a completely exogenous growth caused by the growth in provision of education facilities. Many young females purposefully invested their time, and in some cases their parents invested their money, in education, because they had decided to work in later life and could see the greater rewards that could come from this.

Although this growth in the number of females in further and higher education would have pushed up the MFAR, it had a downward effect on the activity rate for single females. This effect was more noticeable in Britain where most students in full-time education are not included in the labour force, whereas in the USA and Canada it is quite common for students to work their way through college, and thus still to be classed as economically active.

Unemployment

Cross-section and cyclical studies have suggested a negative relationship between the MFAR and unemployment in the short run. Over the longer term in Britain the rapid rise in the male unemployment rate that occurred after 1966, and the rise in female unemployment after 1973 did not appear to have affected the MFAR significantly, which kept rising during this period. However, evidence does suggest that the even more rapid increase in unemployment after 1979 has brought down the number of women in the labour force, although the peculiarities of the British method of counting the unemployed, explained in Chapter 7, make detection of the discouraged worker effect difficult. In the USA unemployment has also risen above the levels of the 1950s, but in the long term the MFAR has not fallen, although the increase in unemployment may have modified the rate of increase.

Wages and demand

It has already been explained that the net effect of the roughly similar increases in male and female earnings has helped to push up the MFAR.

Nevertheless, it is interesting to ask why wages rose. Union agreements or other factors may have influenced some industries but one should not underestimate the effect of demand. The evidence suggests that one reason why female wages were driven up was an increase in demand, rather than contracting supply. Thus wages themselves are not simply exogenous variables influencing female labour supply. Changes in the wage rate are partly the result of the interplay of the demand for and the supply of labour. Thus it can be said that one of the most important factors that caused the number of females in the labour force to increase was an increase in demand, which caused a movement along the supply schedule by raising wages, as opposed to the other factors which caused the whole supply schedule to shift. Oppenheimer (1976) suggested that increased demand was the main reason for the expansion of the US labour force after examining various features of the changes in demand and supply of female labour. Lloyd and Niemi (1978) specifically tested for the effect of increased employment opportunities in female-employing industries and found it to be a significant factor affecting supply.

The way that the tax system operates has also influenced the MFAR because tax thresholds have not fully adjusted to changing income levels. In Britain all workers, including married women, can earn up to a specified amount before becoming liable to income tax. In the 1950s working men with average earnings did not pay any income tax, and so a few hours extra of overtime work would not entail a lower marginal net rate of pay. However, by the 1970s the average worker was paying income tax. Thus even if her gross hourly wage was lower than her husband's overtime rate a married woman might still be able to take home more per hour for a few hours' work than her husband could anticipate receiving from working overtime because his earnings would be taxed and hers would not. Even if the net differential was still in the husband's favour, the relative change over time might still have helped induce more married women to seek employment. Zabalza (1983) and Greenhalgh (1980) allowed for the discontinuity in the budget constraint that the tax system causes when they estimated the determinants of economic participation and hours of work for married women. Greenhalgh concluded that the lowering of marginal rates of tax would have a larger negative effect on wives' supply than would an increase in tax allowance levels for men. Thus a lowering of the real value of tax thresholds and an increase in marginal tax rates, taking into account earnings-related National Insurance payments, which is what has effectively occurred, would tend to push up the labour supply of married women. Using US data, Leuthold (1978) estimated the elasticity of hours supplied with respect to tax, which was found to be negative, its apparently small magnitude being due to any given percentage change in the tax rate having a much larger effect on net income.

Labour-saving changes

Many changes have reduced the time needed to run a home. Domestic appliances obviously make chores quicker and easier to do. Refrigerators and freezers reduces the number of shopping trips necessary. In Britain the replacement of coal fires as the primary domestic heating source by gas, oil and electric heating systems has eliminated the need to light and tend a fire through the winter months. It is sometimes argued that the growth in the number of labour-saving devices was a response to the extra demand that came from women who had decided to enter employment for other reasons and who had the money to pay for these devices. An opposing view is that the growth in provision of these devices was due to technical innovation and production at a commercial cost which then allowed women more time to seek employment. There were probably forces working in both directions and one cannot really separate out which was cause and which was effect.

Other changes that reduced work in the home were more obviously demand-induced rather than being the result of technical innovation. Restaurants, ready-made clothes, and some types of pre-prepared foods existed at the start of the century, and so the increase in the number of meals eaten in restaurants and in 'off-the-peg' clothes sales, and the decrease in home baking and cooking, were primarily demand-induced. It must be remembered, though, that until the Second World War domestic service was the largest single occupation for women in Britain, and for better off families these changes often meant a reduction in the amount of domestic labour employed rather than less work in the home for the wife.

One should not overestimate the extra free time created by all these changes. There are now fewer adults per household to share the work, and higher standards of living are aspired to. As well as the average married woman having more rooms to be cleaned in her home, she is also likely to have to travel further to go shopping or meet friends if she lives in a growing suburban housing estate. Geographical mobility and isolation at home may, on the other hand, have encouraged married women to go out to work to meet people. Martin and Roberts (1984) found that the social aspects of work were very important for many women.

Working patterns

It is not just the wage and the type of work that a woman considers before taking a job. Hours of work are also very important. The growth of part-time employment, the reduction in the standard working week for full-time workers, and the introduction of more flexibility in working hours have all made employment attractive, particularly for married women. Part-time employment, as well as being a demand-side influence on the growth of the female labour force (see Chapter 7), has also influenced supply. For example, many part-time jobs are in retailing, helping to cope with the extended opening hours that many stores now operate. This helps to make it possible for other women to take up employment because if a married couple both work, they still have the opportunity to do their shopping during these extended opening hours. The provision of part-time employment also allows the taking up of otherwise surplus supply from those women who, given current reward packages offered by firms, would only wish to supply a few hours per week.

Changing attitudes

Many people would perhaps cite this as the first reason why more married women now wish to go out to work. It is not just the attitudes of the women themselves that have changed. Parents, schoolteachers, husbands, friends and employers have also changed their attitudes over the years, and the idea of a working married woman is now acceptable to most people, but still not to everyone. Husbands are more likely to help with housework, teachers and parents are more likely to encourage girls to train for a worthwhile career.

Economists, however, do not place great emphasis on the idea that changing attitudes are an explanation of increased labour force participation by married women. It is difficult, if not impossible, to test this hypothesis properly because attitudes cannot be measured, nor their effect distinguished from other influences, although Shapiro and Shaw (1983) did suggest that changes in attitudes, as measured in a questionnaire survey, could account for about 50 per cent of the increase in the US married female labour force between 1967 and 1978. This does not mean to say that most economists think that changing attitudes are unimportant. Attitudes have changed, but one must ask whether the attitudes changed due to some social or other influences that have not been considered by economists, or whether women have been induced into the labour market by the economic factors discussed in this chapter, and as people have become more accustomed to seeing married women at work.

To say that more women are in the labour force because more of them think they ought to go out to work is not a very helpful statement. The campaigning of various women's movements and equal pay legislation have probably changed some people's attitudes, but apart from vague statements like this one cannot really say to what extent changes in attitudes by themselves have increased the female labour supply.

5 The Demand for Female Labour

The last chapter examined the changes in the nature and character of the female labour supply over the post-1945 period, particular attention being given to the increases that have occurred in the Married Female Activity Rate. Empirical studies using statistical analysis have not been widely undertaken to study the labour demand for female workers. Rather the developments in the study of labour demand have been directed at considering the influences on labour demand at the level of the organisation (e.g. Hazledine, 1981), or at the wider economy level (e.g. Henry and Tarling, 1981). This is not to say that economists have not considered the special circumstances which may surround the demand for female labour as against labour demand in general. Oppenheimer (1976) and Hakim (1979) gave consideration to female labour demand but within a narrow context, their approach being to say that historically females have been segregated in a limited number of occupations and/or industries and that female labour demand is therefore related to the relative fortunes of such occupations and/or industries. Each of these two types of approach have extended the understanding by economists of the process of labour demand, but for an understanding of the changing demand for female workers it will be necessary to draw upon both types of approach.

WHY IS THERE A DEMAND FOR LABOUR?

To the economist labour demand differs from the demand for goods and services in that the demand for labour is a derived demand. Labour demand arises from the demand for goods and services and for no other reason. Consequently, employers do not demand labour because of a wish to employ people as such but they employ people when there is a demand for the goods and services these individuals can provide. It is the anticipated demand for goods and services that will determine whether or not employment is generated and a demand for labour exists. The labour demand is therefore said to be derived from the demand for the products of labour. Within the private sector the level of product demand is determined by the willingness or otherwise of individuals, firms or goverment to purchase the goods and services which may be produced. One influence on this willingness is the price of the good or service, and price will reflect the cost of the required labour input.

Economists, in considering the level of labour demand in the private sector, assume that all firms seek to maximise their profits, and therefore labour costs become a significant consideration. In practice firms may not seek to maximise their profits, but seek to achieve other objectives. To say firms seek to maximise their profits is not the same as saying that they are seeking to minimise costs. If a firm closed, its costs would be at a minimum, but, unfortunately, so would its profits. Rather it is assumed that there is a level of operation where it is possible to achieve maximum profits, and at that level of operation firms will endeavour to minimise their costs and this will determine their labour requirements. (A development of the concepts referred to in the last three paragraphs will be found in Lipsey, 1983, 6th edn, Part 5.)

A high proportion of British and American females are not employed in the private sector but take employment with public bodies. The majority of public sector organisations, especially those providing a service like education or medical care, are not expected to make a profit. Rather the level of service, and hence the labour demand, is a political decision, and the national government or a local council determines what will or will not be provided. Their decisions will, it is assumed, take into consideration the wishes of the consumers who periodically spend votes rather than money. Thus in the public sector, unlike the private sector, the operational level will be determined by political decisions which are open to non-economic considerations.

Once the operational level is determined, those responsible for the public sector will wish to keep costs to a minimum. Thus the criteria for determining the level of provision of goods and services varies between the sectors. Once the level is determined, the public sector acts in the same way as the private sector, both endeavouring to minimise their costs. If employers seek to minimise their costs this may have implications for labour demand. It may mean changes to job descriptions, and offering employment to females in preference to males, or it may mean taking advantage of new technology and employing fewer people.

There is another assumption concerning technology that economists make in their labour demand theory. Technology is considered important in determining labour demand, for if technology changes, the quantity of labour required for specific tasks is often modified. Manufacturers of word processors claim, for example, that these are 50 per cent more productive than electric typewriters. If this new technology were to be adopted the demand for word processor operators would be only two-thirds of the labour demand for typists, with final output levels remaining unchanged. Technology, and changes in technology, are major determinants of both the level of labour demand, i.e. the numbers of people in employment, and the nature or character of the labour demand, i.e. the type of workers who will be employed. A considerable proportion of employed females now undertake job tasks that were inconceivable in 1900 given the then level of technology.

Employment of individuals occurs when there exists a demand for their labour services at or above the wage level they are prepared to work for. Theoretically, with exceptions that are allowed for by legislation, all available employment is open to members of both sexes. Robertson and Walton (1979), however, noted that as recently as 1960 in the USA forty-three states had protective legislation which restricted where females could take employment. The implication of the assumption that employment is open to all is that there is not a specific demand for female labour as such, nor is there a specific demand for male labour. Thus in examining the determinants of labour demand a non-sexist approach might be the most appropriate one.

However, within labour markets there are often divisions between differing groups of potential employees, and the criterion for some of these divisions is sex. It is common to talk of 'men's jobs' or 'women's jobs'. It ought to be noted that such forms of classification do not necessary hold for all time. An example of change in the sexual allocation of an occupation is typewriting. When introduced, the typewriter was considered a highly technical piece of equipment and its operation required prolonged training and high skill levels. Given such assumptions it is not surprising that typists tended to be male. Over the last eighty years the mystique has been taken from the typewriter. Typing is not regarded as a particularly special skill and typists now tend to be females. What was a 'man's job' has become a 'woman's job'. Even when allowance for changes of this nature are made, it remains true that certain industries and/or occupations are still heavily reliant on one sex or the other. Thus in the world of work, and hence of labour demand, there are often still sex boundaries, although over the last decade there are indications that these boundaries are being removed (see Rytina and Bianchi, 1984).

Observation would suggest that employers' demand for female labour consists, as Gitlow (1953, p. 551) suggested, partly of a general demand for labour and partly of a specific demand for female labour. This division of female labour demand into two categories arises from the differing degrees of occupational segregation that have developed in the USA and Britain. In certain occupations it makes no difference to a worker's performance what sex the worker is. For example, in the USA in 1980 45 per cent of accountants and bus-drivers were female. When, therefore, there is a demand for an accountant or a bus-driver employers collectively will usually be indifferent as to whether they employ a male or a female worker. For this type of occupation there is a general demand for labour, and within the general demand there will be a demand for female labour. This situation does not hold for all occupations. Again in the USA of 1980, 96 per cent of registered nurses and the same percentage of typists were female. When a US employer is seeking to fill a vacancy in one of these two occupations he or she will almost certainly, but not always, be demanding female labour. While accepting the concept that there is a demand for labour, and that the sex of the worker is irrelevant, occupational segregation has in practice often caused employment demand to be directed at either the specific male or female labour supply.

It is in the labour market that labour demand occurs, and the operation of markets, whether for goods and services or for labour, is at the centre of the study of economics. Labour markets are differentiated from other, commodity, markets for a number of reasons. Unlike commodity markets, where the ownership of the good or service may change, in the labour market the services of the worker are demanded, not the worker him or herself. The implication of this is that workers must be willing and able to go where their labour services are required. Thus any limitations on the ability of workers to do so, e.g. family or household constraints, may restrict the supply of labour and the numbers of workers employed, although it would not reduce actual labour demand.

A second way labour markets differ from other market types is in the participants' perception of what the term means. For those who demand labour, employers, the labour market is often regarded as a specific spatial area. This is often reflected in the way information concerning vacancies is made available. For many of those seeking employment the concept of the labour market being a spatial area is also important. Wright (1979, p. 23) suggests that the ability of married women to participate in the labour market was often constrained by their being unable to work very far from home. Thus labour markets are often considered in geographical terms. The British census, for example, provides data on 'travel to work areas'. The dimensions of the labour market's geographical area vary according to which industries and occupations are considered. The entry into specific industries and/or occupations will be dependent upon a number of considerations, e.g. ability, opportunity, custom and practice; thus these considerations will in their turn affect the nature of the individual labour markets.

The economic theory of labour markets is often explained in terms of the single labour market, but in reality, in examining the demand for females and/or males, it is more appropriate to think in terms of a multiplicity of labour markets. As Cairnes (1874, p. 68) wrote: 'we are compelled to recognize the existence of non-competing individual groups as a feature of our economy'. When employers demand labour it is usually a specific demand, for a typist or an engineer, for example. Thus those without the prescribed requirements are excluded from competing for the specified services, i.e. they are members of the non-competing groups. Kerr (1954) suggested that labour markets not only consist of non-competing groups but that these markets have become highly structured through the development of institutional rules designed to favour certain groups in specific occupations and/or industries *vis-à-vis* other groups. The degree to which such rules have developed will vary between the different labour markets, and they are seen at their highest level in what Doeringer and Proire (1971) term 'primary markets', while in contrast in 'secondary markets' the degree of institutional control in the labour market is limited.

The employment of females, it was seen in Chapter 3, has become concentrated in certain industries and in certain occupations. Thus employment in the labour market(s) of both Britain and the USA, reflecting actual demand for labour, appears to have become highly structured. In most labour markets, whether of a geographical, industrial and/or an occupational nature, males and females often appear to be members of different non-competing groups – a situation which reflects and reinforces views of labour market segregation.

THE LEVEL OF LABOUR DEMAND IN BRITAIN AND THE USA

The changing level of demand for female labour in the British and US economies has to be examined against the background of the total level of demand for labour in each nation, since female labour demand is part of the aggregate labour demand. Male labour demand and the extent to which it is met by the potential supply of male workers must be considered, for the demand of male and female labour are interconnected even when members of the two sexes are not direct substitutes for each other in all jobs. Despite recent downturns in the economies of Britain and the USA, each nation's 'employed civilian labour force' in 1980 had grown in size from 1970. Between 1955 and 1980 the employed civilian labour force in Britain grew by a million, or 4 per cent, a modest growth by US standards, where the increase in the same period was thirty-six million, i.e. an additional 60 per cent. Should the employed civilian labour force be taken to represent realised demand for labour, then labour demand, when measured by the numbers in the labour force, has grown over the last twenty-five years. Consequently, because female demand represents a part of the total demand for labour, then one explanation for the increase in the demand for paid female labour services is that the total demand for labour has been increasing. However, reservations have been expressed concerning the use of the employed labour force as a measure of labour demand (see Oppenheimer, 1976, p. 163).

The British and the US experiences have been quite different over the last few decades. In Britain, while the realised labour demand was a million higher in 1980 than in 1955, this demand was a million lower than it had been in 1966. The realised labour demand in Britain rose over the post-war period to 1965-6, by when it was two million higher than in 1955; thereafter the aggregate total declined, although Figure 5.1 indicates that fluctuations occurred around the upward and downward trends. This was not the pattern in the USA, where, with the exception of the two years 1957 and 1975, the employed civilian labour force has grown from year to year.

While labour demand changed over this period in both nations so did the total labour supply. The 'total civilian labour force', the labour supply, in both Britain and the USA, grew more rapidly than the 'employed civilian labour force'. Consequently the imbalance between the quantity of labour available and the realised quantity of labour demanded increased. The difference between these two figures at any one time, i.e. the excess labour supply, was the number recorded as unemployed.

The changes in the total civilian labour force and the employed civilian labour force are shown in Figures 5.1 and 5.2. Also shown in these diagrams, for Britain and the USA respectively, are the changes in the male and female sub-totals. These particular graphs represent the differing levels of male and female labour supply and the realised level of labour demand for each of the two sexes. In each case the difference between the supply curve, represented by the total civilian labour force, and the demand curve, represented by the employed civilian labour force, represents the recorded unemployed.

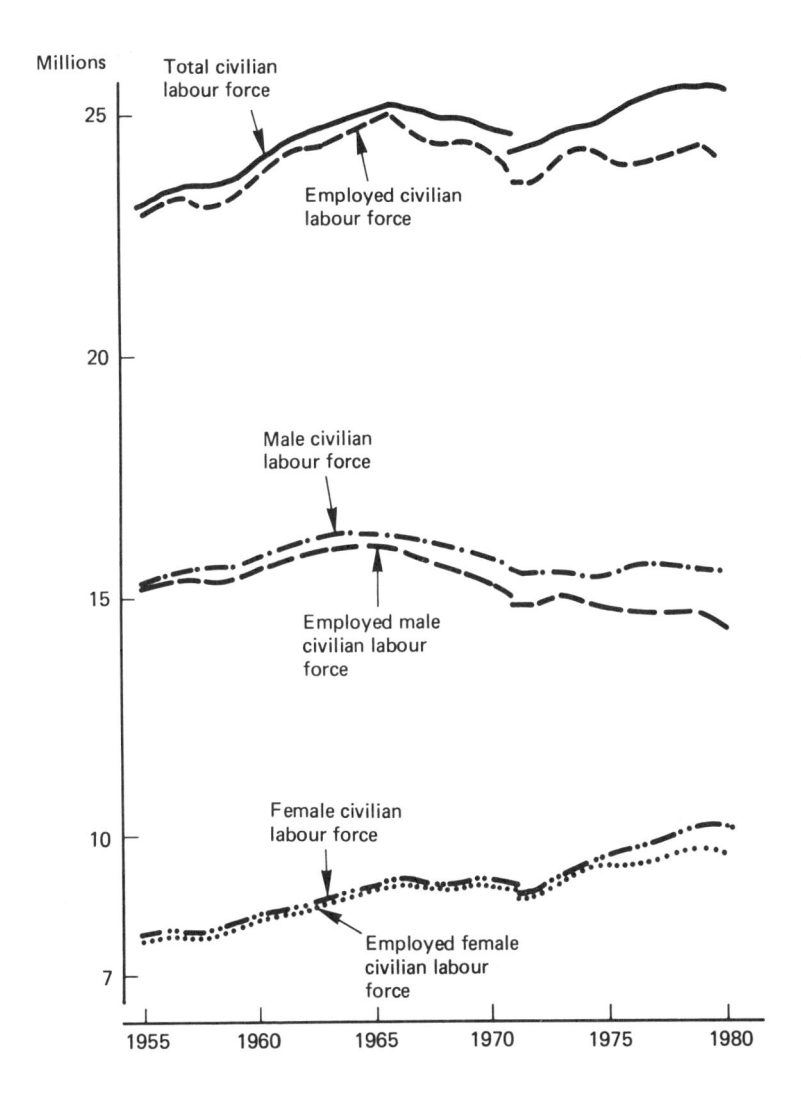

FIGURE 5.1 *Trends in British employment, 1955-80*
SOURCE *Annual Abstract of Statistics*, nos 97 (1960 edn) to 118 (1982 edn).

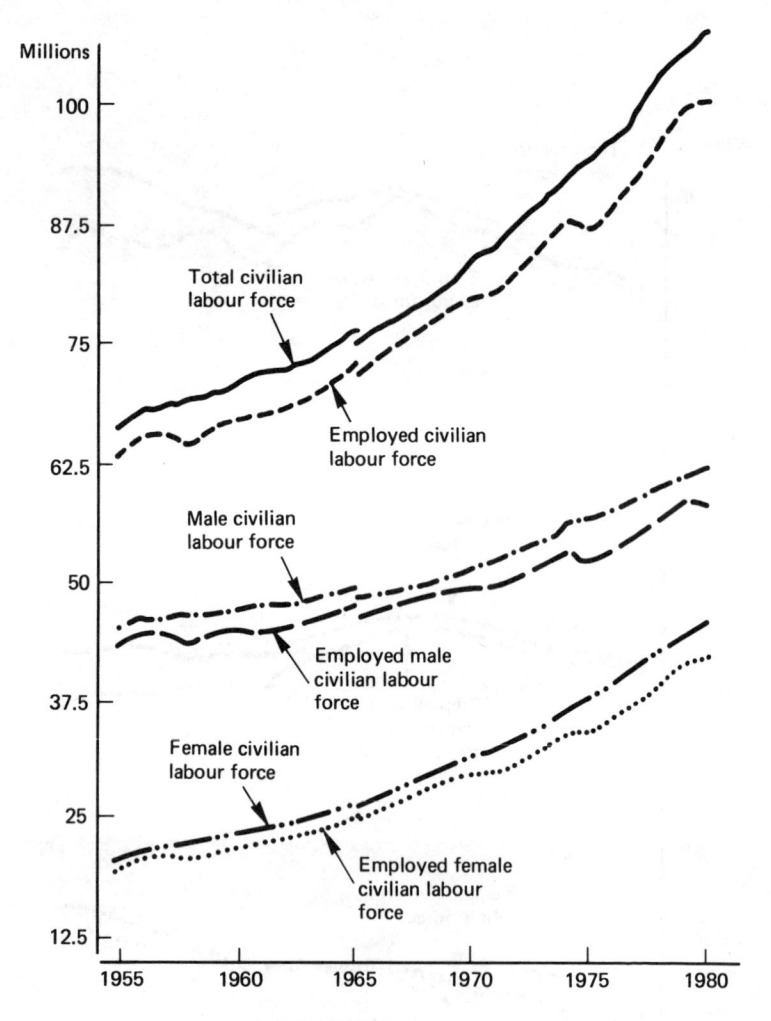

FIGURE 5.2 *Trends in United States employment, 1955-80*
SOURCE *Statistical Abstract of the US*, nos 75 (1955) to 104 (1984).

The British experience

Male labour supply and labour demand have fluctuated considerably since 1955. The general trend for the total male civilian labour force was initially upwards, an increase from 15.3 million in 1955 to 16.2 million in 1965, a 6 per cent growth over the decade. From 1965 the general trend was reversed, and by 1980 male labour supply had contracted to 15.4 million, no higher than in 1955. The employed male civilian labour force, i.e. the realised demand for male labour, also changed, and these changes were of a greater magnitude than those which occurred in the male labour supply. The realised male labour demand grew through the 1950s until it peaked in 1965-6. This growth in male labour demand matched and/or exceeded the increases in male labour supply in most years of this period (see Table 5.1). Since the mid-1960s the realised demand for male workers has declined, and this is reflected in the figures for the employed male civilian labour force. There has been a reduction of one and three-quarter million in the level of realised male demand. This reduction in male demand is nearly 100 per cent more than the simultaneous decline in the male labour supply.

Since 1965-6 total employment in Britain has declined, and by 1980 this reduction equalled a net job loss of 900,000. The decline in male employment has been more rapid and was three times the level which might have been anticipated should the net job losses have been distributed between the two sexes in proportion to the 1955 male/female employment distribution.

The twenty-five year period, 1955-80, divides into two distinct periods. During the first decade male employment grew more rapidly than the male labour force. A proportion of young males who might have contributed to the male labour supply did not do so either because they were continuing their education or undertaking compulsory military service. This loss, though, was partially offset by older male workers remaining in the labour force. For those males beyond the retirement age of 65 years the activity rate in the 1950s was 31 per cent. Consequently any shortfall in male labour supply in the 1955-65 period had to be made up from other potential sources of labour supply, for example females or immigrants. All available data suggest that the male labour market was, in the economist's language, tight, and until at least 1965 the British economy only maintained its expansion, when measured in terms of numbers employed, by increasing the demand for female labour. That there was a desire, or preference, on the part of employers to employ male labour at this time is reflected in the low levels of registered male unemployment. Until the early 1960s registered male unemployment, which included those unsuitable for work or in the process of job change, never exceed 2 per cent of the male civilian labour force.

In the subsequent period, 1966-80, the levels of both male labour supply and demand were quite different (see Figure 5.1). The male population aged 15-64 years continued to increase but at a modest rate com-

TABLE 5.1 Principal trends in British employment, 1955–80*

	Civilian labour** force		Male civilian labour** force		Female civilian labour** force		Total** *** productive industry employment (millions)	Total** † service industry employment (millions)
	Total (millions)	Employed (millions)	Total (millions)	Employed (millions)	Total (millions)	Employed (millions)		
1955	23.1	22.9	15.3	15.2	7.81	7.75	11.55	8.22
1956	23.3	23.1	15.4	15.3	7.90	7.84	11.67	8.35
1957	23.5	23.2	15.5	15.4	7.95	7.88	11.66	8.46
1958	23.5	23.1	15.6	15.3	7.90	7.79	11.49	8.50
1959	23.6	23.2	15.6	15.3	7.99	7.89	11.50	8.65
1960	24.0	23.7	15.8	15.5	8.25	8.16	10.85	10.19
1961	24.3	24.0	15.9	15.7	8.39	8.32	11.00	10.37
1962	24.6	24.2	16.1	15.8	8.52	8.42	10.94	10.49
1963	24.7	24.3	16.2	15.8	8.56	8.44	10.80	10.84
1964	24.9	24.6	16.2	16.0	8.69	8.61	10.99	11.00
1965	25.0	24.8	16.2	16.0	8.84	8.78	11.13	11.12
1966	25.2	24.9	16.2	16.0	9.01	8.96	11.19	11.23
1967	25.0	24.5	16.1	15.7	8.92	8.83	10.80	11.25
1968	24.9	24.3	15.9	15.5	8.93	8.86	10.60	11.36
1969	24.9	24.4	15.8	15.4	9.00	8.93	10.62	11.42
1970	24.7	24.2	15.7	15.3	9.01	8.93	10.46	11.40

1971	24.2	23.5	15.5	14.9	8.63	8.60	9.50	11.65
1972	24.3	23.5	15.4	14.8	8.82	8.70	9.25	11.99
1973	24.6	24.1	15.5	15.0	9.16	9.08	9.36	12.45
1974	24.7	24.2	15.3	14.9	9.38	9.30	9.34	12.60
1975	24.9	24.0	15.4	14.7	9.49	9.34	8.96	12.86
1976	25.2	23.9	15.5	14.6	9.63	9.32	8.71	12.98
1977	25.3	24.0	15.5	14.5	9.80	9.42	8.73	13.06
1978	25.5	24.1	15.5	14.6	9.93	9.53	8.69	13.22
1979	25.5	24.3	15.4	14.5	10.08	9.68	8.63	13.43
1980	25.4	23.8	15.4	14.3	10.05	9.55	8.25	13.41

*Until 1970 statistics derived mainly from counts of national insurance cards, from 1971 *Census of Employment* data. Figures are not therefore strictly comparable. Mid-year estimates throughout.

**Until 1973 persons over 15 years and over included, 1974 onwards 16 years and over.

***Productive Industry Sector consists of All Manufacturing, Mining and Construction Industries.

†Services other than those provided by Transport, Communication and Public Utilities but including all Public Administration.

††1955–1959 based on 1948 Standard Industrial Classification (SIC)
1960–1965 on 1958 SIC and 1966–1980 on 1968 SIC.

SOURCE *Annual Abstract of Statistics*, nos 97 (1960 edn) to 118 (1982 edn).

pared with the previous decade. However, rising participation by young males in education led to a higher proportion than previously being temporarily withdrawn from the labour market; part of the increase was permanently withdrawn as a result of policies leading to earlier retirement in some industries. Census data indicate a decline in the numbers of males of 65 years and over in the civilian labour force. Consequently the effect on the labour force of the growth in the male population aged 15-64 was outweighed by the increasing numbers in education and retirement, resulting in the potential male labour supply declining continuously between 1966 and 1980. Simultaneously, the employed male civilian labour force, i.e. the realised male labour demand, also declined over this period, the total reduction being double the increase experienced in the previous decade. While male labour demand fell against the background of a reduced male labour supply, the decline in the demand for male labour was both more rapid and larger, and resulted in a higher percentage of the male labour force being unemployed in 1980 than in 1965, the figures being 7 per cent and 1.3 per cent respectively.

The trends in aggregate employment in Britain would suggest that, in part, the increase in the demand for female labour has been a consequence of the overall rise in labour demand. The employed civilian labour force grew by 900,000 between 1955 and 1980. Since females represented one-third of the labour force in 1955 it could be anticipated that female employment might increase as total employment did. Secondly, in examining the trends in male employment the evidence might suggest that the 'tightness' of the male labour supply until the mid-1960s could have acted to induce employers to increase their demand for substitutes for male labour, and the most immediately available substitute was female labour. Against this background the changing character of the realised female labour demand, i.e. the employed female civilian labour force, can be analysed.

The trend in aggregate female labour supply delivered to the labour market, i.e. the total female civilian labour force, has been sharply upwards throughout the period, with only minor variations about the trend in 1967-8 and 1971-3. Over the period 1955 to 1980 the female labour supply in Britain increased by nearly 30 per cent, from 7.8 million to 10.1 million. Half of this increase occurred during the course of the first decade, the period when the male labour market was exceptionally tight. The remainder of the increase was between 1966 and 1980 when male labour supply came increasingly to exceed male labour realised demand. The female labour supply continued to grow, especially after 1971, against a background of rising male unemployment. While an increasing proportion

The Demand for Female Labour

of the British male labour force has registered as unemployed, a simultaneous growth in the numbers of females offering to supply paid labour on the labour market has taken place. Further, as Figure 5.1 indicates, until 1975 at least 99 per cent of those females who supplied labour, the total female civilian labour force, could expect to gain employment in the employed female civilian labour force, for throughout the entire period 1955 to 1980 the realised demand for female labour increased.

In the decade 1955-65, the realised demand for females increased by over one million. This growth in female employment was both relatively faster than male employment growth and was absolutely greater than the male increase, although the male increase may have been constrained by demographic and institutional factors. Thatcher (1979, p. 280) takes the view that given the rising demand for labour and the static male labour supply, the extra labour could only be obtained by employing married women; that is to say, females were substituted for males. In the period 1965 to 1980 the numbers of females in employment continued to increase, by an overall addition of three-quarters of a million while male employment fell by 825,000. When considering the realised demand for females the period again divides into two parts. There is an early period, 1955-65, when female labour supply moved in parallel with the rapid growth in the realised demand for female labour, and the consequence was a low level of recorded female unemployment. Then there is a later period, 1966-80, when realised female labour demand, reflected in the employed female civilian labour force totals, continued to grow, but at a rate of only half the average annual percentage increase previously recorded, against a background of accelerating female labour supply growth and rising male unemployment. Between 1955 and 1980, against a changing demographic and social background, e.g. changing attitudes towards education and retirement, a decisive change in the character of the realised labour demand in Britain occurred. Total realised labour demand grew by nearly a million, but within that increase realised male labour demand fell by 900,000 or 6 per cent, and the realised female labour demand increased by 1.8 million, a 25 per cent increase over the numbers employed in 1955.

The US experience

The magnitude of the change in employment levels in the US economy and the direction of those changes are quite different from the British experience, for while in Britain civilian employment rose by 4 per cent, in the USA the increase was 60 per cent. In analysing the growth of female employment it is of value initially to examine the employment trends for each sex as shown in Figure 5.2.

Observation of the curves for males reveals that both the level of supply, the total male civilian labour force, and the realised level of demand, the employed male civilian labour force, rose almost continuously throughout the period, although with occasional fluctuations about the trend for the realised demand. The male labour supply rose from 45 million in 1955 to 61.5 million in 1980, this rise occurring despite the exclusion after 1966 from the total of the 14-16 year-old age group. Thus in twenty-five years the US male labour supply rose by one-third, this growth being due to both natural growth and of migration to the USA. Unlike Britain, even when account is taken for growing numbers in both education and retirement, the US male labour force grew by an average of 1.5 per cent per annum.

While the male labour supply increased, a simultaneous growth in the realised labour demand for US males took place. The employed male civilian labour force grew from 43 million in 1955 to over 57 million in 1980, a 14 million increase. The employment trend rise was almost continuous, and only occasionally was realised male demand in one year lower than in the previous year. Although the economic circumstances were different in the USA, one feature was the same as in Britain, namely a faster growth in the total male civilian labour force, i.e. the male labour supply, than the numbers in the employed male civilian labour force, i.e. the realised labour demand. The difference is reflected in the male unemployment level which rose by two-thirds from 4.2 per cent in 1955 to 6.9 per cent in 1980.

In the USA, until the early 1960s, the male population aged 15-64 years was smaller than the number of males in the total male labour force, which included the male civilian labour force and young males still 'in school'. Also as in Britain, the US economy depended in part for its male labour supply on those aged 65 years and over. While the rate of US male unemployment was higher than in Britain, it would appear nevertheless that the US male labour market was also 'tight'. If there was to be employment growth in the US economy, then it was only possible if substitutes to US male workers were available. In fact two close substitutes did exist, male immigrants and females, and Woytinsky (1967, p. 105) found that females in fact contributed two-thirds of the increase in the total workforce during this early period. As the 1960s progressed this no longer held true; total male labour force plus the 'in school' group by 1980 represented only 90 per cent of the male population aged 15-64. Over time not only did the level of unemployment rise by two-thirds, but there was a simultaneous withdrawal by males from the male labour supply. There developed in the USA a situation similar to the one which had occurred in Britain, although with one essential difference. In the USA realised demand for males continued to grow. From the mid-1960s, when the 'tightness' of male supply in the labour market was decreasing, the average percentage growth in realised male employment was double that experienced in the earlier period when the male labour market was tight. In the USA, as a potential male labour supply became available the demand for male employees accelerated; in Britain there had been a decline.

During the quarter of a century, 1955-80, the total female civilian labour force in the USA, i.e. the female labour supply, more than doubled, from under 21 million to over 45 million, even after taking into account the withdrawal after 1966 of the 14-16 year-olds. The timing of this growth in the female labour supply is worthy of note. In the first ten-year period, 1955-65, when it has been suggested that the male labour market was tight, the female labour supply rose by 25 per cent. In the subsequent period to 1980, when the tightness went out of the male labour market, the female labour supply grew by a further 95 per cent of the 1955 total. In this instance the US experience has been the reverse to that of Britain. In the latter nation the fastest growth in the female labour supply was in the first decade when the male labour market was tight, but in similar circumstances the percentage increase in the USA was lower.

With respect to the realised demand for female labour, as reflected in the employed female civilian labour force, the pattern of growth was somewhat similar, but not entirely so. Over the period being considered the employed female civilian labour force grew by 113 per cent, from 19.8 million to 42.1 million, an absolute growth one and a half times that of the employed male labour force. In the early period there was an increase in female employment of 27 per cent, a marginally higher percentage increase than in female supply, which resulted in a decline in female unemployment. This growth in female employment could be taken to imply that there was some substitution of females for males within the tight labour market situation. Of the increased realised demand within the US economy at this time 60 per cent was met by females, and the average percentage rate of increase of female employment was three times that experienced by males. It is an open question as to whether more males or females would have gained employment if the supply of either sex had been higher. R. E. Smith (1977) believed it was the consequence of the high level of aggregate labour demand in the USA that caused the female labour supply to increase. Given the tight male labour market,

TABLE 5.2 Principal trends in US employment, 1955–80*

	Civilian labour** force		Male civilian labour** force		Female civilian labour** force		Total***** productive industry employment (millions)	Total**† service industry employment (millions)
	Total (millions)	Employed (millions)	Total (millions)	Employed (millions)	Total (millions)	Employed (millions)		
1955	65.8	62.9	45.0	43.2	20.8	19.8	20.5	30.2
1956	67.5	64.7	45.8	44.0	21.8	20.7	21.1	31.3
1957	67.9	65.0	45.9	44.0	22.1	21.0	20.9	32.0
1958	68.6	64.0	46.2	43.0	22.5	20.9	19.5	31.9
1959	69.4	65.6	46.6	44.1	22.8	21.5	20.4	32.9
1960	70.0	66.1	47.0	44.5	23.6	22.2	20.4	33.8
1961	71.6	67.0	47.4	44.4	24.2	22.5	19.8	34.3
1962	71.9	67.8	47.4	44.9	24.5	23.0	20.4	35.1
1963	73.0	68.8	47.9	45.3	25.1	23.8	20.6	36.0
1964	74.2	70.4	48.4	46.1	25.8	24.2	20.9	37.2
1965	75.6	72.2	49.0	47.0	26.6	25.1	21.8	38.6
1966	75.8	72.9	48.5	46.9	27.3	26.0	23.1	40.8
1967	77.3	74.4	49.0	47.5	28.4	26.9	23.3	42.6
1968	78.7	75.9	49.5	48.1	29.2	27.8	23.6	44.2
1969	80.7	77.9	50.2	48.8	30.5	29.1	24.2	46.0
1970	82.8	78.7	51.2	49.0	31.5	29.7	23.5	47.4

1971	84.4	79.4	52.0	49.2	32.1	29.9	22.6	48.3
1972	87.0	82.2	53.3	50.6	33.3	31.0	23.5	50.2
1973	89.4	85.1	54.6	52.0	34.4	32.7	24.7	53.1
1974	91.9	86.8	55.7	53.0	36.2	33.8	24.7	53.7
1975	93.8	85.8	56.3	51.9	37.5	34.0	22.5	54.4
1976	96.2	88.8	57.2	53.1	39.0	35.6	23.4	56.0
1977	99.0	92.0	58.4	54.7	40.6	37.3	24.3	58.1
1978	102.3	96.0	59.6	56.5	42.6	39.6	25.6	61.1
1979	105.0	98.8	60.7	57.6	44.2	41.2	26.5	63.4
1980	106.9	99.3	61.5	57.2	45.5	42.1	25.7	64.8

*Beginning 1960 figures include Alaska and Hawaii.
**1955–65 includes persons 14 years and over; 1966–80 includes persons 16 years and over.
***Productive industry sector consists of all manufacturing, mining and construction industries.
†Services other than those provided by transport, communications and public utilities but including government employees where appropriate.
SOURCE   Statistical Abstract of the US 75th Edition (1955) to 104th Edition (1984) inclusive.

employers appeared to switch their labour demand to females to the extent that the female labour market itself began to experience lower levels of unemployment.

While the increase in the realised demand for females was substantial between 1955 and 1965, this was to be insignificant when compared with the following period. Between 1965 and 1980 the realised demand for female labour grew from under 25 million to over 42 million, a 70 per cent increase and an annual percentage rate of growth of double that experienced in the previous decade.

The increase in the realised demand for female labour took place when both male and female labour supply were increasing rapidly. In the latter case the total female civilian labour force rose from 23.25 million in 1965 to 45.5 million in 1980. This increase in the female labour supply was faster than the growth in the realised demand for female labour, and the percentage rate of female unemployment rose.

The rise in the realised demand for female labour, reflected in the numbers of females employed, was of a greater magnitude, in both percentage and absolute terms, than occurred among males. The consequence of this in the USA was the same as in Britain, although for quite different reasons, namely employed females came to represent a higher proportion of the employed civilian labour force. Females in 1955 in the USA contributed 31.5 per cent of the employed labour force. After ten years of 'tightness' in the male labour market this had risen by 1965 to nearly 35 per cent, a modest shift but at the time considered to be significant. In 1980 the percentage had risen to 42.4 per cent. The growth in the female contribution to the US employed labour force was fastest when there was no shortage of potential male employees, which was also the British experience.

WHY THE DEMAND FOR FEMALE LABOUR GREW

The employment patterns and industrial experiences of the USA and Britain between 1955 and 1980 appear on examination to be different. In the USA, the level of realised labour demand, reflected in the numbers employed, grew continuously for males and females on a year-to-year basis. In Britain a similar pattern, but at a lower level, was identifiable for the period 1955–65, but subsequently male and total employment declined, although female employment continued the earlier pattern of growth, at a slower pace.

Similarities did exist. Until 1965 the growth in male employment in both nations may have been constrained by tight labour market conditions which reflected demographic, social and political circumstances. The tightness in the male labour market in each country may have caused employers to seek substitutes for male workers. In both the USA and Britain immigration levels rose, and in both the USA and Britain the employment of females grew. The increased demand for female employees reflected an increasing demand for labour and was not the result of a desire to employ females specifically. Wright (1979, p. 57), while accepting that the increased number of females in the labour market did reduce certain labour shortages, believed their contribution was limited by their willingness to enter only a few occupations.

However, in both countries after the mid-1960s differing sets of circumstances are identifiable. In the USA, aggregate demand for civilian labour, measured in the numbers employed, continued to grow, while in Britain employment demand fell. In both countries the demand for male labour slackened. The previously tight male labour markets now experienced higher levels of unemployment, for in this period there was an increasing male labour supply relative to the level of demand. The previous need to substitute female labour for male labour, *ceteris paribus*, ceased to be necessary. Nevertheless the labour demand reflected in the number of females employed continued to increase, although not as fast as the available potential female labour force. In both the USA and Britain the female contribution to the employed civilian labour forces grew in relative significance.

In the period 1955-65, and possibly for some years earlier, there was a growth in the demand for female employees as a consequence of a constrained male labour supply. From 1965 onwards, when different economic conditions existed, there occurred a shift in the character of labour demand and this induced a rapid expansion of the realised demand for females at the apparent expense of male workers.

The explanation for this aggregate shift in the character of labour demand lies not with the numbers of males and/or females willing to work but rather with the changes that were taking place in the underlying influences of labour demand.

To consider the changing influences on labour demand it is assumed that the economies of the USA and Britain are both two-sector economies with a productive industry sector and a service industry sector. Other sectors, i.e. agriculture and transport, communications and the public utilities, are excluded from this examination. In Britain the two sectors being considered provided 86 per cent and 91 per cent of the realised

108 Women and the Economy

civilian labour demand in 1955 and 1980 respectively. For the USA the comparative figures were 81 per cent and 91 per cent respectively. These two sectors combined were the dominant influence on the size and character of the realised civilian labour demand on both sides of the Atlantic. Therefore the employment performance of the two sectors may possibly explain the shift in the character of labour demand. The trend in the relative employment demand in the two sectors is shown in Figure 5.3.

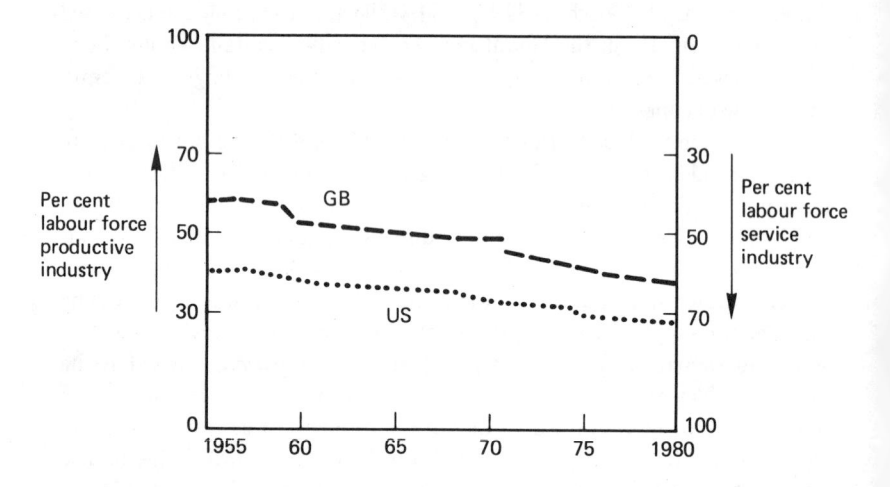

FIGURE 5.3   *Percentage of labour force in productive industry and service industry, Great Britain and the USA*
SOURCE   Table 5.1 and Table 5.2.

The direction of the trend is clear. In both countries the employment significance of the productive industry sector was in continuous decline, while the employment significance of the service industry sector grew. It is important to appreciate that it was the *relative* significance that was changing. Employment in the productive industry sector in Britain grew in absolute terms through the 1950s (see Pollard, 1979, p. 430), as it did in the USA (see Sample, 1974, p. 121). Other writers, though, e.g. Morgan (1966, p. 31) have drawn attention to a change in the sector away from producing capital goods to an expansion of consumer goods industries, a shift which might have facilitated greater employment opportunities for females. While the relative decline in the productive industry sector was faster in Britain than in the USA, the rate of decline varied little between the pre- and post-1965-6 periods. In the USA the decline in the productive industry sector's relative employment was more rapid post-1965, which possibly reflected the ending of the availability of an alternative labour reserve pool from the agriculture sector. Of greater significance are the aggregate figures of realised labour demand. Until 1965-6 productive industry and service industry employment in Britain grew, while after that date the former sector's employment declined. In the USA the productive industry sector labour demand grew over the entire twenty-five year period, but the relative growth was below that achieved in the service sector.

While total employment in the productive industry sector declined relative to employment in the service sector industries, the character of the available employment was also in the process of change. Elliot (1977) attributed this to technical change which led to the substitution of white-collar for manual workers, and Woytinsky (1963, p. 113) believed that these changes within industries favoured the employment of females. Waldman and McEaddy (1974) went so far as to attribute the expansion of female employment to a tidal wave of paperwork that occurred in the industrial world after the Second World War.

Figure 5.3 shows that a change was occurring in the character of the derived demand for labour, there being a relative decline in demand from the productive industry sector and a growth in demand from the service industry sector. The reasons for this employment shift are complex. Metcalf and Richardson (1982, p. 251) have attributed the change to increases in labour productivity in the productive industry sector, reflecting investment in technology which partially favoured female employment, and changes in consumer demand, which were a consequence of rising real incomes. Whatever the cause, the derived demand for labour has changed, and even if aggregate labour demand had been constant between 1955 and 1980, the character of the labour demand changed. Some industries and occupations in the productive industries declined while simultaneously some industries and occupations in the service sector increased in size.

These changes in derived demand need not have caused an increase in the demand for females at the expense of the male labour demand, unless there were other considerations, and three factors suggest that a switch in the character of labour demand was a possibility.

First, while in the 1950s females were a minority of the labour force of both sectors, females represented a smaller proportion of the productive industry labour force than of the service sector. In 1950, females contributed 25 per cent and 20 per cent of the labour in the productive industries of Britain and the USA respectively, while their contribution to the service industries exceeded 40 per cent in both countries (see Tables

3.4 and 3.5). Consequently growth in the service industry sector which occurred at the expense of the productive industry sector would, *ceteris paribus*, lead to a shift in labour demand which favoured females.

In theory there was no reason why males should not have sought employment in the expanding service industry sector as the productive industry sector's employment declined relatively. In practice the location of the growing service sector industries was often other than the location of the declining productive industries, and this reduced the opportunity of males to transfer between sectors. Even where no locational problems existed the range of job skills offered in the labour market often differed between the sexes. Those with clerical skills, an occupation where 60 per cent of the workers in 1951 were female in both countries, could more easily transfer between sectors than those with machine-related manual skills. In both countries the fall in employment in the productive sector consisted mainly of males, while most of the increase in employment in the service sector consisted of females. The view of Urquhart (1984), based on a study of labour flows, is that there has been no real net migration of workers from the productive sector to the services sector; rather the primary source of new employees to the service sector was women who had not previously, or recently, held jobs. There are then *a priori* grounds for expecting that the relative rise in the service sector employment *vis-à-vis* the productive industry sector would lead to the increase in the female demand noted above. If Urquhart is correct, and he is not alone in his views, then those females now entering the service sector, which previously employed a higher percentage of females than the productive industry sector, were further reinforcing the occupational segregation which already existed.

Two features of potential female employees made them attractive employees to the growing service sector industries. Females were cheaper to employ than males, average wage rates for females being below those for males. The desire to keep labour costs at a minimum has been especially important in the service industry sector, where demand for the services being provided is often highly responsive to price movements. Demand for many service sector activities, e.g. recreation, entertainment, vacations, meals outside the home, etc. is more dependent upon the cost to the consumer than the demand for goods like food and housing. The labour costs associated with this type of service represent a high proportion of the costs of provision and hence the price charged. Growth in employment in the service sector industries requires the level of prices charged, and hence the wages actually paid, being kept at a minimum. Only service sector industries that have achieved this have maintained their employment

The Demand for Female Labour

growth. Thus employment growth has been dependent upon containing labour costs, and this requirement has encouraged employers to take on female workers.

Finally, the 'production cycle' requirements of the service industries differ from the productive industry sector where output can flow continuously throughout a shift and/or a day. In many of the service sector industries there are peak periods when demand is high, for example midday in financial institutions and distribution, or evenings in hotels and restaurants, with corresponding troughs when demand is relatively low. Thus the conventional working day for productive industry, e.g. eight hours continuous working, is not necessarily appropriate in the service sector. Rather an appropriate working day might be four hours' work at mid-day, then a four-hour break, followed by four hours' work in the evening. This unconventional pattern of working hours would hold few attractions for either male or female workers. If such a working day was divided between two employees, or over a seven-day week shared between four, it could simultaneously meet service sector employers' labour requirements and offer the opportunity for those who might not otherwise enter the labour market, in particular married women, to combine employment with work in the home. Fearn (1981, p. 78) believed the service sector labour demand for part-time work and more flexible hours was a better match for those with household commitments. The willingness of females to accept part-time employment, (half the females working in the service sector in Britain in 1981 were employed part-time), ensured that there was a female labour supply to match the increasing labour demand being generated by the relative growth of the service sector industries.

One result of this willingness of females, especially those re-entering the labour market, to accept part-time employment in a limited number of occupations, which often require skills similar to those used in the home, e.g. serving food and cleaning, is to strengthen further labour market segregation.

Wider questions relating to female part-time employment are examined in Chapter 7. One aspect of the growth of female part-time employment requires to be noted in the context of this chapter, however. Should an employer require an additional forty hours of labour input and employ one worker full-time, the total labour force will increase by one; if those hours were split between two part-time workers the total labour force would increase by two, although the additional hours of labour input would be the same. In Britain, between 1971 and 1981, the Annual Employment Census shows that female employment rose by 790,000. In the same period full-time female employment fell by 213,000, while female part-time employment rose by 1,003,000. Over the past generation the number of females employed part-time has grown rapidly, often at the expense of full-time employment for females as well as males, this type of work pattern reflecting the derived demand for labour in service sector industries. One consequence of the growth of part-time working is that the aggregate size of the employed female civilian labour force, the realised demand for female labour, has grown more rapidly than if the measure of labour demand was in the form of either working days equivalent or total working hours demanded. Indeed, Bosworth and Wilson (1980) suggest that the growth in female employment is partly an illusion caused by considering the labour input only in terms of heads and not hours. A similar conclusion was reached by Kuhn (1956, p. 330), who in noting the fast growth of female part-time employment expressed the view that the upward trend in the number of 'whole' workers in the US economy may have been an illusion.

CONCLUSION

The demand for labour is derived from the demand for goods and services. If shifts occur in labour demand that is because society collectively changes its demand for goods and services. In the post-Second World War era the real incomes of the population in both the USA and Britain have risen. Initially that rise generated a high demand for consumer goods, causing employment levels to increase in manufacturing, especially in the new light manufacturing sectors. Such an increase in employment levels created labour bottlenecks which reflected the limited number of males available to enter the labour market. One solution to the labour market tightness was to encourage other groups to enter, or re-enter, the labour market, and one such group was women. This should not be taken to mean manufacturing industry went out of its way to recruit females. The process was often far more complicated, but always at the end of the process there existed jobs, usually in the service sector, which would not be filled unless females were employed. Such employment was often in what Doeringer and Prior (1971) termed the secondary labour market, from which males were only too happy to escape, leaving an increasing number of women in a limited range of often low skilled occupations in selected industrial sectors. This increase in occupational and industrial segregation, the nature of which Oppenheimer (1976) examines, became only too apparent. This early period was of importance in establishing a higher level of demand in peace time for female labour than had occurred before 1940. Both Knudsen

(1970) and Lewenhak (1980, p. 228) attributed the change to a combination of demographic factors and labour shortages. Metcalf and Richardson (1982, p. 251) have examined other alternatives but concluded that the growth in female demand was attributable to the unprecedented and persistent tightness of the male labour market.

As real incomes continued their unprecedented rise through the 1960s, consumer demand began to grow in the area of service activities, although where the activities were funded by public bodies, e.g. education and medical care, the growth had begun earlier. This growth in the service sector created new labour demands, and females who had become increassingly established in the service sector, where their willingness to work flexible and unsocial hours for wages which were relatively low by productive industry standards had made them satisfactory employees, were to be the main beneficiaries of this rise in labour demand. The result was an increase in labour market segregation. At the same time, though, increasing numbers of females were, as a result of legislation and increased educational opportunity, able to enter into primary labour market jobs, thus beginning the process of reducing the degree of industrial and occupational segregation in that type of market.

The demand for female labour cannot be looked at in isolation. It is created within a dynamic economic system and continuously changes in response to consumer tastes and preferences and in response to technological development which leads to both new productive methods and new products. There are economic explanations for the changing nature and increasing demand for females within the labour market, but equally of importance is the change that has had to occur in social attitudes which now allow women to work in areas of employment where the traditional labour demand was for males only.

6 Equal Opportunity and Pay

The question of whether or not females have equality with males in the labour market remains contentious. It is necessary to recognise that inequality is a concept with many facets. Firstly, there is the possibility of 'pre-entry discrimination', whereby females are denied equality of opportunity to enter some occupations and/or industries. Secondly, when a female has successfully gained employment she may face 'post-entry discrimination'. One form of post-entry discrimination is a poorer reward package for female employees, i.e. lower pay, often accompanied by fewer holidays, less sick pay and pension rights, etc. Post-entry discrimination may also take the form of denial of equal opportunity for training and/or promotion.

It is therefore possible to identify three specific areas where discrimination may occur. Before seeking economic and/or other explanations, it is necessary to establish whether or not inequalities in these areas do exist. Discrimination can, of course, be directed not just against females but this is the only aspect that is investigated here.

THE EVIDENCE OF INEQUALITY

Pre-entry discrimination

In Chapter 3 an outline was provided of female employment patterns in contemporary Britain and the USA, and it is unnecessary to repeat this at length here. However, it is appropriate to highlight certain features.

From Table 6.1 it is clear that females are overrepresented in the service sector of the economy, and are underrepresented in manufacturing industries. Similarly, it is necessary to take note of the occupational divisions

TABLE 6.1 *Deployment of male and female employees by key industrial sector, 1980–1*

	Female employment (000's)	Male employment (000's)
Britain (1981)		
Manufacturing industry	1 921	5 878
Service sector*	6 671	5 495
United States (1980)		
Manufacturing industry	7 652	15 899
Service sector*	33 394	28 500

*Service sector excludes transport and communications.
SOURCES *Census of Population*, 1981; *US Census of Population*, 1980.

between the sexes. In Britain in 1981 over 50 per cent of all female employees were in the two occupational categories of clerical and related and catering, cleaning, hairdressing and other personal services; in these occupations males represented less than a quarter of the workforce. A report by the Office of Manpower Economics (1972) noted that one-third of female employees were in occupations where males represented less than 10 per cent of the workforce; by 1981 male representation in the occupations where 50 per cent of women were employed was 12 per cent.

The obvious inference from Tables 6.1 and 6.2 is that employees are not randomly distributed between occupations and/or industries, but rather each occupational group and industrial sector has distinctive characteristics, of which sex is one. Even in industrial sectors where females represent the majority of the labour force, clear segregation still occurs. Robinson and Wallace (1977) drew attention to the employment patterns within the distribution industry, where females represent 55 per cent of the total labour force. There was a high female concentration in 'groceries and provisions', 'clothing and footwear', 'other non-food' and 'general stores', but women represented only one-third of the labour force in 'furniture, carpets and electrical goods'. Waldman and McEaddy (1974) suggested that while both men and women find employment in the fast growing sectors of the economy, somehow the men obtain the more prestigious, better paying professional-technical jobs. Thus there appears to be evidence to support the hypothesis that there is inequality of opportunity in the initial distribution of employment.

TABLE 6.2 *Deployment of male and female employees in selected occupations, 1980-1*

	Female employment (000's)	Male employment (000's)
Britain (1981)		
Professional and related		
Education, welfare and health	1 232	652
Science, engineering and technology	87	896
Catering, cleaning, hairdressing, and other personal service	1 959	496
Processing, making, repairing and related (metal and electrical)	145	2 531
United States (1980)		
Managers and administrators (except farm)	2 850	8 069
Clerical and kindred	14 502	3 603
Craft and kindred	752	11 777
Operatives, except transport	4 149	6 197

SOURCES *Census of Population*, 1981; *US Census of Population*, 1980.

Post-entry discrimination: pay

When comparing male and female pay one has to make clear whether one is talking about hourly rates of pay or total earnings. As many more women than men work part-time, total earnings would consequently on average be lower for females even if the hourly rate was the same as the male rate. One can, of course, argue that it is total earnings that matter, and discrimination, in the home and at work, forces many females into part-time employment. Nevertheless, it is important to keep the distinction between hourly pay and total earnings in mind.

Figure 6.1 shows the earnings profiles of manual and non-manual male and female employees in Britain, by age cohort. Certain features can be identified, although in doing so it has to be remembered that these curves cover all industries and occupations.

Firstly, and most significantly, the 'average' pay of females, whether manual and non-manual is always below the levels achieved by males in each age level. Secondly, while male earnings continue to rise until the recipients are in their 30s or 40s, the rise in female earnings ceases abruptly when the recipients are in their early 20s. For the average woman, earnings stabilise from the usual age when family formation starts.

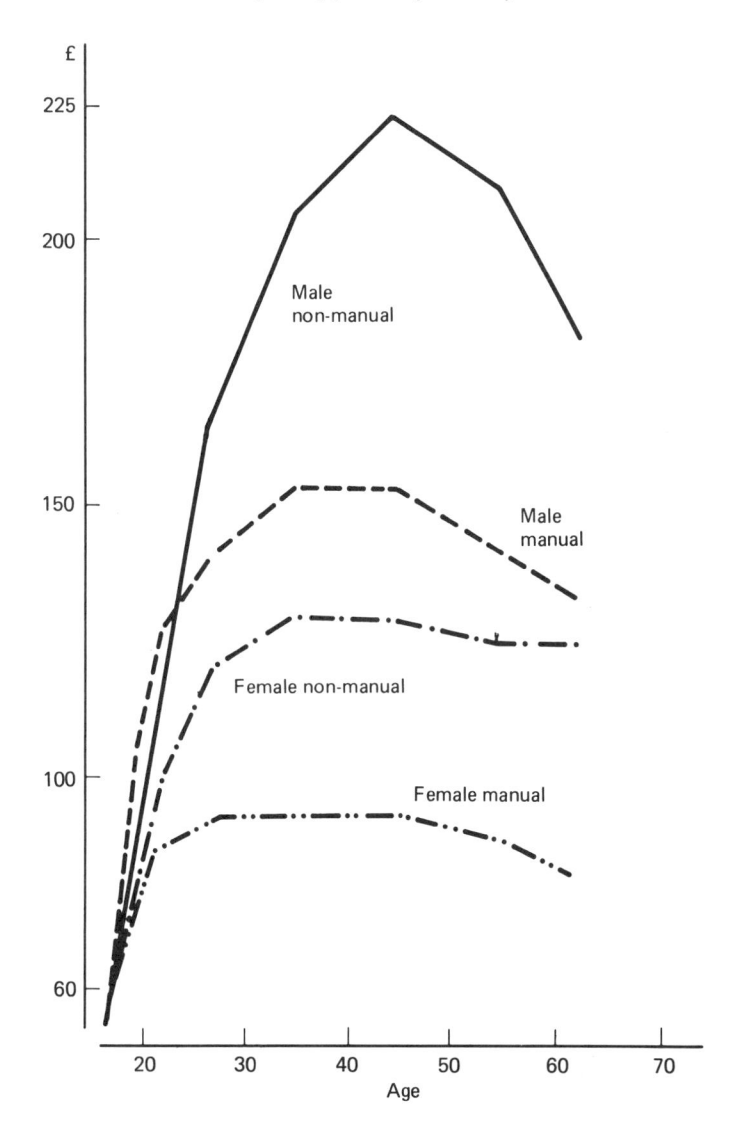

FIGURE 6.1 *Profile of full-time adult gross weekly earnings by age, sex and status, 1983*
SOURCE *New Earnings Survey*, Part A, 1983.

Figure 6.1 would, therefore, appear to provide evidence that there exists inequality of earnings between the sexes in Britain. This, of course, not a recent feature. During the twenty-year period 1950-70 weekly female earnings remained within a band of 50-55 per cent of male earnings, this stability occurring at a time of changing supply and demand conditions in the labour market.

Hacker (1983, p. 148) has provided an analysis of the relation of US females' income to that of males, by occupational class, which indicates that in the majority of classes female income was between 60 and 66 per cent of male income. This figure is confirmed by the *Statistical Abstract of the US* (1984, Table 76), where the median weekly earnings for females in 1981 and 1982 are shown as being 63 per cent of the male median weekly earnings.

This inequality in pay is not a uniquely British or American feature; it is common in most Western industrial nations. The OECD (1979) noted that in member nations hourly female earnings were usually 70-75 per cent of the male level, regardless of the relative size of the female labour force. In Britain in 1982 the average hourly female earnings were 74.8 per cent of those received by males, although the percentage of women receiving 'equal pay' had risen considerably from the 11 per cent of the female labour force in 1966, which was noted by Paterson and Armstrong (1972).

Although in Britain average female earnings are below male average earnings, the actual spread of earnings between the lowest and highest deciles is virtually the same for the two sexes (see Table 6.3). Thus the structure of earnings for each sex is nearly identical, the only difference being that the female one is at a lower level.

TABLE 6.3   *Dispersion of full-time adults' total earnings, 1983*

	Lowest £	Decile % of median	Median £	Highest £	Decile % of median
Males					
Manual	91.2	68	134.8	204.5	152
Non-manual	106.3	60	176.1	300.2	170
Females					
Manual	57.9	69	84.1	122.2	145
Non-manual	69.1	60	104.7	172.4	165

SOURCE   *New Earnings Survey,* 1983.

Post-entry discrimination: promotion

This is an area of potential inequality which is one of the most difficult to identify, for while the census analyses of occupations provide some clues to suggest that equality of opportunity may not exist (e.g. in Britain only 19 per cent of all managers and administrators and only 20 per cent of all supervisors are female), it would be valuable to have detailed information on specific cases. This is regrettably not readily available for the private sector of the economy, but there is limited evidence for the public sector in Britain, where equal pay policies have operated for over twenty years.

In England and Wales in 1982, females provided 59 per cent of the total number of schoolteachers. However, 77 per cent of primary schoolteachers were female but only 45 per cent of the teachers in secondary schools. While all teachers start their careers at the same point as probationers, as Figure 6.2 shows, their subsequent career prospects diverge greatly. In the basic grade (Scale 1) the number of female teachers is higher than might be anticipated, whereas in subsequent grades to which teachers may be promoted the proportion of female teachers declines to below their percentage level in the profession. Thus while teachers may begin their careers as equals, as their careers progress males tend to achieve promotion to the higher posts. A situation not dissimilar to the British one has been

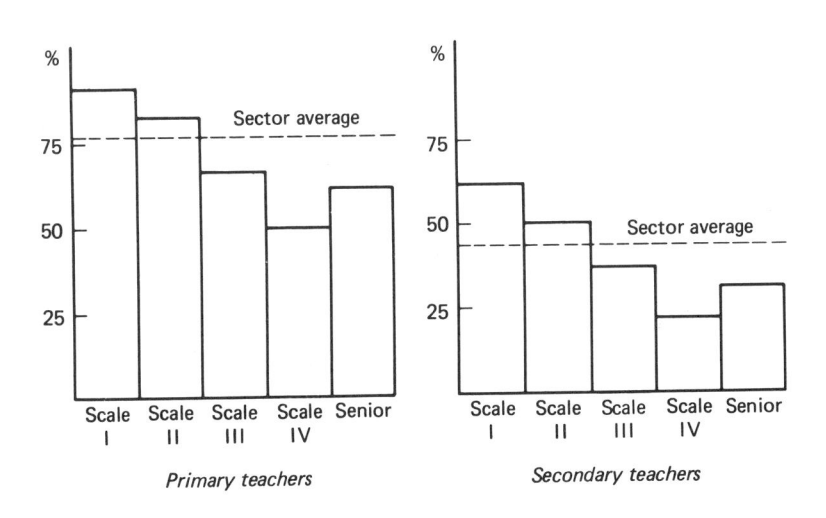

FIGURE 6.2 *Percentage distribution of female schoolteachers by level of post, 1982*
SOURCE *Statistics of Education*, 1982.

noted in the USA. Gross (1968) observed that while most men teach in high schools and women mainly teach in the elementary schools, the school principals and other administrators tend to be men.
Information published on clearly defined grades within the British Civil Service show a similar situation. Recruitment to the Civil Service clerical grades (i.e. Clerical Assistant and Clerical Officer) and to the Executive Officer grade have shown a bias towards females. Subsequent promotion from these grades, however, shows a bias towards males. A female Clerical Officer has only 60 per cent of a male Clerical Officer's chance of becoming an Executive Officer, and only 73 per cent of the chance of promotion to the Higher Executive Officer grade that males have. This is not to say that fewer females are promoted. Indeed, the reverse is true in terms of absolute numbers, with more female Clerical Officers gaining promotion than males, but their relative chance of gaining promotion is less. Drawing upon available Civil Service data, one of the Civil Service trade unions, the First Division Association (1982), suggests on the basis of cohort analysis that the careers of those who entered the Civil Service in the period 1950 to 1959 and were still employed in 1980 had developed as follows:

> Of male entrants to the Clerical Officer grade, 26% had become Senior Executive Officers, and only 6% remained in the Clerical Officer grade. However, of female entrants 23% had gained no promotion and only 8% had become Senior Executive Officers . . . of entrants to the Executive Officer grade, all but three percent of the males gain gained promotion, but 19% of the females remained in the grade.

These data refer not to those who have only limited employment history and/or experience, but to employees who with continuous employment of twenty to thirty years have experienced very different promotion patterns. These findings in the British Civil Service tend to confirm those of Chiplin and Sloane (1976, p. 45) some years previously.

There does appear, therefore, to be evidence to support the hypothesis that even where there is equal opportunity of entry to employment, and equal pay for the work undertaken, there may subsequently be discrimination on the basis of sex with respect to future prospects.

EXPLANATIONS OF THE OBSERVED INEQUALITIES

Even if the evidence indicates inequality of treatment of females within labour markets, that by itself is insufficient to substantiate the existence of discrimination against females as such. Clearly evidence of inequality of treatment is a necessary requirement, but it is not sufficient. There may well be other economic explanations for the observed inequalities.

In the study of microeconomics it is often assumed that labour is homogeneous. It is obvious, however, that in considering females *vis-à-vis* males within the labour market the total labour supply is not always homogeneous. There are very obvious differences. In particular it is thought males have greater strength, whilst females have greater manual dexterity. Thus one possible explanation for part of the observed inequality may flow directly from the different qualities the two sexes bring to the labour market. One may, of course, still call this discrimination but it is a question of definitions. Economists usually refer to unequal treatment of females just because they are females as discrimination, but others would say that unequal treatment because their labour is different is still discrimination. Recognising that there may be differences in the capabilities of males and females it must be stressed that these apply to manual work which, with technological developments and the changing structure of the economy, is decreasing relative to non-manual work. Discrimination is sometimes a legacy from the days when heavy manual work was more widespread and male-dominated, despite the fact that automation and the growth of non-manual work now provide jobs that males and females are equally capable of doing.

It has already been pointed out that when considering the inequalities of payment there is a need to exercise special care to ensure only like is compared with like. For example, one reason why the average weekly male earnings are higher than the average weekly female earnings is the simple fact that males on average tend to work longer and/or different hours. When males work longer hours, this is in part often paid for at enhanced overtime rates. Similarly, if males are employed on shift work, and female workers' opportunity to do the same has been restricted by the 'protective' legislation in both Britain and the USA, male workers will expect a premium payment which is denied to females. Figures from the Equal Opportunities Commission (1982) in Britain confirm the situation described above. In 1981 the average gross hourly earnings of full-time female employees were 75 per cent of the male hourly earnings, but when average gross weekly earnings are compared the figure was 65 per cent.

One interesting point related to the above is that in the post-1945 era trade unions in Britain and the USA have successfully negotiated reductions in the basic working week, while simultaneously, until quite recently, the total average hours worked by males remained fairly constant. Thus over a thirty-five-year period, females, who generally do not participate in working overtime, have been employed on a steadily decreasing basic week. Consequently, the hours worked by full-time working females have steadily declined relative to the hours worked by males. Chiplin and Sloane (1976, p. 21) found that in 1951 the average full-time female worked 90 per cent of the average hours worked by males. By 1974 this had fallen to 83 per cent. In this situation, *ceteris paribus*, female weekly earnings would have fallen relative to males.

There is some, be it limited, evidence discussed by Lord (1979) that in manufacturing males are more concentrated in large employing units, while females are found in smaller employing units. Furthermore, the larger units tend to be in industries which exhibit a greater degree of market concentration. Hence the firms have a greater control over their prices and may be able to pass on to the consumer, at least in part, the higher costs associated with paying higher wages. Unionisation is also greater in large manufacturing units, which could also lead to higher wages. The female-employing firms usually have relatively less market power over price, and indeed are often to be found in industries where product demand is price elastic, e.g. clothing and food processing. In this type of environment the firm is more likely to seek to minimise costs with the consequential depression of wages. Even where females are employed in male-dominated manufacturing industries they are often found to be working for relatively small sub-contractors who will be under pressure from large, and male-dominated, firms to minimise costs. Thus the apparent inequitable treatment of women may well be partly a consequence of the fact that they frequently work for small firms.

The major non-discriminatory explanation, however, relates to the differing supply and demand conditions exhibited by or for males and females. Indeed some observers have expressed the view that the occupational distribution by sex reflects the operation of supply and demand. From the supply side females exhibit differing characteristics to males with respect to their attachment to the labour force and the qualities they bring to it.

There is statistical evidence which can be taken to suggest that females are both less attached to the labour force as such, and to employing firms in particular. The information exhibited for each age group in Figure 6.3 provides clear evidence that at each age level the male activity rate is higher than the female activity rate. The obvious implication to be drawn is that female attachment to the labour force is less than that of males. However, as noted in Chapter 2, the activity rate is calculated on the basis of the whole of the age group at risk. Thus, if a significant proportion of the age group withdraws from the labour market, e.g. because of family formation,

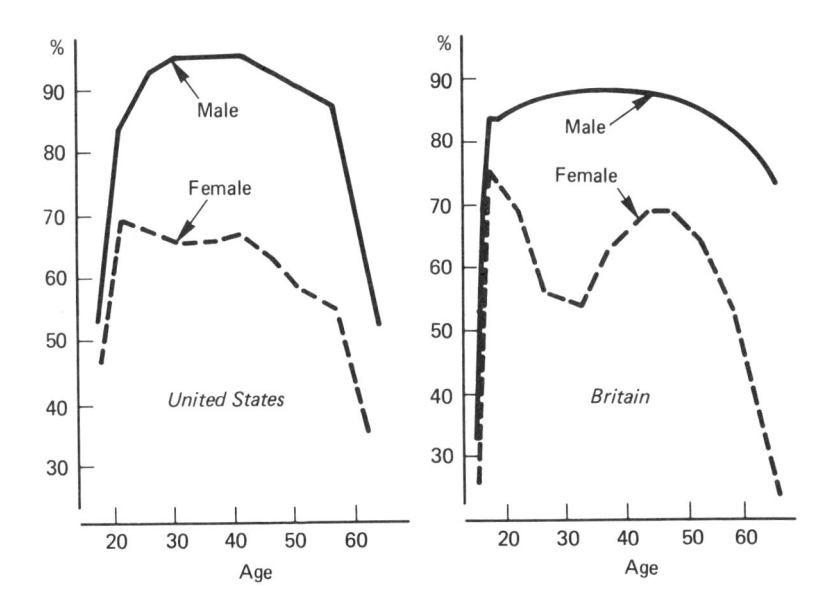

FIGURE 6.3 *Male and female economic activity rate by age, Britain and the United States, 1980-1*
SOURCES *Census of Population, 1981; US Census of Population, 1980.*

this will depress the activity rate. However, those females who remain in the labour force may well have as committed an attachment as any male. Fearn (1981) noted that there was a striking similarity in the activity rates for single males and single females. Thus the information shown in Figure 6.3 could be misleading.

From Table 6.4 it is clear that females do not exhibit the same degree of attachment as males, and this assumed lack of commitment may cause employers to be less willing to offer employment to, and/or to contemplate promotion of, females.

Willingness to offer employment may further be influenced by the qualities females bring from the educational system when they first seek employment. Schooling is one of the few areas of life where both sexes begin equal. It is no surprise that at the end of schooling children leave school with different levels of qualification, but what is surprising, and what has a significant impact on their future employment prospects and careers, is the bias of males towards science and mathematics. This bias clearly widens the range of potential occupations open to young males,

TABLE 6.4 *Length of Employment with current employer, 1979 (% of total number of employees)*

	Under 1 year	1 to 3 years	Over 3 years
Males			
Manual	11.1	22.3	66.6
Non-manual	8.0	19.7	72.3
Females			
Manual	13.8	30.4	55.8
Non-manual	15.0	31.7	53.3

SOURCE *New Earnings Survey*, Section E, 1979.

while simultaneously 'crowding' young females into a very limited range of clerical occupations.

Frank (1978) has suggested that personal characteristics that are unobservable to academic researchers may be observable to employers who are faced with a female supply of doubtful attachment to the labour force in general, and to specific employers in particular, and whose educational experience is liable to restrict occupational choice. An employer's demand for labour will be influenced by the firm's anticipated productivity, and high turnover and low qualifications usually make workers on average less productive. There is evidence by Phelps Brown (1951, p. 138), although now dated, which suggests that in occupations which require physical effort — and these are getting scarcer each year — female output levels are some 75-80 per cent of male levels. Similarly, given the weaker attachment of females to the labour force, it is sometimes thought that their

TABLE 6.5 *Selected subjects successfully attempted at summer examinations, 1982*

	Obtained at 'O' level (in 000's)		Obtained at 'A' level (in 000's)	
	Male	Female	Male	Female
English	121.2	159.7	11.0	32.5
French	37.8	58.6	4.9	13.5
Mathematics	149.3	98.8	46.6	18.2
Physics	81.3	30.3	30.6	7.9

SOURCE *Statistics of Education, 1982*, 'School leavers', Tables C31 and C32.

attitude to employment will lead to lower levels of production. Further, should employers believe that female output levels are below those obtainable by males, this may cause the employer to be less willing to offer training, which might ultimately open the door to promotion. In this latter situation the employer may believe that female workers' productivity will be below the male level, not only because of the physical strength element but also as a consequence of assumed higher labour turnover.

If it were the case that the productivity for females were below the anticipated male level, this would lead employers to offer a lower wage. Such a difference in wage levels ought not to be regarded as discriminatory, using the economist's definition, for it would reflect the difference in value of the relative levels of productivity achieved.

THEORIES OF DISCRIMINATION

A series of possible explanations, therefore, exists for the inequality of treatment experienced by females within the labour market. However, it has to be acknowledged that these do not entirely explain the situation that exists on both sides of the Atlantic.

A number of economists have sought, by the use of statistical techniques, to evaluate the consequences of removing the causes of inequality discussed above. If the assumption were made that the female labour force is distributed through the economy in an identical way to the male labour force, i.e. if all barriers to entry and promotion in occupations and industries were to be removed, and allowance were made for length of work experience, differing levels of productivity and variations in the number of hours worked, then Chiplin and Sloane (1976, chapter 8) and the OECD (1979, p. 76) believe that some 50 per cent of the observed differences in wage earnings could be explained. Oaxaca (1973) believed that the unexplained residual, after correcting for the factors above, amount to roughly 20 per cent of the average female wage rate, which given the then US pay structure approximated to the 50 percent of the wage differential that the observers noted above. Thus, if all the variables identified earlier were to be equalised, a proportion of the observed earnings variation would still remain, and it is assumed that this residual is the consequence of discrimination against females in the labour market.

A number of theories has been developed to provide explanations for discrimination, but this work is still in its infancy. Much of the pioneer work originated in the USA and was often initially devoted to the explanation of the operation of racial discrimination within the US labour market.

It has, however, proved possible to apply the concepts to explain sexual discrimination within labour markets, and the ideas behind three such approaches are considered below.

'Taste' for discrimination by employers

This approach, which comes closest to 'traditional' economics in providing an analysis of discrimination, is the one initially outlined by Becker (1971), who assumes that discrimination is merely the consequence of the tastes of various economic agents and that these tastes are formed outside the market place, i.e. they are exogenous. To put it simply, employers will discriminate against employing females because they dislike the idea of employing women!

In the Becker model the normal neoclassical economic assumption is retained, namely that economic agents (i.e. employers) will attempt to maximise their income, profits, etc., but with the taste for discrimination incorporated. Thus should an employer have a 'taste' for discriminating against employing females, he or she will act as if he or she is willing to pay not to employ females, even if this should mean employing males at a higher wage. This line of reasoning enables Becker to introduce a 'discrimination coefficient' which places a monetary value on the taste of not employing females.

When applied to an employer, the discrimination coefficient can be illustrated in the following way. Let the money wage of females equal Wf; then employers with a distaste for employing females will act as though $Wf(1 + di)$ is the net wage to females. In this instance di is the discrimination coefficient and is assumed to be positive. The actual value of di will be determined by the degree of intensity of the taste held, i.e. the greater employers dislike employing females, the higher the value of di.

The implication of this approach by Becker can be briefly outlined, and it will be assumed that:

Wf = female wage without discrimination
Wm = male wage
di = discrimination coefficient
and Wf is always less than Wm

If the employer discriminates against females he or she will act as if the female wage is $Wf(1 + di)$. Becker's analysis suggests employers will attempt to minimise their money costs, although this will be subject to the degree of their intensity to discriminate against females. Thus if male and female workers are perfect substitutes and $Wm < Wf(1 + di)$, only males will be employed. Should $Wm > Wf(1 + di)$ only females will gain employment, and when $Wm = Wf(1 + di)$ members of either sex will be employed. Thus if employers have a taste not to employ females they will prefer to employ males, even if the male is less productive, since the discrimination coefficient will make up the difference between male and female employees. The employer is effectively willing to forego an element of his potential profits to satisfy his taste of not employing females.

Dual labour market

The second distinct analysis of discrimination is the approach initially associated with Doeringer and Poire (1971) concerning the structure of labour markets and in particular the concept of the dual labour market. This analysis places stress on structural and institutional constraints which perpetuate sex discrimination.

The dual labour market theory recognises the existence of two, quite distinct, labour markets in an economy, the primary and the secondary. The primary labour market is characterised by stable, secure working conditions, favourable job prospects, scope for promotion and high wages. In contrast, the secondary market is characterised by unstable working conditions, poor prospects and low wages.

The behavioural patterns of the secondary sector, i.e. high labour turnover, absenteeism, etc., are reinforced by working in this sector, and workers who are 'mistakenly' allocated to this sector will as a consequence adopt those habits. The segmentation of the labour market proceeds along sexual lines and hence females come to be confined to the secondary market with the sex division occurring at both occupational and industrial levels. Workers will be allocated between the two market sectors on the basis of their assumed suitability for job requirements. However, as employers are initially unaware of the potential job applicants, they will be allocated to jobs in either the primary or secondary markets on the basis of past experience and assumed productivity characteristics. Thus employers will discriminate on the basis of previous experience of labour turnover, absenteeism, productivity levels, etc., and this will lead to a concentration of females in secondary market jobs with all that that implies.

The obvious implication of the dual market analysis with its emphasis on institutional mechanisms within firms is that regardless of legislative initiatives the practice of discrimination against females will continue. The economic implications for employers, however, are different from those identified in the Becker analysis.

Within the dual market it is again true that male workers will still benefit by higher earnings but it is also now assumed that there is a 'payoff' for employers, namely they will incur reduced costs by the initial screening of job applicants, via lower labour turnover. Simultaneously, employers in the secondary sector benefit by having a higher labour supply than might otherwise occur if potential employees had the opportunity of stable primary employment. Indeed, the great advantage flowing from the dual market approach is the obvious fact that everyone benefits, except for the females and those males who are forced into the secondary market!

Human capital

The third model to explain discrimination, and one that has been developed by Mincer (1962b) and Becker (1975) is based on the concept of 'human capital accumulation'. A worker, regardless of sex, becomes more valuable to an employer, can command a higher wage and have the opportunity of higher grade jobs, if he or she has pursued relevant educational and training programmes and/or has extensive employment experience.

The acquiring of education, job skills, and the gaining of experience can all be regarded as investments in human capital. As investments they obviously have to be paid for. From the workers' side the 'payment' may take the form of lower wages during an apprenticeship, or no wage as a student. The employer makes a 'payment' in the form of lower profits as a result of providing training facilities and wages during the non-productive training period. In seeking to explain discrimination by reference to human capital accumulation, recognition is given to the fact that those who have invested in human capital subsequently benefit by higher wages and greater opportunities compared with those who have not invested.

In the academic year 1981-2 there were in Britain 1.73 times as many men as women on full-time advanced courses in higher education. Similarly, in the same year the number of male full-time university students was 1.5 times the number of females (*Annual Abstract of Statistics*, 1984, Tables 5.9 and 5.10). This pattern of higher education take-up does not occur in the USA, where there is equality between the sexes in aggregate in colleges and universities. However, it is not only in the aggregate figures of students that a difference may exist between the sexes. Undergraduate students in education on both sides of the Atlantic are predominantly female, 61 per cent in Britain and 74 per cent in the USA. In contrast, in engineering only 21 per cent of US students are female and only 5 per cent in Britain. The reasons for this situation arising are complex. In part it is the result of the experience within schools where an element of sex stereotyping appears to occur in subject choice (see Table 6.5).

Schooling alone, though, is not the only explanation, and it does seem apparent that young females are less willing to make an investment in post-school education. This could arise through lack of encouragement from schools and/or family, but it could also arise because the anticipated returns females may expect from such investments are lower than those received by males who make similar investments. In the initial discussion with respect to teachers it was seen that males come to dominate the more senior, and high paid posts, thus gaining a greater return on investment. Higher education as such is often used as a screening device by employers prior to further investment in training. If employers believe that the anticipated returns for such training will be limited, due to family formation, etc., they may be unwilling to offer, and pay for, such training. This would effectively deny females the opportunity of using their education to gain entry to high status jobs with the consequential reduction in the return on their investment.

With respect to skill, as against academic, training in Britain, figures prepared by the Equal Opportunities Commission (1982) show that in the spring of 1981, for every female undertaking an apprenticeship there were 32.5 males. Again, schooling might have an influence. After all, a two-year school course on typewriting enables the recipient to apply for a job using that skill without further training, while two years of metalwork or technical drawing may be a useful experience prior to an apprenticeship but is not a prerequisite for such training or entry to a job using that skill.

There does seem to be evidence on both sides of the Atlantic that a higher proportion of female school-leavers expect to start 'real' work, without extended training, upon leaving school compared with male school-leavers. How far this is the result of sex stereotyping within the labour market or the result of feedback from the experiences of previous generations in the labour force is hard to say.

From the female's viewpoint there is a vicious circle. If a schoolgirl observes that women get paid less than men, and have fewer chances of promotion, she may decide (or her parents may decide for her) that it is not worth investing time and effort getting qualifications. The more girls that do this the less women will earn, and the circle continues. In considering the limited opportunity for young British females to pursue apprenticeships it could be argued that employers are acting rationally with respect to where they invest. Claydon (1980), reporting a National Training Survey undertaken in Britain, revealed that while 75 per cent of males who had gained an apprentice qualification were working in the same or related occupation, the figure for females was only 25 per cent. Indeed, 48 per cent of females with apprentice qualifications were not in employment, compared with only 4 per cent of the males.

The majority of training and human capital accumulation, however, does not take place in colleges or universities or on apprenticehsips. It is after all a continuous process while the worker is employed, and thus the longer the period of employment the greater the human capital accumulation. Thus those employees who are older and in regular employment will in fact benefit as their length of service extends. As they gain experience, develop new skills and thus accumulate human capital, they become more valuable to the employer who will reward them accordingly.

There is evidence, then, to suggest that differing levels of human capital accumulation lead to discrimination in the employment market. The indications are that females on average receive less education and job training, and there does exist a strong correlation between education and training and the level of earnings. There would also be a strong relationship, one assumes, between education and training and the opportunity for advancement.

Females are at a disadvantage in the human capital accumulation process. As was noted above, the majority of job training is acquired as the result of years of accumulated experience, and in this process, because females tend to break their employment for family reasons, they are at a disadvantage. Indeed, Mallier and Rosser (1982) conclude that training facilities appear to be designed to accommodate the male work-cycle and not to cope for those who withdraw and re-enter. Thus job tenure is a key dimension of job experience and training which is essential for human capital accumulation, but the existing pattern of the division of labour within families disadvantages women.

CONCLUSIONS

There continues to exist a degree of inequitable treatment for females in both the American and British labour markets. This inequality is the result, in part, of discrimination by employers and employees. However, to many people such discrimination is unacceptable and legislation has been passed through the United States Congress and the British Parliament to try to bring about its elimination.

In certain European nations, e.g. France and Germany, discrimination by sex is forbidden by their constitution, a route not available to the

British with their reliance on an unwritten constitution and a route not followed in the USA. An alternative approach is adopted in Sweden whereby employers and trade unions have negotiated discrimination away. This was the approach desired by the British trade unions, who through their Trades Union Congress have passed forty resolutions advocating equal pay, the first in 1888. However, failure to achieve its objectives caused the Trades Union Congress in the 1960s to request legislative changes similar to the 1963 amendment to the Fair Labor Standards Act in the USA, which provided for 'equal pay for equal work'. In passing legislation both nations have taken the middle way between constitutional measures and reliance upon collective bargaining.

The British legislation, which was pre-dated by that in the USA, came in two stages, the first being the Equal Pay Act 1970, although a five-year period was allowed for the implementation of equal pay before it came into force. The Act did not allow for equal pay for all, but rather specified situations where it was required. The subsequent guidelines from the Department of Employment (1973a) specified:

> An individual woman has a right to equal treatment with men when she is employed on like work, i.e. work of the same or a broadly similar nature to that of men, or in a job which though different from those of men, has been given an equal value to men's jobs under a job evaluation exercise.

One consequence of specifying the relevant situations in this form is that it enabled employers during the lead-in period to adjust the way in which they allocated their labour force, thus reducing the application of the Act by removing possible areas of overlap.

The relevant US statute, the amendment to the Fair Labor Standards Act, has now been operative for twenty years, the British one for ten. Over those periods some of the inequalities in pay that had previously existed have been reduced, but they have not been eliminated.

Since the legislation was passed there have been improvements in the relative earnings of females *vis-à-vis* males, and these improvements have occurred rather faster than previous trends would have indicated, although it is unclear in the British case to what extent it was the Equal Pay Act or other government incomes policies which bought the change about. In Britain progress was slow in the early 1970s because of employer avoidance, while subsequently the general economic recession has been a significant factor. The slowness of changes in Britain led the European Court (1982) to express the view that 'the Equal Pay Act was inconsistent with the requirements of the European Community Equal Pay Directive', and this judgement has led the British government to amend the original 1970 Act.

A detailed study by Snell *et al.* (1981) of the working of the Equal Pay Act 1970 expresses the belief that the legislation has been reasonably successful in removing the most obvious excess of sex discrimination in pay, but it had not achieved equal pay, nor equal opportunities.

It can be said that the Equal Pay Act was not designed to achieve equal opportunity, as this was the objective of later legislation, the Sex Discrimination Act 1975. It is of interest that in the USA there was a greater appreciation of the relationship between equal pay and equal opportunity. The relevant legislation for equal pay and for equal opportunity, the latter being the subject of the Civil Rights Act 1964, passed through Congress coincidentally. The objectives of the British Sex Discrimination Act was explained by the Home Office (1975) as being to:

> make sex discrimination unlawful in employment, training and related matters, in education, in the provision of goods, services and in the disposal and management of premises.

Two features require to be noted. As with the US civil rights legislation, the British Act goes beyond employment, and indeed the Equal Opportunities Commission established under the Act is not responsible to employment ministers. Secondly, the Act is equally applicable to males, i.e. it aims to eliminate discrimination against males as well as against females. However, it is realistic to regard this second piece of legislation as an essential complement to the Equal Pay Act, in the same way as the two US Acts complemented each other. Each of the Acts seeks to tackle those areas of discrimination previously covered, thus improving the position of females as a general group in employment.

The far-sighted nature of the Civil Rights Act and the Sex Discrimination Act are such that even now it is too early to enable an adequate evaluation of their operation, especially when their implementation has occurred against a background of the worst economic recession for fifty years and when technological innovation is radically changing the character of available employment. Indeed, against such a background it is possible that the most valuable contribution such legislation will have is the elimination of discrimination in training. The results, and consequences, will only emerge in the long term. It must always be remembered that no single policy instrument can lead to the achievement of equal opportunities; it can only seek to prohibit sex discrimination.

7 Issues of the 1980s: Part-time Employment, Unemployment and the New Technology

In recent years the three related issues of part-time employment, unemployment and new technology have had a significant impact on the female labour market, and are likely to play an important part in determining future trends. Britain, and to a lesser extent the USA, has in the last decade experienced an increase in both part-time working by females and in the female unemployment rate. Most of the new part-time jobs have provided employment for married women, many of whom have been attracted back into the labour force by this type of work being made available. Meanwhile, a relative scarcity of full-time employment opportunities has developed, and one argument is that these new part-time workers have gained their jobs at the expense of higher unemployment, particularly among younger females who are looking for full-time work. The issue is not quite as clear-cut as this, though, and other factors influencing part-time employment and unemployment are examined here. Technical innovation, in particular the development of the microprocessor, has already had some effect on work patterns and employment levels in several industries and occupations, and research suggests that in the near future it will have an increasing impact on female employment.

PART-TIME EMPLOYMENT

The remarkable post-war growth of the female labour force, when measured in terms of numbers, exaggerates the actual increase in the amount of paid work done by women in both Britain and the USA. This is because although the total number of females in the labour force has risen, the proportion of part-time workers within this total has also increased. This phenomenon has occurred in several economies in Europe and North America but it has been much more noticeable in Britain than in the USA. Mallier and Rosser (1979) estimated that the growth of part-time employment, together with a reduction in the length of a normal working week, meant that despite an increase of 2.1 million females in the British female labour force between 1951 and 1976, there was hardly any change in the total number of hours worked by females.

Definitions of part-time working

Part-time employment could be defined as anything less than full-time employment, but this is rather vague: one still has to define what a full working week is. In practice official statistics used a defined cut-off point for the maximum number of hours per week that someone can work and still be classed as a part-time worker. In Britain the usual definition of a part-time worker is someone who works less than thirty hours a week; in the USA it is someone who works less than thirty-five hours. However, when someone is normally employed on a full-time basis but is currently working below the cut-off point due to involuntary short-time working, they may still be classified as a full-time worker. Other exceptions exist, and classification may depend on the method used to collect statistics. For example, a continuous survey may count as part-time those workers who normally work part-time but who are temporarily working full-time, whereas a one-off survey might just be concerned with hours worked in the survey week. The average weekly hours of female part-time employees aged 18 and over in Britain is approximately twenty (*New Earnings Survey*), and in the USA Leon and Bednarzik (1978) also found median weekly hours for adult females working part-time to be close to twenty.

The first census of population in Great Britain to use the Department of Employment definition of a part-time worker as someone working less than thirty hours a week was in 1971. Figures from earlier censuses are not strictly comparable because different definitions were used, e.g. in the 1961 census respondents were asked if they worked 'less than a normal week', although no definition of a normal week was given. Bearing in mind these qualifications of the figures, the censuses of population indicate that the proportion of females working part-time in Britain rose from 25 per cent in 1961 to 39 per cent in 1981. Before 1971 the Department of Employment published statistics only for part-time employment in manufacturing industries, which showed a gradual increase in the percentage of women working part-time from around 10 per cent in the early 1950s to nearly 20 per cent by 1971. The Department of Employment (1973b) used information from the Family Expenditure Survey (FES) to estimate a continuous series of statistics for all industries, which showed an increase in the proportion of women working part-time from 37.5 per cent to 45.5 per cent between 1963 and 1972.

From 1971 on, details of part-time employment in all industries can be obtained from the census of employment. This data source does not cover the self-employed or those employed in private domestic service, and before 1981 many small businesses were not included in the survey. These omissions, plus the fact that it is conducted in one specific week, partly explains why the percentage of women working part-time shown in Table 7.1 is lower than the FES figure given above. On the other hand, as census of employment returns are made by employers, there can be some double counting and overestimation of the number of part-time workers when a person works for two separate employers.

Although the census of employment may not give completely accurate statistics, one cannot mistake the general trends that are apparent from Table 7.1. From 1971 to 1981 the proportion of all employees working part-time rose steadily from 15 per cent to 21 per cent, and the proportion of female employees who worked part-time grew from 33.5 per cent to 42 per cent. Since 1981 Department of Employment estimates suggest that the number of females working part-time has continued to grow, while full-time female employment has fallen, thus pushing up the part-time percentage of the female labour force even further. It is not widely appreciated that two in five of all female employees, and one in five of all employees, are now part-time workers. Although there has been some growth of male part-time employment, the vast majority of the new part-time jobs have been taken by women and the proportion of part-time employees who are female has remained fairly stable at around 83 per cent.

In the USA data are collected monthly in the Current Population Survey (CPS), and a part-time employee is defined as someone who works less than thirty-five hours during the survey week. Part-time workers are classed into those working part-time voluntarily and those working part-time involuntary. Voluntary part-time workers are in the majority, making up approximately 85 per cent of the total number of part-timers. Involuntary part-time working covers those who normally work full-time but who only worked part of the survey week because of short-time working at their place of employment or because they started or terminated a job mid-week. Included also are those who work part-time only because they cannot find full-time work. Although the US figures for part-time working

TABLE 7.1 Part-time employment in Great Britain, 1971–83 (June each year 1971–8, September 1981–3; thousands, except percentages)

	1971	1972	1973	1974	1975	1976	1977	1978	1981	1982*	1983*
Part-time employees	3 341	3 477	3 828	4 110	4 248	4 284	4 298	4 384	4 499	—	—
Total employees	21 648	21 649	22 182	22 296	22 212	22 047	22 125	22 253	21 148	20 678	20 238
Part-time as % of total	15.4	16.1	17.3	18.4	19.1	19.4	19.4	19.7	21.3	—	—
Female part-time employees	2 757	2 877	3 163	3 421	3 551	3 585	3 617	3 680	3 759	3 769	3 833
Female total employees	8 224	8 331	8 705	8 934	8 951	9 050	9 158	9 013	8 875	8 839	8 973
Female part-time as % of total	33.5	34.5	36.3	38.3	39.6	40.1	40.0	40.2	41.7	42.5	43.4
Females part-time as % of total part-time	82.5	82.7	82.6	83.2	83.6	83.7	84.2	83.9	83.6	—	—

*Department of Employment estimate.
SOURCES 1971–81 *Census of Employment*; 1982–3 Department of *Employment Gazette*, February 1984, Table 1.4. There was no Census of Employment in 1979, 1980, 1982 and 1983.

are collected on a different basis to that used in Britain, some broad comparisons can still be made using US voluntary part-time work statistics. Deutermann and Brown (1978) reported that between 1954 and 1977 the number of non-agricultural part-time employees grew at twice the annual average rate of growth for the number of full-time workers, and the part-time proportion of the non-agricultural workforce rose from 15 per cent to 22 per cent. Voluntary part-time workers grew in number more rapidly over this period than involuntary part-timers. However, since the end of the 1960s the proportion of part-timers in the workforce has remained fairly constant at around 21-22 per cent, as has the ratio of voluntary to involuntary part-timers, at just under six to one.

In Table 7.2 more recent trends in US voluntary part-time working are shown. Since 1970 the voluntary part-time proportion of the total workforce has stabilised at around 14 per cent, and the proportion of adult females in employment working part-time has also stayed almost unchanged, at just over 20 per cent. The majority of part-time employees are women, but the proportion is only 70 per cent compared with a British figure of over 80 per cent. The figures in Table 7.2 show a slight increase between 1965 and 1983 in the US proportion of part-timers who are females aged 20 and over, up from 55 per cent to 57.5 per cent. The

TABLE 7.2 *Part-time employment in the USA, 1965-82 (persons working part-time voluntarily)*

	Total (000's)	Employed part-time			Part-time employed as % of all employed		
		% Female 20 yrs+	% Male 20 yrs+	% Persons 16-19 yrs	Total	Female 20 yrs+	Male 20 yrs+	Persons 16-19 yrs
1965	7 952	55.0	19.2	25.8	11.2	19.3	3.5	40.7
1970	10 814	53.7	19.6	26.7	13.7	21.5	4.7	47.0
1971	10 990	53.3	19.8	26.9	13.9	21.6	4.7	47.7
1972	11 443	53.2	19.7	27.1	14.0	21.6	4.8	46.2
1973	11 839	53.6	19.3	27.1	14.0	21.7	4.8	44.3
1974	12 070	53.8	19.1	27.0	14.0	21.6	4.8	44.0
1975	12 251	53.7	19.4	26.9	14.3	21.4	5.0	46.4
1976	12 528	54.3	18.7	26.9	14.3	21.5	4.8	46.4
1977	13 028	54.3	19.1	26.6	14.4	21.3	5.0	45.5
1978	13 549	54.5	18.7	26.8	14.4	21.0	4.9	45.5
1979	13 843	55.1	18.3	26.5	14.3	20.8	4.9	46.0
1980	14 275	55.4	18.9	25.8	14.7	20.5	5.1	47.7
1981	14 271	56.8	18.7	24.5	14.2	20.5	5.0	48.4
1982	14 239	57.5	19.4	23.1	14.3	20.4	5.2	50.1

SOURCE *Statistical Abstract of the US.*

proportion of adult males in the part-time employee total has remained almost unchanged at around 19 per cent, and the proportion aged under 20 has fallen by 2 per cent. One of the most striking differences between the USA and Britain is that a substantial percentage of part-time jobs in the USA are held by young people. In 1981 the proportion of part-time employees who were aged under 20 was 24.5 per cent in the USA compared with only 1.4 per cent in Britain (Table 7.3).

TABLE 7.3 *Part-time employment in Great Britain, 1981*

	No. employed part-time (000's)	% of total part-time employed
Females	3 543	90.7
Males	362	9.3
Married females	3 066	78.5
All under 20 years	55	1.4
Females under 20 years	38	1.0
Males under 20 years	17	0.4
Females 20 years plus	3 505	89.8
Males 20 years plus	345	8.8
Males 65 years plus	203	5.2

SOURCE *Census of Population, 1981.*

Characteristics of part-time workers

Given that most part-time workers are female, what other characteristics are typical? As mentioned above, the age distribution of part-time employees in the US differs from that in Britain (see Table 7.4). Deutermann and Brown (1978) reported that 56 per cent of US females aged 16-19 in employment worked part-time voluntarily, whereas in Britain the 1981 census of population showed that only 5 per cent of working females in this age group were part-timers. One major reason for this difference is that many American young people work part-time while still at school or college. In Britain a relatively smaller percentage of the population continue their education past the age of 16, and courses in higher education are generally shorter and more intensive than in the USA, leaving less time for regular part-time employment. Most British students on degree courses are entitled to some form of government grant to help cover living costs,

TABLE 7.4 *Age distribution of female part-time workers*

(a) *Great Britain 1981: Part-time workers as a % of total employment*

	All 16+	16-19	20-24	Age groups 25-34	35-44	45-54	55-59	60-64	65+
All females	38.7	4.7	8.7	39.1	51.6	47.0	42.7	63.9	71.8
Married females	51.2	15.1	16.8	49.2	56.9	52.1	54.2	68.0	76.4

SOURCE *Census of Population*, 1981.

(b) *USA, 1977: Voluntary part-time workers as a % of total employment*

	All 20+	Under 20	20-24	Age groups 25-34	35-44	45-54	55-59	60-64	65+
All females	21.3	55.9	17.4	19.0	23.2	20.1	19.5	26.7	56.4

SOURCES Leon and Bednarzik (1978); Deutermann and Brown (1978).

which eliminates some of the financial necessity to work for money as well as studying.

Above the age of 20 the age distributions of female part-time employees display some similar characteristics. In both countries the percentage of employed women working part-time increases until it reaches a peak in the 35-44 age group. It then declines slightly in the following age groups and then rises again for those aged over 60. Below the age of 25 the American figure is above the British one, reflecting the relatively higher number of students in this age group and the higher propensity of US students to take part-time work. Part-time employment increases over the 25-44 age range, which contains many women with children, a feature which places a constraint on the time available for paid employment. Although the proportion of women with very young children is highest in the 25-34 age group, the percentage of this age group working part-time is lower than the 35-44 age group. This is because between the ages of 25 and 34 those women without children will usually work full-time, whereas those who have small children will often stop working completely.

Past the age of 45, when most mothers' children have grown up, full-time work becomes relatively more common again until old-age, failing health and pension payments cause part-time work to become the norm for those women remaining in the labour force after the usual age of retirement. Part-time employment in both Britain and the USA is more common among married women than non-married women. In 1981 in Britain 51 per cent of employed married women worked part-time compared with 15 per cent of non-married females in employment. Leon and Bednarzik (1978) reported that in the USA one in four married women who worked was a voluntary part-time employee, compared with one in six widowed, separated or divorced females, and one in seven adult single women.

Part-time workers tend to be concentrated mainly in service sector, female-dominated industries. In 1981 in Britain 87 per cent of all part-time employees worked in the service sector. The industrial sectors with the highest proportion of women working part-time were miscellaneous services (60 per cent), distributive trades (51 per cent) and professional and scientific services (49 per cent), which includes educational services (57 per cent) and medical and dental services (44 per cent). In total these three industrial sectors accounted for 75 per cent of all part-time employees, both male and female. In the USA decennial censuses have reported that over 80 per cent of female part-time employees work in service-producing industries and that the three industries wholesale and retail trade, personal services, and professional and related services employ over 80 per cent of all female part-time employees.

Part-time employees on average are relatively poorly paid compared with full-time employees when earnings per hour are compared. Robinson and Wallace (1981) explain how, despite equal pay legislation in Britain partially closing the gap between male and female earnings, part-timers' pay has not improved relative to that of full-timers. The relatively low average hourly earnings of part-time employees are usually not due to blatant discrimination between full- and part-time employees doing the same job. They are a consequence of the concentration of part-time workers in the less well paid industries and occupations, and in the lower grades within each occupation. Owen (1978) confirms that the same pattern occurs in the USA. Elias and Main (1982), reporting on the 1975-6 National Training Survey in Britain, point out that two out of five part-time female employees work in 'other personal service' occupations. These are nearly all low paid, low status and low skill jobs, including, for example, unskilled catering staff and cleaners. Elias and Main also found that these jobs were more likely to be done by middle-aged women than younger females. Ballard (1984), in her summary of those aspects of the Department of Employment 1980 Women and Employment Survey relevant to part-time employment, highlights the fact that some 70 per cent of manual jobs in the service sector are done by part-time workers. One reason for the relatively low employment status of most part-time workers is that employers tend to neglect the training of part-time employees and give them little chance of promotion. As Mallier and Rosser (1982) explain, although some part-time employees only join a company late in life and only work a few hours a week and thus may not pay back to the company as much from training as a full-time worker, many employers underestimate the benefits that they could get from a proper training programme to suit the requirements of part-time workers.

Explaining the growth of part-time employment

As with the growth of the female labour force in total, one must take into account both supply and demand influences to explain the growth of part-time employment.

Several of the cross-section studies of the labour supply of married females mentioned in Chapter 4 identified the factors that affect the hours of work supplied. The presence of those factors that are likely to decrease the number of hours supplied, e.g. children, will therefore tend to encourage part-time work if a woman does actually work in the first place, whereas those factors that increase labour supply will, if present, make full-time working more likely. Some studies, e.g. Long and Jones (1981), specifically test for the factors influencing the decision between full-time and part-time working. Results confirm that the same basic set of variables that influence the probability of economic activity also influence the choice between full-time and part-time work.

It is, however, more difficult to explain why the supply of women wishing to work part-time may have increased more rapidly than the supply of females wishing to work full-time. One could argue that the fastest growing section of the female labour force has been the one that is most likely to wish to work part-time, i.e. married women, and this has been the main cause of the growth in part-time employment. On the other hand, it could be argued that part-time jobs do not just appear because people want them, and it is the increased availability of part-time work, discussed below, that has actually been the cause of the largest proportion of the overall growth in the female labour force coming from the married female population.

There are several reasons for the growing demand for part-time workers common to both Britain and the USA. However, in Britain, where the growth of part-time employment has been greater, a number of factors have operated which do not apply to the US situation.

Total employment in both countries has grown most in those industries where part-time employment has always been common, mainly in the service sector. In Britain between 1971 and 1981 the total number of employees in the service sector, where 23.6 per cent worked part-time in 1971, grew by 15.3 per cent, whereas in the manufacturing sector, where the proportion working part-time had only been 6.8 per cent, total employment fell by 23.2 per cent. In the USA Deutermann and Brown (1978) reported that employees in the service-producing sector were five times more likely to work part-time by choice than employees in the goods-producing sector, and that between 1969 and 1977 total employment in the service producing sector rose by 33 per cent compared with an increase of only 4.4. per cent for the goods-producing sector. Since 1977 employment in some goods-producing industries has actually fallen, while most service industries have continued to expand. Thus changes in industrial structure can account for some of the growth in demand for part-time workers.

A second feature of the growth of the part-time labour force is that part-time working has become more common within nearly all industries, in both the manufacturing and service sectors. Mallier and Rosser (1980b), considering the British case, suggest that there are a number of factors that have made part-time employees more attractive from an employer's viewpoint. After the 1970 Equal Pay Act came into operation in 1975, women could claim pay parity with males who did the same work. Because in many firms part-time jobs are done only by women, it has been more difficult for them to use this means of increasing their wage than for full-time female employees. Unit labour costs can also be lower when part-time employees are used because an employer usually does not have to pay them overtime premiums or a special rate for working anti-social hours, which would often be the case if full-time employees were used. The 1975 Employment Protection Act, even after the modifications extending its coverage in 1978, denied certain rights, e.g. regarding redundancy conditions, to employees working less than eight hours a week, or under sixteen hours a week if they had been with the same employer for less than five years. This gave an incentive for employers wishing to have a greater control over their workforce to employ part-timers who did not have the protection of this legislation. Disney and Szyszczak (1984) found that employers tended to alter the pattern of hours worked by part-timers to bring them below this threshold rather than get rid of those who worked sufficient hours to qualify for the rights granted in the Employment Protection Act. Robinson and Wallace (1984) found evidence which suggested that the continued growth of part-time employment after 1979, when full-time employment was falling, was primarily due to an increased demand for part-time labour on the grounds of greater flexibility and cost savings. The British income tax and national insurance (NI) systems have also operated in such a way as to make part-timers relatively cheaper. Below a specified earnings level, which has fallen relative to the average full-time weekly wage over the years, an employee does not have to pay income tax or make NI contributions. Thus employers will not have the expense of administering payments, or of making NI contributions for employees who fall into this category, who will mostly be part-time workers.

Apart from those factors affecting the growth of part-time employment that only apply to the British case, in both the USA and Britain there have been improvements in many industries in the non-monetary benefits received by full-time employees in the form of holidays, pension rights, sickness benefits, etc. These have often been denied to part-timers, or at least not given to the same extent, even in proportion to hours worked, and this has helped to make part-timers relatively cheaper to employ. Mallier and Rosser (1980c) give some specific examples of this happening in Britain.

Furthermore, part-time employees are less unionised and less likely to oppose management decisions on staffing or operational matters. Bosworth and Dawkins (1982), reporting on a sample survey of employers in Britain, found that the flexibility of a part-time labour force was a major reason for using this type of labour. In recent years, though, as Mallier and Rosser (1983) explain, there has been some increased union participation among part-time female employees, while full-time union membership has fallen back in Britain as full-time jobs have been lost.

There has also been a growing awareness among businessmen on both sides of the Atlantic of the advantages of employing part-time workers. Management journals have contained a number of articles extolling the virtues of employing part-timers, e.g. Werther (1975), Clutterbuck (1979) and Tavernier (1979). This might simply be due to the factors listed above coming into effect and being recognised. However, it also seems that there used to be a myth that part-timers tended to be unreliable and inefficient and costly to employ, which it has taken a long time to dispel. Although some of the advantages of employing part-time workers have existed for some time, in the period of relatively high profitability before the 1970s recession there was less incentive to exploit them. Since then declining profitability in the last decade or so, particularly in Britain, has spurred management into implementing more effective cost-cutting exercises.

Part-time work and equality in Europe

The growth of part-time employment has been a feature of most European economies although, apart from the Scandinavian nations, it has not reached the same extent as in Britain. Robinson (1979) provides a detailed description of part-time employment patterns in EEC member states. It is, in fact, from the EEC that much of the impetus has come for changes in the legislation in Britain with respect to part-time employees. Although Council Directives from the EEC Commission do not automatically become law in member states, there is pressure placed upon individual governments to implement the Directive. Thus, when the EEC Commission (1982) published a proposed Directive advocating that part-timers should be granted the right to receive, in proportion to the hours they worked, equal pay and other non-monetary benefits received by full-time employees, the House of Lords Select Committee on the European Communities (1982) responded with an investigation into the possible impact that the implementation of this proposed Directive would have in Britain.

It may not be widely realised, but this move to put part-time employees on an equal footing with full-time employees with respect to hourly pay, promotion prospects, job security, etc., may well be one of the most important steps that has been taken towards bringing about economic equality between the sexes. Although many married couples now agree that both should have a job, their home and children still have to be cared for somehow. A large number have realised that if both work full-time and then also try to look after the home, too much work is involved and a compromise solution is adopted. One partner will work part-time, nearly always the woman, and take on most of the domestic responsibilities. The reason why they do not both work part-time, say two-thirds of a normal week each, is that most part-time work is relatively poorly rewarded and insecure with few prospects, and for most people reducing their working week by one-third would mean a drop of more than one-third of the rewards from working. The fact that, on average, males earn more than females often influences the decision that it is the wife who should only work part-time. The reluctance of many men to take on a greater share of domestic responsibilities is also a factor, however. One viewpoint is that if work patterns could be altered so that men and women could both work less than a full working week without losing out in pay, chances of promotion and other benefits more than in proportion to their reduction in hours, then more men would be willing to work part-time. They would then have more time to take on responsibilities in the home, and women working part-time would receive more equal treatment at work. True equality can only be achieved by ensuring that women have the same opportunities as men to enter employment and at the same time also taking measures to improve equality of work effort within the home. The moves towards equal rights for part-time workers may bring this a step nearer.

UNEMPLOYMENT

From Figures 7.1 and 7.2 it would appear that there have been some substantial differences between the British and US patterns of female unemployment since 1950. In Britain the number of unemployed females remained close to 100,000 for two decades. Then, in 1975, it started to climb, and by 1983 it was nine times its 1974 value. Apart from a few years in the early 1950s, the percentage rate of female unemployment has remained substantially below the male rate. Cyclical swings in female unemployment have mirrored the cyclical swings in male unemployment but with less severe fluctuations. In particular, when male unemployment grew substantially between 1967 and 1972 female unemployment was only marginally affected.

This contrasts with the USA where, until 1982, the percentage rate of female unemployment had exceeded the male rate throughout the previous three decades. The number of unemployed females grew, with a few fluctuations in the 1950s, stabilised in the 1960s, grew substantially in the early 1970s, apart from a recovery in 1972-3, fell back in the late 1970s, and then shot up again in the early 1980s. The percentage rate of female unemployment followed a similar pattern, although the stabilised number of unemployed in the 1960s translates into a drop in the percentage rate of female unemployment because the total size of the female labour force grew over this period. Although the rate of female unemployment usually exceeded the male rate, the number of unemployed females only exceeded the number of unemployed males in one year, 1969.

The British and US unemployment statistics used in Figures 7.1 and 7.2 are not comparable, however. This is because the British official unemployment figures for females have, over the years, been substantially below the numbers that would have been recorded if a method of collection similar to that used in the USA, and most other Western economies, had been used. In the USA, Canada and many European countries, unemployment figures are calculated from the results of questionnaire sample surveys, whereas in Britain, until October 1982, only individuals who registered with the government Employment Service were counted. Because of the

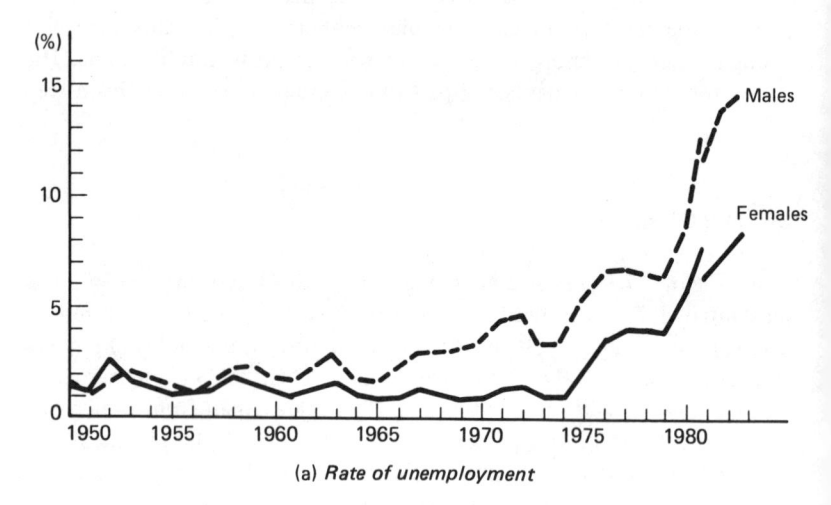

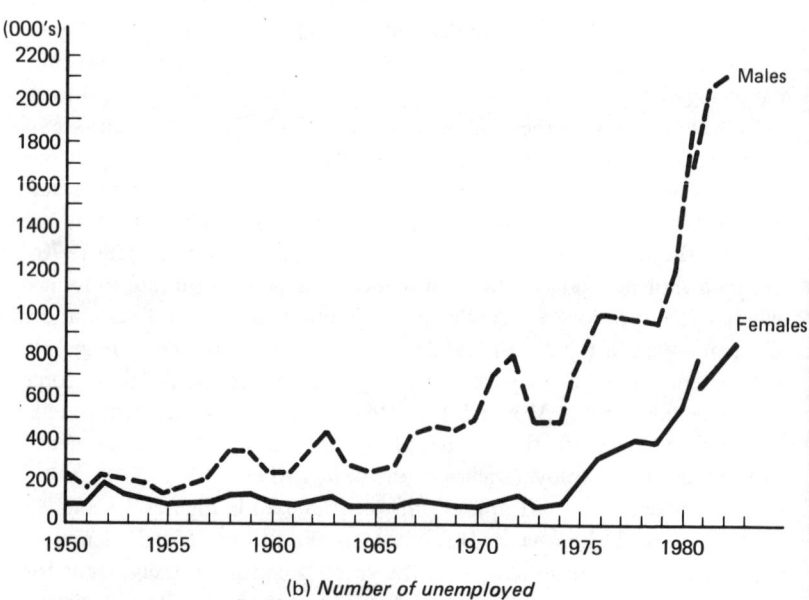

FIGURE 7.1 *Unemployment in Great Britain, 1950-83*
SOURCE *Department of Employment Gazette.*
NOTE discontinuity after 1981 is due to changes in method of counting unemployed introduced in October 1982 (see *Department of Employment Gazette*, December 1982, pp. S.20 for details).

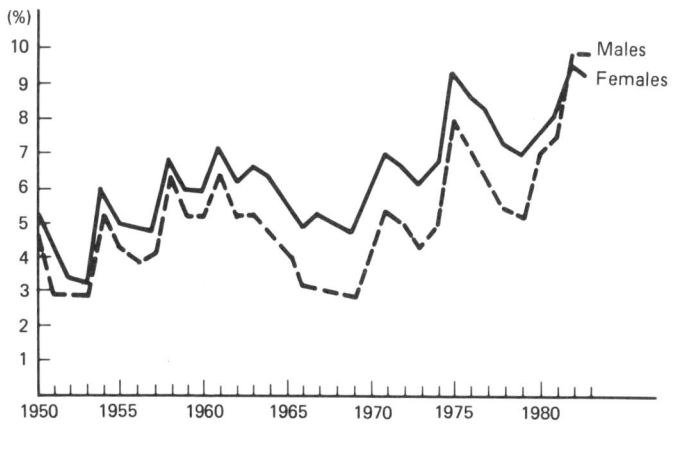

(a) *Rate of unemployment*

(b) *Number of unemployed*

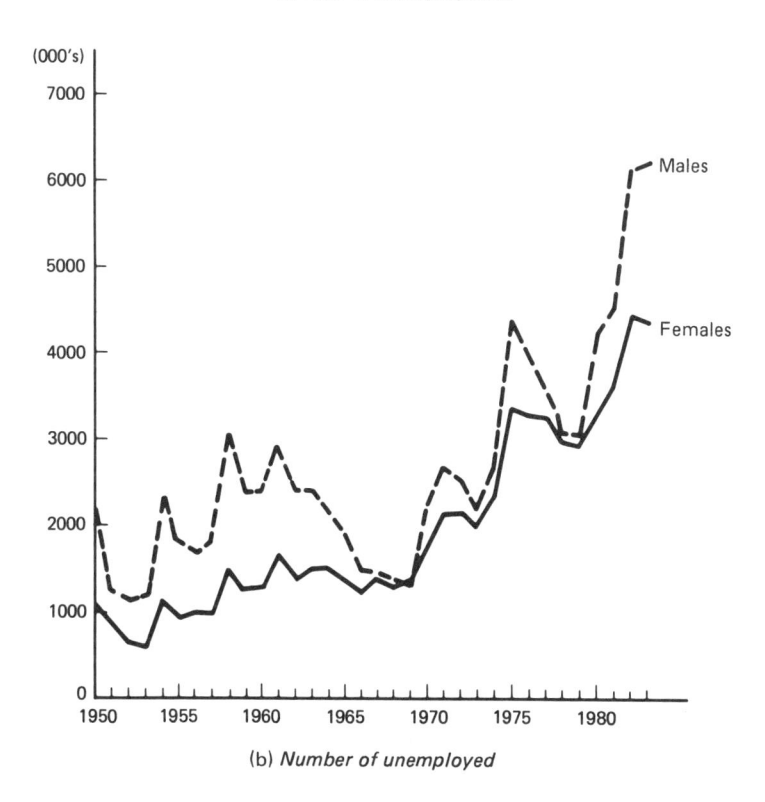

FIGURE 7.2 *Unemployment in the USA, 1950-83*
SOURCES *Employment and Earnings Monthly; Statistical Abstract of the US.*

peculiarities of the British unemployment benefit system, explained below, a large number of females had little incentive to register even though they were seeking work. Thus, as Paukert (1984) explains, Britain has been an exception to the usual OECD pattern, where female unemployment rates have been consistently above male unemployment rates for the last few decades in most member countries.

In Britain the government Employment Service is a source of job vacancies but the help that it can give is limited. Many individuals have found other sources, such as newspaper advertisements or personal contacts, more useful. The reason why many individuals registered as unemployed with the government Employment Service was that it was a precondition for claiming unemployment benefit, or in some cases supplementary benefit. Not all who registered were claiming benefit, though, and some of those who did register were not counted in the unemployment figure, e.g. those seeking part-time employment who were not receiving benefit.

Unemployment benefit and supplementary benefit are the two main categories of state benefit that are paid to unemployed people in Britain. Unemployment benefit can be claimed by those who have worked in the preceding financial year and made sufficient contributions under the British national insurance (NI) scheme, and it is paid for up to twelve months. Supplementary benefit is a basic welfare payment which is payable under certain circumstances to unemployed individuals who do not qualify for unemployment benefit, and to others on low incomes, to ensure that a specified minimum family income is received. Until 1977 working married women could choose to pay reduced NI contributions in return for forgoing their right to receive unemployment benefit, and many took up this option. Married women, and single women 'living as man and wife' with a male, were unable to claim supplementary benefit in their own right if they were unemployed. If their husbands were working then household income was usually above the minimum threshold for claiming supplementary benefit, and if it was not, or if their husbands were unemployed, then it was the man who made the claim for benefit. Since 1983, though, couples have been able to choose whether it is the husband or wife who makes the claim for supplementary benefit if both are unemployed. Thus for most of the post-war period unemployed married women have usually not been able to claim supplementary benefit, and only those who have recently been in employment and paid the full NI contribution have qualified to claim unemployment benefit, and there were relatively few of these. Registering as unemployed did also mean entitlement to be credited with a special NI contribution that would count towards one's retirement pension, but most married women are eligible for a pension on the strength of their husband's NI credits. Therefore, for a variety of reasons, most married women have had relatively little incentive to register as such if they are unemployed. Single females, though, are usually entitled to claim some form of benefit and so are more likely to register if unemployed.

From October 1982 the requirement to register as unemployed with the government Employment Service in order to receive benefits was dropped, except for young people, and unemployment statistics are now calculated from the computer records of those who have claimed and are receiving benefits from the Department of Health and Social Security. The Department of Employment (1982) estimated that with the new method the total 1982 unemployment figure would be almost 190,000 lower than under the old method, although more females than males disappeared from the figures. Over the years there have been other adjustments in the method of calculating total unemployment, although they have not affected the female unemployment figure so significantly.

Estimates of unregistered unemployment in Britain can be made using data from the censuses of population, or sample surveys such as the General Household Survey. Who exactly should be counted as unemployed depends on how one defines unemployment, and different definitions are sometimes used. How, for example, should one classify someone who says that they want to work but who has not actively sought employment, or someone who wants to work only part-time, or someone who has already fixed up a job or a place at college to start at some date in the future?

The 1971 census of population asked those persons aged 15 and over who did not have a job if they were 'seeking or waiting to take up a job' to determine if they should be classed as unemployed. Using these figures the Department of Employment (1976) estimated that the total 'true' figure for female unemployment in 1971 was close to 350,000, i.e. over three times the figure officially published. During the 1970s, though, the ratio of unregistered to registered unemployed is thought to have fallen. One reason for this is that much of the expansion in female employment was taken up by married women, often working on a part-time basis, and most of these married women would not previously have been included in the registered unemployed total. At the same time there was an increase in unemployment among younger single females who were usually entitled to claim benefit and hence included in the published unemployment statistics. There were also heavy full-time female job losses in certain industries, particularly in the manufacturing sector, despite the overall growth in female employment, and those women who lost their jobs were more likely to register as unemployed than those married women who used not to be in the labour force. The propensity of married women to register as unemployed increased after 1977 when the option to pay a reduced NI contribution was removed for new entrants and re-entrants to the labour force. It is also true that some of the social stigma that used to be associated with 'signing on' has now disappeared, whereas in earlier years this had deterred some women from registering. However, Cragg and Dawson (1984) found that a high proportion of women out of work were largely ignorant of what registering entailed and were sceptical about any advantages that might arise from doing so. When the 1981 census of population figure of 645,000 for the number of economically active females seeking work is compared with the June 1981 Department of Employment figure of 593,000 for registered female unemployment in Great Britain, it would appear that hidden unemployment as a percentage of the official figure fell to under 10 per cent in 1981 from 250 per cent in 1971. However, the measurement changes introduced in 1982 and the 'discouraged worker' effect of the current recession have probably pushed up this ratio again.

In the USA unemployment statistics are calculated from data obtained from the CPS (Current Population Survey). This is a monthly sample survey that classifies as unemployed those who are available for work but did not work for pay or profit during the survey week and who took active steps to find work in the preceding four weeks. Although this method is not totally accurate, it provides a much more realistic picture of female unemployment than the British system.

The differences in enumeration methods do account for some of the difference between the British and the US female unemployment figures, and an increase in the propensity to register accounts for some of the rapid growth in recorded female unemployment in Britain after 1974, but there have also been other factors that have influenced female unemployment levels. It is not possible to ascertain the exact contribution of each separate influence, but some general trends can be discerned in the four main ones, which were:
1. The general economic climate and demand for labour in general.
2. Structural changes in industry that specifically affected the demand for female labour.
2. The supply of female labour.
4. Female wage levels relative to male wages.

In Britain the story is basically one of an economy which from 1950 until 1966 had a low stable total unemployment rate close to 2 per cent. Then, partly due to inherent economic structural problems and partly due to government policy changes - explained more fully by Hughes and Perlman (1984) - unemployment started to grow rapidly and has since continued to do so, with only two brief recoveries, in the early and late 1970s. The initial effect of the growth in unemployment which started in 1967 was felt most strongly in manufacturing industries, which mainly employed males, while the service industries, where most women worked, continued to expand. When the recession began to bite again in the mid-1970s women were hit much harder, and in some manufacturing industries more women than men lost their jobs, as Werneke (1978) explains. However, in the brief economic recovery in the late 1970s male unemployment dropped more sharply than the female rate. This illustrates that it is in the male-dominated manufacturing industries that employment responds most significantly to cyclical fluctuations in economic activity. Female unemployment kept to a more steady upward trend.

Although total female employment grew until 1979, the number of full-time female employees started to decline after 1974, and by 1983 it was over 600,000 less than its 1974 level. The significance of this last point is brought home in Figure 7.3. The total supply of female labour (using the Department of Employment definition of employees plus unemployed officially recorded) grew steadily until 1980 and then started to decline. Until 1974 the growth in the number of jobs kept pace with the growth in the female labour force, although it is not really possible to say how much these two variables influenced each other. The creation of more jobs may have encouraged some women to enter the labour force, while the entry of some women into the labour force in itself may have increased the number of jobs done by females, e.g. if a female worker entered the labour force and replaced a male worker. From 1975 until 1983 the growth of around 700,000 in the female labour force was largely matched by the growth in part-time employment of over 500,000. On the other hand the fall in the number of females in full-time employment of over 600,000 could possibly account for three-quarters of the growth in female unemployment of 800,000. Thus although there were many other complex relationships at work, an overview of the situation suggests that most of the growth in the female labour force came from married women taking up part-time employment and that the rapid growth in recorded female unemployment was largely due to the loss of full-time jobs. This lack of full-time employment was felt particularly strongly by young females who were entering the labour market in the late 1970s in increasing numbers as a result of the early 1960s 'baby boom'. Many of the new part-time jobs did not require a high degree of skill and training, and much of the work could have been done by younger women on a full-time basis if it were not for the switch to part-time labour. In some cases, though, the new part-time jobs did require certain skills, e.g. typing, and employers were able to save

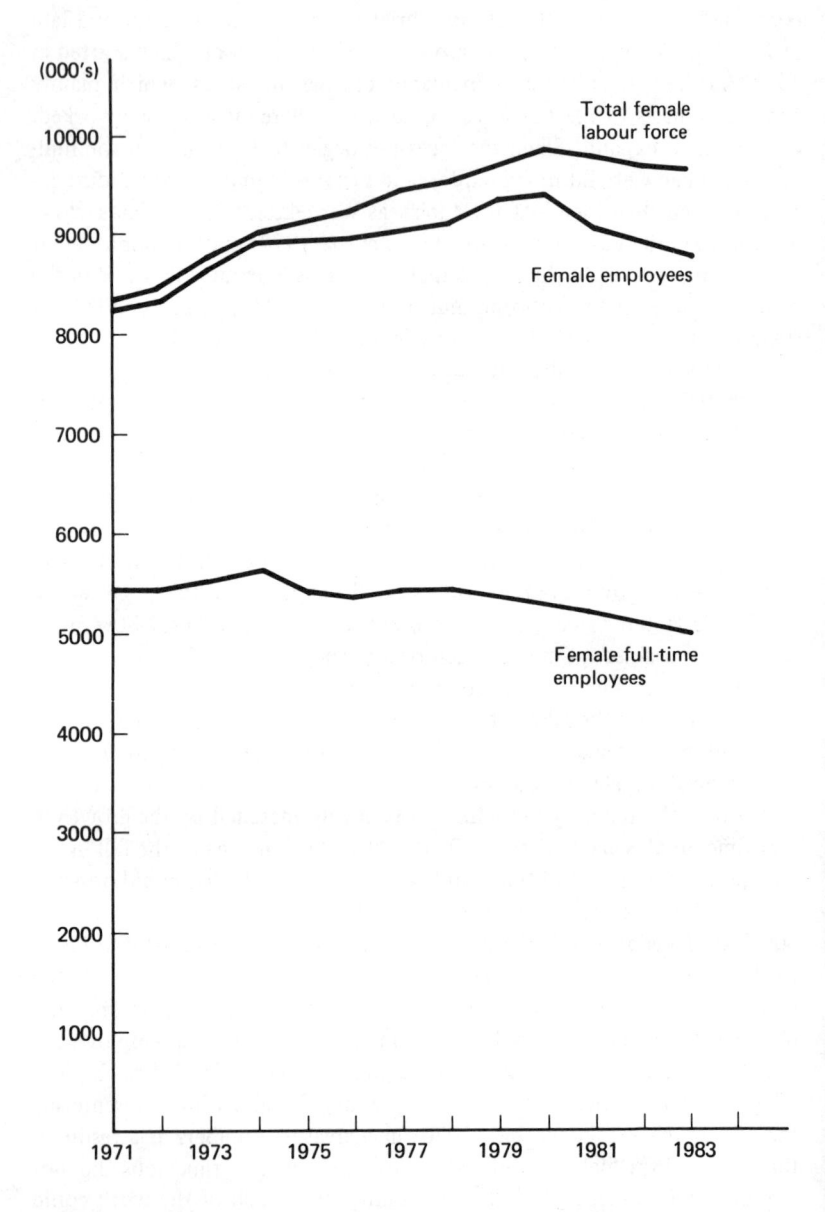

FIGURE 7.3 *Female labour supply in Great Britain, 1971-83*
SOURCES *Census of Employment, Department of Employment Gazette.*

on the costs of training unskilled school-leavers by employing on a part-time basis older, usually married, women who already had these skills.

Another factor that has been cited as a cause of the post-1974 growth in female unemployment is the coming into force in 1975 of the 1970 Equal Pay Act. Female wages rose relative to male wages and microeconomic theory suggests that this would cause both an increase in the number of females wishing to work and a drop in the number that firms will wish to employ, i.e. an increase in female unemployment. Countering this viewpoint it could be argued that microeconomic theory cannot fully explain a macroeconomic situation such as this because it ignores the feedback effects, such as the increased demand for goods and services, and thus labour, that might result from higher female wages. It is difficult to measure the extent to which the demand for female labour has been affected by equal pay legislation, partly because of the effects of the 1975 Sex Discrimination Act. One should, however, be careful not to fall into the trap of reasoning that if one believes that sex equality of wages is a good thing then no undesirable effects will result from this coming about. It is perfectly logical to accept the value judgement that men and women should get equal pay for work of equal value and yet accept, if evidence proves it, that this could cause female unemployment to rise. The evidence, however, is not conclusive.

The pattern of aggregate demand for labour in the USA, and consequently the unemployment level, has differed considerably from the British situation. Hughes and Perlman (1984) explain how both government policy and economic structural changes have contributed to what has happened, as has been the case in Britain.

From Figure 7.2 it was observed that the fluctuations in US female unemployment were not as great as the fluctuations in male unemployment, although the same general trend was followed. This is because, as in Britain, cyclical fluctuations in economic activity tend to have a greater effect on manufacturing industry, which is male-dominated, than on the service sector, where most women work. The whole situation in the USA is, of course, different to the British case in that the total population and workforce grew each year and a recession usually meant slower growth in employment rather than a decrease, but not always. Between 1980 and 1982 total employment in manufacturing (68 per cent male) and construction (92 per cent male) fell by 500 000 and 1 700 000 respectively, while in service industries (61 per cent female) total employment grew by 1 500 000, helping explain the growth in male unemployment over this period.

154 Women and the Economy

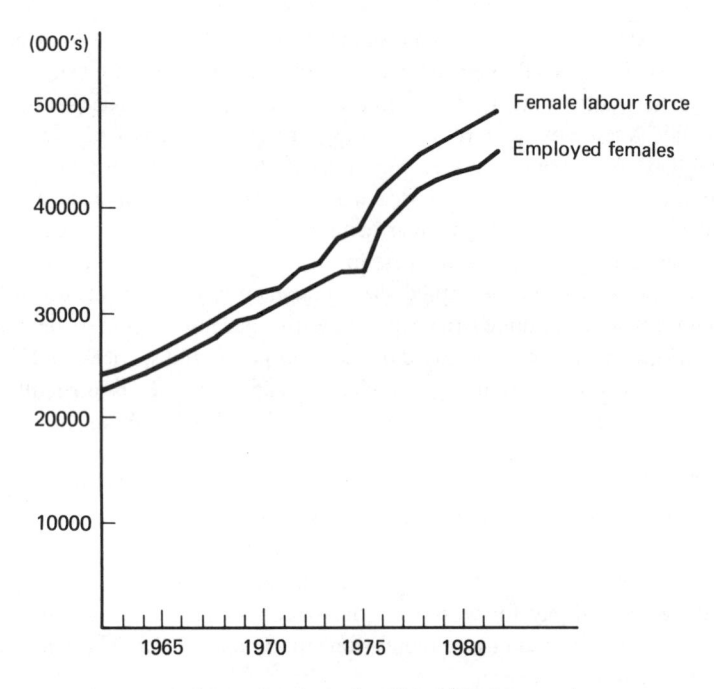

FIGURE 7.4 Female labour supply in the USA, 1962-82
SOURCE *Statistical Abstract of the US.*

Unlike the British case, the number of females in employment in the USA has increased each year over the last decade or so. However, the total female labour force has also increased, at times at a faster rate (see Figure 7.4) leading to rise in unemployment. Vickery *et al.* (1978) argue that structural imperfections in labour markets have contributed to the high rates of female unemployment over the years, and that if women were given greater access to a wider range of occupations then female unemployment would be lower. Lloyd and Niemi (1978) also suggest that the growth of the female labour force, coupled with the constraint of females being concentrated in a relatively small number of occupations, has pushed up female unemployment. However, Johnson (1983) points out that the percentage rate of female unemployment has only exceeded the male rate because the total size of the female labour force is smaller than the total size of the male labour force. As the number of unemployed females is usually less than the number of unemployed males, she argues that there should not be undue concern over the relatively high female percentage unemployment rate.

A glance at Figures 7.3 and 7.4 might suggest that if only the female labour force, in both Britain and the USA, had not expanded quite so rapidly, the increase in jobs would have wiped out any unemployment. This line of reasoning, however, results from a misconception of what unemployment actually is. Unemployment is a stock with people flowing in and out, and it is not always the same people that make up the total, although in Britain at the start of 1984 27 per cent of unemployed females and 41 per cent of unemployed males had been unemployed for more than a year. In 1980, when unemployment was rising and there were no changes in the method of counting unemployment, on average every month the number of females leaving the unemployment register in Britain was 87 per cent of the number of new entrants, and the figure for males was 81 per cent. In the USA the average time spent in each period of unemployment is less for females than for males. Females, however, are more likely to experience a spell of unemployment because they tend to be concentrated in the less secure secondary labour market jobs, and because they leave and enter the labour force more quickly than males. Over 30 per cent of unemployed females are re-entrants into the labour force (Table 7.5). Sandell (1980) estimated that the average length of a spell of unemployment for females, after allowing for certain characteristics that affect earning power, was correlated with their reservation wage, i.e. the higher the minimum wage that they would be willing to accept the longer the time spent searching for a job. Many females in the sample observed in this study thought that it was not worth searching longer because they believed that they would not stay long enough in a job to pay back the cost of the extra time spent searching, but the evidence suggested that greater search time would have paid off for most of them.

The age distribution of female unemployment has also altered in Britain, the USA, and most other industrialised countries. Youth unem-

TABLE 7.5 *Unemployment by sex and reason, USA, 1970 and 1982 (% of total number unemployed, annual averages of monthly figures)*

	1970 Female	1970 Male	1982 Female	1982 Male
Job losses	33.1	53.6	44.2	69.2
Job leavers	14.4	12.6	10.0	6.3
Re-entrants	37.5	23.8	32.0	15.3
New entrants	15.0	10.0	13.8	9.1

SOURCE *Statistical Abstract of the US.*

TABLE 7.6 *Unemployment by sex and age group, Great Britain, 1971 and 1981*

Age groups	% Unemployed*				Unemployed in age group as % of total unemployed			
	Females		Males		Females		Males	
	1971	1981	1971	1981	1971	1981	1971	1981
Under 20**	6.2	16.7	8.7	18.9	18.8	25.6	15.3	13.9
20–24	4.2	10.9	5.6	15.9	15.2	22.8	15.9	17.9
25–34	4.2	6.7	4.0	10.0	18.2	21.6	19.9	23.4
35–44	3.0	3.7	3.2	7.7	16.1	12.2	15.3	15.4
45–54	2.7	3.6	2.9	7.4	16.4	11.1	13.3	13.4
55–59	3.0	4.2	3.1	8.6	6.9	5.6	6.9	7.6
60–64	2.8	1.2	6.1	13.2	3.9	0.6	11.6	8.1
65+	4.7	1.7	2.3	1.5	3.9	0.5	1.8	0.3
Totals	3.6	6.5	4.2	10.3	100.0	100.0	100.0	100.0

*Per cent unemployed calculated as % of total economically active who were out of work and seeking employment.
**Aged 15+ for 1971, 16+ for 1981.
SOURCE   *Census of Population.*

ployment became a serious problem in the 1970s, particularly in Britain (see Table 7.6). It is still a problem, although the ratio of youth unemployment to total unemployment has fallen in the last few years. This is partly because of a rise in adult unemployment and partly because a large number of unemployed young people are 'hidden' on various government youth training schemes.

Although this section has explained the trends in female unemployment that are discernible from published statistics, simple head counts can never give an accurate picture of the total potential labour force that is untapped. If a woman is asked, 'Would you take a job if one was offered?' the response might be first to ask 'At what wage? What type of work? How many hours per week?' Of course, it is impossible to compile a complete picture of unemployment that would take into account all these qualifications to the figures, but some indication of the potential female labour force is provided by Martin and Roberts (1984). Reporting on the 1980 Women and Employment Survey in Britain, they found that only 36 per cent of nonworking women, and 12 per cent of all women, expected not to work again or were unsure if they would work again. All of the rest, including many of those not working and not currently seeking work, expected to work at some time in the future.

THE EFFECTS OF THE NEW TECHNOLOGY ON FEMALE EMPLOYMENT

Female employment is likely to be affected quite significantly in the future by technological advancement, and in particular by developments in the field of microelectronics. The development of the microprocessor has started to open up a vast range of possible applications in computer-controlled production and information processing. It is not just the technological advances that are important but also the ability of computer companies to manufacture equipment on a mass scale and at a cost low enough for even small firms to afford. The introduction of this new technology has already led to significant changes in employment patterns in some areas. There are two main areas of application of the new microelectronic technology which may have a significant effect on female employment. Firstly, mainly in manufacturing industries, microprocessors can be used to control machinery, particularly where repetitive mechanical tasks are performed, and certain manual jobs may disappear. Secondly, mainly in the service sector, new developments in information processing will mean the elimination of much clerical work, particularly in those occupations involved in the recording, storing, retrieval and processing of information. The ETUI (1980) give a more detailed account of the different ways in which the new technology can be applied in these fields. Women are particularly heavily concentrated in those occupations that are most likely to be affected by these new developments. Before examining the effects of the new technology on female employment in more detail, it is first necessary to say something about the effects of the new technology on employment in general.

Technological advancement has been progressing since the invention of the wheel. Some writers, however, have been making predictions about the effects of the new technology without any reference to what has happened in the past when other labour-saving innovations have been implemented. One line of reasoning is that if machines can do the work of humans then the labour input will drop and either workers will lose jobs or working hours will be reduced. This latter possibility has particular appeal for female workers. If automation reduces unit costs, why not share the benefits with workers by reducing hours without a corresponding drop in pay? Shorter hours would be welcomed by many women, not just because they would prefer less time in paid employment themselves because of the disproportionate share of domestic responsibilities that they take on, but also because if men also worked shorter hours then they too would be able to help more in the home. In a competitive world, though, this is unrealistic.

Unless all employers are forced to cut hours without loss of pay, e.g. by government legislation or trade union pressure, then any that do would be undercut and forced out of business by those that do not. Hours of work tend only to drop slowly over the long term, although there are several different ways in which a drop in hours resulting from the new technology can come about. Blandy (1984) gives some examples, e.g. holidays may be increased.

The assumption that labour demand will drop at all has been questioned. One view is that in the past advances in technology have decreased labour demand in some areas but a new demand has arisen elsewhere, and this will also happen with the latest phase of technological advancement. However, explanations of the precise economic mechanism that will bring about this sort of adjustment are sometimes rather vague. Another view is that economic conditions have changed and there is no inevitable reason why the free market will automatically adjust to provide employment opportunities elsewhere. Employers sometimes argue that the instalment of new technology will enable them to improve the quality of the service that they provide and/or increase output without a reduction in their workforce. However, Arnold *et al.* (1982) give several examples of this being contradicted. One reason, perhaps, is that employers forget that their competitors may also be thinking along the same lines and, unless the whole market is expanding, not everyone can sell more. Some markets can expand, but in those that cannot a drop in labour demand is likely. There may also be spin-offs for other industries if the investment expenditure resulting from the instalment of the new technology creates jobs and helps fuel an economic recovery, but it is not inevitable that the number of jobs created in this way would equal, or exceed, the number of jobs that disappeared.

On an international scale the same reasoning can be used. Industrialists, politicians and others often advocate the rapid application of new technology on the grounds that this will help industry in general to produce more cheaply and thus increase exports. But if other countries are doing the same then they will tend to cancel out each other's competitiveness and output will not necessarily expand. This, however, does not mean that a country should not be too concerned about the speed of introduction of the new technology. If one country is slow at taking up the new technology there will be others who are not and who will be able to steal markets from the first country. Thus in some cases there is a need to take up the new technology simply to keep one's market share rather than to rapidly expand sales.

It is impossible to make precise estimates of the effects of the new technology on employment levels. The speed of implementation, further technological advances, as well as market demand and other economic factors can all affect employment in the industries in which the new technology is used. There will also be unquantifiable effects on employment as the implementation of new technology in one industry affects output in other industries, e.g. more reliable electronic goods mean less repair work is required, and throughout the economy in general, e.g. if investment and exports are stimulated. It is possible to predict in which industries and occupations the immediate effects of the new technology are most likely to be felt, and Williams (1984) surveys some of the forecasts that have been made. Some researchers, even though their figures are only tentative, have even attempted to quantify predicted job losses in specific occupations. Many changes, of course, have already taken place, but all agree that the main impact of the new technology is yet to come.

Manual employment in manufacturing industry

In manufacturing industries computer-controlled production processes have been in use for many years. These, though, have mainly been large-scale production processes with long production runs where the high investment costs of mainframe computer control could be recouped. The new generation computer technology can bring down the costs of computer control dramatically, making it profitable to use in small-scale production. The jobs that will tend to disappear will be those that involve repetitive tasks that can be done by computer-controlled machinery, e.g. assembling, welding, cutting, painting, drilling and packaging. Because only a minority of women work in manufacturing industry the number affected in total will be less than the number of men. However, the effect of the new technology is likely to hit those jobs done by women relatively harder than those done by men. This is because females employed in manufacturing industry tend to be concentrated in those jobs involving repetitive tasks, some skilled and some unskilled, that offer potential for automation. For example, from Table 7.7 one can see that although repetitive assembly of electronic goods makes up only a small proportion of total female employment, it is a female-dominated occupation and likely to see many changes as the new technology is diffused.

TABLE 7.7 Females in selected occupations, Great Britain, 1981

	No. of females in employment	Female % of all employed	% of total females employed	% females unemployed*
All occupations	9 151 470	39.9	100.0	7.4
All clerical and related occupations	2 877 270	74.4	31.4	2.7
Secretaries and typists	750 600	98.3	8.2	3.5
Clerks	1 591 650	70.0	17.4	3.5
Telephone operators	72 780	87.6	0.8	4.9
Shop assistants	701 020	84.4	7.7	5.0
Catering, cleaning, hairdressing and other personal services	1 958 670	79.8	21.4	3.8
Textile winders and reelers	9 910	86.7	0.1	14.0
All textile workers	48 650	53.0	0.5	11.2
All painting, repetitive assembling, product inspection, packaging and related	376 540	42.8	4.1	9.7
Repetitive assemblers of electrical and electronic goods	51 900	78.5	0.6	11.0
Machine tool operators	44 650	16.2	0.5	10.6
Press and machine tool setters	620	1.3	0.01	12.7
Electronic engineers	1 050	3.6	0.01	3.7

*Calculated as percentage of all economically active. Unemployed are classified in the census according to previous occupation. As 43 per cent of all unemployed females were classed as inadequately described or occupation not given, these figures can only be taken as a rough guide.
SOURCE *1981 Census of Population*, Economic Activity Table 3.

Although repetitive manual jobs will disappear, there may be a greater demand for skilled workers able to set up for production runs, to monitor production and to carry out maintenance. At present these skilled jobs are often done by men, and unless more women are trained to be able to cope with these changes in job requirements the male-female ratio in manufacturing will increase. An example of where this is likely to happen is in machine tool setting. If machine tools are computer-controlled then there will be less need for machine tool operators but there will not be such a great drop in the demand for machine tool setters who set specifications before a production run. Looking at Table 7.7, one can see that females make up 16 per cent of machine tool operators but only 1 per cent of

TABLE 7.8 *Females in selected occupations, USA, 1982*

	% female of all employed	% of total females in employment
All occupations	43.5	100.0
Clerical and kindred workers, including:	80.7	34.4
Secretaries	99.2	8.8
Typists	96.6	2.1
Telephone operators	91.9	0.6
Computer and peripheral equipment operators	63.3	0.8
Key punch operators	94.5	0.8
Assembler operatives	53.8	1.4
Textile operatives	63.0	0.4
Computer specialists	38.6	1.0
Electrical and electronic engineers	4.0	0.04

SOURCE *Statistical Abstract of the US, 1984.*

machine tool setters. Thus jobs will disappear where women are more significantly represented and be maintained in occupations where there are hardly any women.

One area where there will be a fast growing demand for highly skilled specialists is electronic engineering, but only 4 per cent of electronic engineers in both Britain and the USA are female. In a comprehensive survey of available evidence Arnold *et al.* (1982) summarise the likely effects of the new technology on different manufacturing industries in Britain. In the engineering industry female employment has already fallen substantially, particularly in the assembly of electronic goods, such as televisions and telephone equipment. The microelectronics industry itself does not offer much scope for expansion of employment. A large proportion of microelectronic components are imported into Britain from the USA. As Keller (1983) explains, employment in the microelectronic industry is polarised into highly skilled technical jobs and relatively unskilled assembly work, which is still reasonably labour-intensive. Some of this labour-intensive assembly work is in fact not carried out in the USA, but in South East Asia, where labour is cheaper. Continual developments in the technology, and the secrecy requirements in military contracts, mean that there are limits to the extent that companies can rely on this 'off-shore sourcing' of production. In the USA the assembly side of production in the new technology industries is relatively poorly paid, and a large proportion of the work is done by women and migrant workers. Within the US electronics industry as a whole, according to Snow (1983), after falling from a peak in 1966 employment grew through the 1970s, particularly in semi-conductor production, despite this off-shore sourcing of some production. However, the blue-collar proportion of the workforce has fallen, and although the percentage of female workers has not altered substantially, a smaller proportion are employed in production and more are employed in clerical and related occupations. Whatever growth there has been in female employment in this industry has had a negligible effect on total female employment compared with the effects that the application of this new technology has had, and will have, in other industries. Only a tiny proportion of the female workforce is employed in the new technology industries, and most expansion has been concentrated in a small number of geographical areas, such as 'Silicon Valley' in California. Riche, Hecker and Burgan (1983) found that employment in US high technology industries grew faster than average industry growth between 1972 and 1982, and they estimated that this relatively faster growth rate would continue into the future. However, even when broadly defined, the high technology industries only account for a small proportion of total employment, and the projected increase in the number of scientific and technical workers to 1995 is only 6 per cent of the projected total increase in employment.

One manufacturing industry where female employees are in the majority is the textile industry. In the British textile industry heavy job losses in recent years have been due to the introduction of new technology as well as the recession. Although automation has been taking place for many years, new developments allow even more tasks to be controlled by computer. For example, weaving and knitting machines can now be controlled by programmes that allow patterns to be easily altered. Dyeing is now literally a dying craft. Dye recipes have been coded, using the knowledge of the now redundant skilled dyers, and a greater success rate than before can be achieved in colour matching. Improvements in textile quality resulting from computer-controlled operations also mean job losses among those workers involved in finding and rectifying faults. In the clothing industry the cutting of material can be fairly easily controlled by computer, but not the final sewing and assembly.

The printing industry is one of the few industries where the introduction of new technology is likely to cause an increase in the female-male ratio of employees. In Britain nearly all the skilled jobs involved in manually setting up text for printing are done by men. New technology now allows automatic setting up for printing by simply typing text on to a visual display unit. In the USA these developments have already had an impact, and during the 1970s there was an increase in female employment and a slight fall in male employment in the newspaper industry. In Britain the highly organised male-dominated trade unions in the printing industry are resisting these changes.

Service industries and non-manual occupations

Although most of the changes that are already under way are affecting manual employment in manufacturing industries, it is in the service industries and non-manual occupations in the manufacturing sector that the most significant effect on female employment is likely to take place. This is not just because this is where most females work, but also because, for various reasons, capital investment and the introduction of technical innovations have been relatively low in the past. The effects will be felt more heavily in some occupations than others. In particular clerical and related occupations, where over 30 per cent of females in both Britain and the USA work and where three-quarters of all employees are female, offer much scope for the introduction of the new technology. In some areas of female employment, though, such as services like hairdressing or office cleaning, few changes are expected as a result of new technology.

Word processors can reduce substantially the time required from typists for a given output. Bird (1980) predicted a loss of 21,000 secretarial and typing jobs in Britain by 1985 (about 2 per cent of the total employed) and a maximum of 170,000 jobs (17 per cent of the total) displaced by 1990. Although some new jobs will be created in selling and customer support for word processors, the majority of these jobs tend to be done by males, especially selling, although some females are involved in customer support. This is yet another example of where existing women's jobs will disappear and any new jobs that are created will tend to be male-dominated unless there are radical changes in the training and employment of women in technical and sales areas.

In addition to typing, nearly every other clerical related job will be, or already has been, affected by the new technology. Storage, processing and transfer of information by computer is already the norm in large organisations, and soon most smaller concerns will also be moving in this direction. This eliminates the need for filing clerks and other clerical staff engaged in routine tasks. For example, in 1970 annual premiums for motor insurance policies were still being calculated manually in some insurance companies, but now everything is calculated and printed by computer. In some large supermarkets information from checkout registers feeds directly to a warehouse so that the correct re-stocking requirements can immediately be known, cutting down the need for stock-taking and the compiling of orders. In banking the market in Britain is growing and is expected to continue to expand in the future, but the new technology will allow business to expand without a significant change in total labour requirements. However, traditional female occupations, e.g. cashiers and routine clerical work, will diminish and there will be a growth in the higher management echelons and in computer staff, where at present women are underrepresented. A study by the Institute of Manpower Studies (1984) explains that, even though there may be some increase in employment in the initial stages of implementation of new technology in an expanding market, in the long run employment in financial institutions is likely to fall. Past trends cannot always be assumed to continue into the future. In Britain the initial expansionary phase is now almost over in insurance, and in the next decade banks and building societies will follow a similar path.

Evidence from the USA signifies that the changes are already underway. Remembering that this is a growing economy where total employment increased by 13 per cent between 1972 and 1982, data (*US Statistical Abstract*) show that over this period the number of all clerical and kindred workers grew by 29 per cent, but within this broad occupational group there were three occupations where employment fell: book clerks and storekeepers (down 3 per cent), telephone operators (down 28 per cent) and typists (down 8 per cent). On the other hand, the number of computer operators grew by 195 per cent, and the number of key punch operators was up 28 per cent. New automatic telephone exchange equipment has also led to a drop in the number of telephone operators in Britain over the last decade. Although in terms of total numbers female employment will be most affected by the new technology in clerical jobs, the effects of the new technology will also permeate into other service occupations. One example is the catering industry. In Britain and the USA the growth in the number of single households, and in the number of working wives, and a long-term rise in living standards, have contributed to a growth in eating out. In restaurants and other prepared food outlets, changes such as greater control over cooking times and temperatures, and microwave ovens allowing the serving of off-premises mass-prepared food without a great deal of point-of-sale labour involved, have reduced costs and increased productivity. Thus the need for staff expansion to cope with growth in turnover has been diminished. However, in some service sector industries, such as education, employment levels will depend more on government expenditure policy than the introduction of the new technology.

Another way that the new technology can affect female employment is through the growth of home-working. Huws (1984) gives some examples of the use of remote working, which is already spreading in the USA. Information transfer systems, e.g. via cable, enable basic tasks such as data inputting, as well as more skilled jobs such as programming, to be done from home. One of the major savings for employers is office space, which can be costly in city centres. Flexibility of hours and being at home to look after small children are some of the advantages of this system. However, some women do not like the solitude or the intermingling of work and home life, and if work is only done on a piece-rate basis, without job security or fringe benefits and with little hope of promotion, then this development could hamper progress towards equality. Bissett and Huws (1984) found evidence that home-workers in the new technology industries received on average substantially less per hour than other employees doing the same work.

Summing up this brief overview of the vast literature on the impact of new technology on female employment, several conclusions can be drawn. In many industries women are concentrated in occupations that involve routine tasks which makes them more likely to be affected by the new technology than men. Because of the present distribution of female employment, and the state of technological development, the greatest effect on female employment in terms of numbers will be in clerical and related occupations. Unless women acquire new skills, they are going to lose out to men in the competition for those new jobs that are created in implementing and supervising computer control systems. Thus although it is impossible to predict the net effect on total employment of the new technology, there is a possibility that it could swing the balance of employment away from women.

8   International Comparisons

This chapter is in two sections. In the first some comparisons are made between Britain and the USA and other free market industrialised nations. Most developed market economies have experienced a growth in the female labour force, but there have been variations in the patterns of growth. In the second section the structure of the female labour force in a planned economy, the Soviet Union, is studied. Despite the different economic system it appears that in this centrally planned economy there are some similarities with the patterns of female employment found in capitalist economies.

FEMALE EMPLOYMENT IN FREE MARKET INDUSTRIALISED ECONOMIES

Although differences in methods of data collection and classification of labour force statistics make precise comparisons between different countries difficult, it is nevertheless obvious from Tables 8.1 and 8.2 that there has been a significant increase in female labour force participation in most, but not all, of the countries included. There is some variation in both the rate of growth of the proportion of females in the labour force and in the female economic activity rate. Also, even where growth rates are the same, variations in the base year value mean that the 1980 figures are different. However, what is important is not these variations but the fact that the phenomenon of a growing female labour force has been a common feature of most industrialised nations and has not just been confined to Britain and the USA.

Between 1950 and 1980 in both Britain and the USA the female proportion of the labour force grew by about one-third, and the female economic activity rate grew by just over one-third in Britain and just over a half in the USA. Out of those countries where comparable data are avail-

TABLE 8.1   Females as a percentage of total civilians in employment

	1950	1960	1970	1980
Australia	*	28.2 (1964)	28.8	34.1
Belgium	28.7	30.7	32.7	35.9
Canada	21.8	26.8	33.6	39.7 (1979)
Denmark	*	31.6	39.4	43.6
France	*	*	35.2	38.0
West Germany	35.6 (1951)	37.8	36.6	38.3
Ireland	26.0	*	26.7	28.5
Italy	*	30.1	28.3	32.1
Japan	*	40.7	39.3	38.7
Norway	27.8	29.0	30.8	41.1
Portugal	23.0	18.7	*	38.8
Spain	16.1	*	25.0	29.0
Sweden	*	36.1 (1962)	39.4	45.0
UK	32.6	34.4	36.3	40.1
USA	29.4	33.3	37.2	42.4

*Data not available.
SOURCE   OECD Labour Force Statistics, country tables.

TABLE 8.2   Female activity rates

	\multicolumn{4}{c}{Total female labour force as % of female population aged 15–64 years}
	1950	1960	1970	1980
Australia	*	38.9 (1964)	46.5	52.6
Belgium	33.4	36.4	40.2	48.0
Canada	26.2	32.0	43.2	57.3 (1979)
Denmark	*	43.5	58.0	70.8
France	*	*	47.5	52.5
West Germany	*	49.3	48.1	49.3 (1979)
Ireland	37.2 (1951)	35.5 (1961)	34.3	34.6
Italy	*	36.7	33.5	39.8
Japan	*	60.1	55.4	54.9
Norway	36.6	36.3	38.8	63.2
Portugal	26.3	20.1	30.8	55.7
Spain	17.7	23.6 (1962)	29.2	31.9
Sweden	*	53.3	59.4	74.1
UK	42.9	48.6	50.8	57.6
USA	37.6	42.6	48.9	59.7

*Data not available.
SOURCE   OECD Labour Force Statistics.

able for the whole of this period, these growth rates were exceeded in Canada, Portugal, Spain and Norway, and were roughly the same in Belgium. Exceptions to the general upward trend are found in West Germany, Japan, Italy and Ireland, where growth was negligible and, in a few instances, negative. These aggregate figures, though, do hide some variations in the pattern of change, which are discussed later.

Changes in the female labour force are the net result of a complex set of relationships between different economic, demographic, political, social and cultural factors. It would, therefore, be difficult to provide a full explanation of why growth rates have varied from country to country, although Winegarden (1984) does attempt to estimate the relationship between female economic activity and a set of explanatory variables using data from ten different countries, producing results similar to those described in Chapter 4. However, one important influence that can be identified fairly easily is the degree of 'economic maturity' of a nation. Most of the world's industrialised nations have gone through three main stages of economic development. All countries once had the major part of their labour force employed in agriculture, as many developing nations still do. In Europe and North America employment in agriculture declined relatively as manufacturing grew and, more recently, employment in manufacturing has declined relatively as the service sector has expanded. As the manufacturing and then the service sectors expand, they have to draw labour from somewhere. In its early stages manufacturing usually starts with the textile industry and then progresses to the 'heavy industry' type which has mainly been a male preserve. Thus the growth of manufacturing has usually drawn both men and women, previously employed in agriculture, from the countryside into the cities but has provided employment mainly for males, with the exception of the textile industry, where both males and females are usually employed. In most economies the service sector has begun its expansionary phase while most males are employed in manufacturing, and has thus provided employment opportunities for females. Even when growth in manufacturing slackens off, employment segregation by industry often persists, and so the growth of the female labour force is closely related to the growth of the service sector.

This sequence of economic development can be observed in Table 8.4, where the OECD industry groupings 'agriculture', 'industry' and 'other', correspond approximately to the three sectors agriculture, manufacturing and services. The only countries where the proportion of the labour force in manufacturing increased were those that still had a relatively large agricultural workforce in 1960, which then declined in the next two decades, i.e. Japan, Italy, Greece and Finland. In all the countries listed,

TABLE 8.3 *Females in civilian employment by industrial sector, 1980 (%)*

	Agriculture*	Industry**	Other†
Australia	4.2	16.0	79.8
Belgium	1.8	17.8	80.4
Canada	3.1	15.6	81.2
Finland	9.9	21.9	68.1
West Germany	8.0	30.3	61.7
Greece	42.4	19.3	38.3
Italy	16.0	27.6	56.4
Japan	13.2	28.4	58.4
Norway	6.1	13.6	80.3
Spain	17.9	20.7	61.4
Sweden	3.1	16.2	80.6
Switzerland	5.5	25.7	68.8
UK	1.4	22.5	76.1
USA	1.6	18.5	79.9

*Agriculture = agriculture, hunting, forestry and fishing.
**Industry = mining and quarrying; manufacturing; electricity, gas and water; construction.
†Other = wholesale and retail trade, restaurants and hotels; transport, storage and communications; financing, insurance, real estate, and business services; community, social and personal services; activities not adequately defined.
SOURCE *OECD Labour Force Statistics.*

though, the service sector grew, and those with the highest proportion of all employment in the service sector tend to have the greatest female labour force participation. That the service sector tends to be the main source of employment for females is confirmed in Table 8.3. Only in the less developed industrialised nations, such as Greece, did agriculture employ more females than the service sector in 1980. The relatively high proportion of the labour force employed in agriculture is one contributory factor to countries like Japan and Italy being exceptions to the typical pattern of growth in female labour force participation. Although statistics for the numbers employed in agriculture can often be inaccurate, it is usually the case that in peasant families women do a significant proportion of the work on the land. Thus a decline in agricultural employment may release for other work more females than there are opportunities available in manufacturing or services. In Japan, for example, in 1955 some 42 per cent of the recorded female workforce were unpaid family workers in the agricultural sector, but this number had declined to 10 per cent by 1980. A similar pattern occurred in Italy, where the proportion of unpaid family

TABLE 8.4 *Total civilian employment by industrial sector (%)*

	Agriculture 1960	1980	change	Industry 1960	1980	change	Other 1960	1980	change
Australia	11.3	6.5	− 4.8	40.9	31.0	− 9.9	47.7	62.4	+14.7
Belgium	8.7	3.0	− 5.7	46.8	34.8	−12.0	44.6	62.3	+17.7
Canada	13.3	5.5	− 7.8	33.2	28.5	− 4.7	53.5	66.0	+12.5
Finland	36.4	11.6	−24.8	31.9	34.4	+ 2.5	31.7	54.0	+22.3
West Germany	14.0	6.0	− 8.0	48.8	44.8	− 4.0	37.3	49.2	+11.9
Greece	56.6	28.5	−28.1	17.7	30.6	+12.9	25.7	40.9	+15.2
Italy	32.8	14.2	−18.6	36.9	37.8	+ 0.9	30.2	48.0	+17.8
Japan	30.2	10.4	−19.8	28.5	35.3	+ 6.8	41.3	54.2	+12.9
Norway	21.6	8.5	−13.1	35.6	25.7	− 9.9	42.9	61.8	+18.9
Spain	42.3	18.9	−23.4	32.0	36.1	+ 4.1	25.7	45.1	+19.4
Sweden	14.9	5.6	− 9.3	42.6	32.2	−10.4	42.5	62.2	+19.7
Switzerland	13.2	7.2	− 6.0	48.4	39.5	− 8.9	38.4	53.3	+14.9
UK	4.1	2.7	− 1.4	48.8	38.1	−10.7	47.0	59.2	+12.2
USA	8.3	3.6	− 4.7	33.6	30.5	− 3.1	58.1	65.9	+ 7.8

NOTE: for definitions of industrial sectors see note to Table 8.3.
SOURCE *OECD Labour Force Statistics.*

agricultural workers in the total female workforce fell from 30 per cent to under 5 per cent between 1955 and 1980. In both cases this was offset by a growth in paid employment in the manufacturing and service sectors, but the net effect was only a very small growth in the female labour force as opposed to the significant net growth in countries like Britain, where the growth in female employment in the service sector was not counteracted by a noticeable decline in female employment in agriculture. In the USA there was a substantial decline in the percentage of females employed in agriculture but this was outweighed by the expansion of employment opportunities in other industries.

As in Britain and the USA, the rise in the female economic activity rate in other countries has largely been due to the increased economic activity of married women. However, the increased economic activity rates for married women shown in Table 8.5 have in most cases been partially counterbalanced by a drop in the economic activity rate for single women, due partly to an increase in the numbers staying on in full-time education beyond the legal minimum school-leaving age. This is particularly noticeable in West Germany, where the net increase in the overall female economic activity rate has been negligible. In most other cases, however, the growth

TABLE 8.5 *Employment of married women*

	Married females in employment as a percentage of married female population	
	1970	1980
Austria	29.8	39.8 (1979)
Denmark	49.0	64.4 (1979)
Finland	58.3	64.9 (1979)
West Germany	35.8	40.0
Japan	48.4	48.9
Sweden	50.5	64.2
USA	40.8	50.3
Great Britain	40.7 (1971)	45.0 (1981)

SOURCES *OECD Labour Force Statistics*; Great Britain *Censuses of Population*, 1971 and 1981.

in the economic activity rate of the relatively large married female population has been sufficiently large to outweigh any decrease in the economic activity rate of the relatively smaller single female population.

The way in which the economic activity of females in different age groups has altered is shown in Figures 8.1 to 8.14. In most economies after the war the female economic activity rate was typically high for the younger

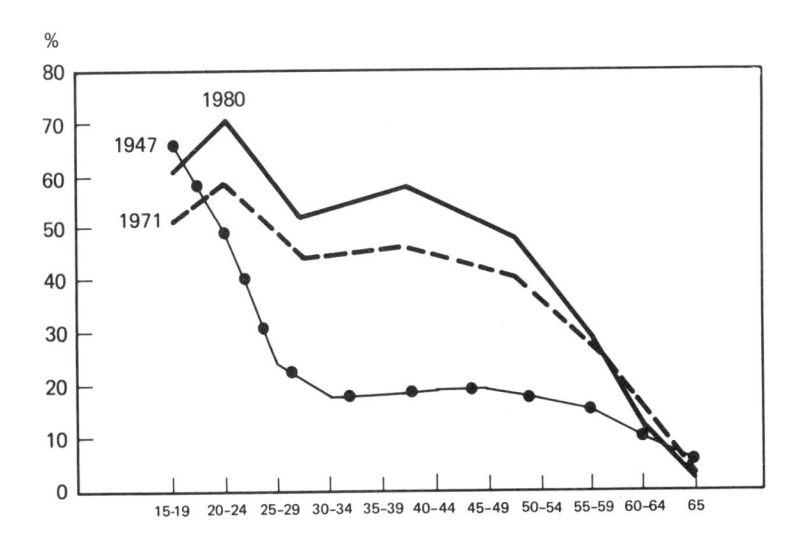

FIGURE 8.1 *Female labour force participation by five-year age groups: Australia*

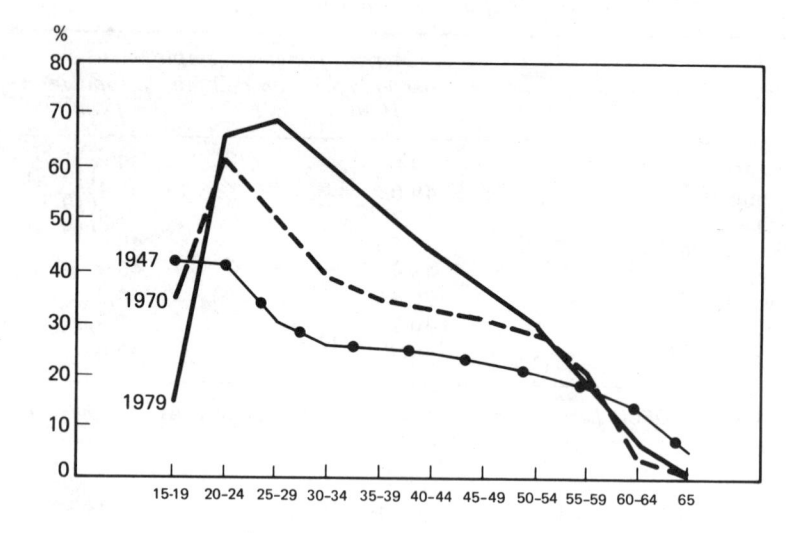

FIGURE 8.2 *Belgium*

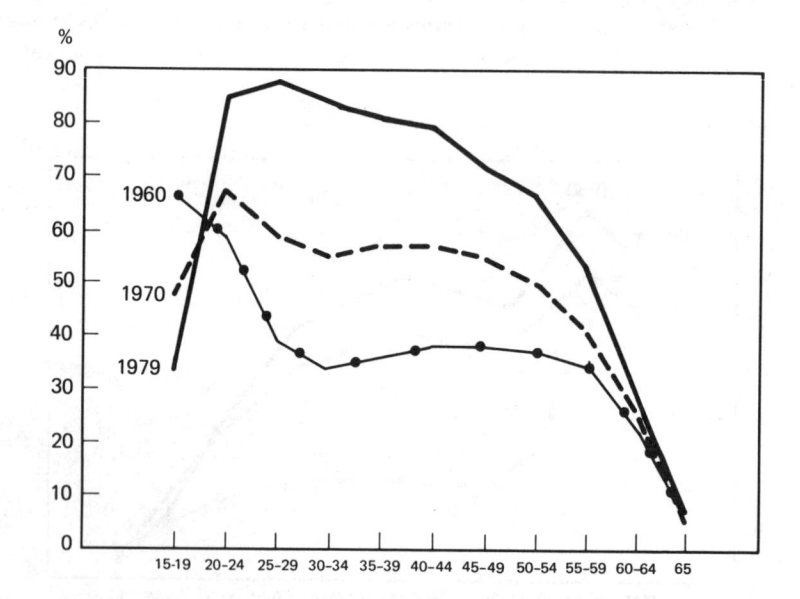

FIGURE 8.3 *Denmark*

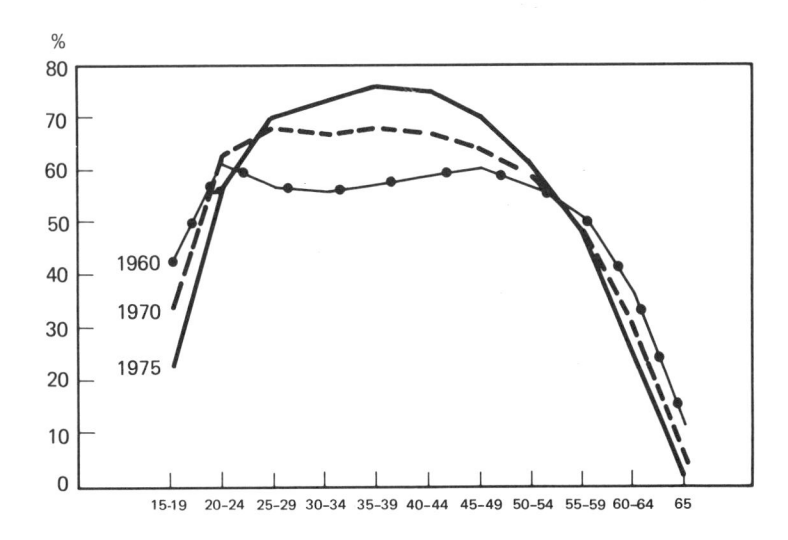

FIGURE 8.4 *Finland*

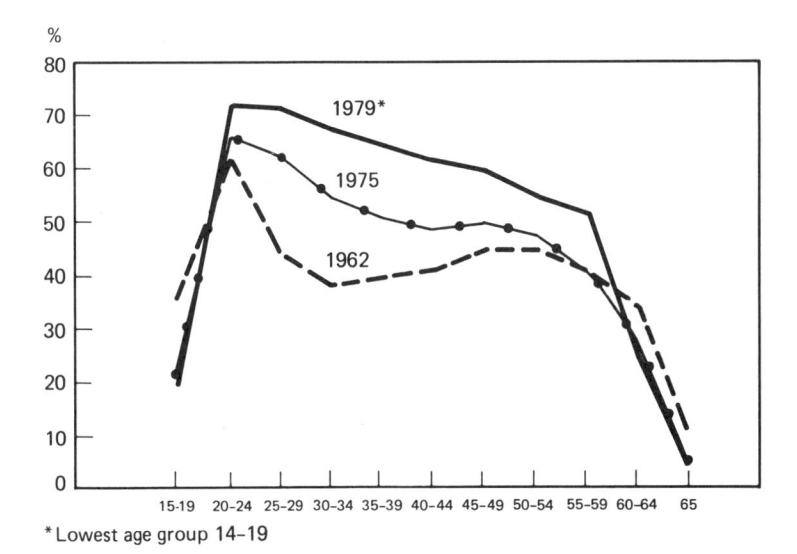

FIGURE 8.5 *France*

*Lowest age group 14–19

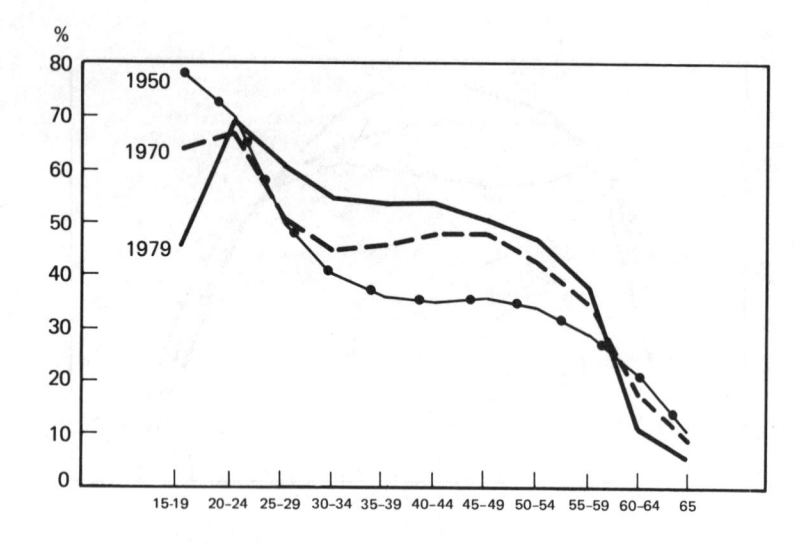

FIGURE 8.6 *West Germany*

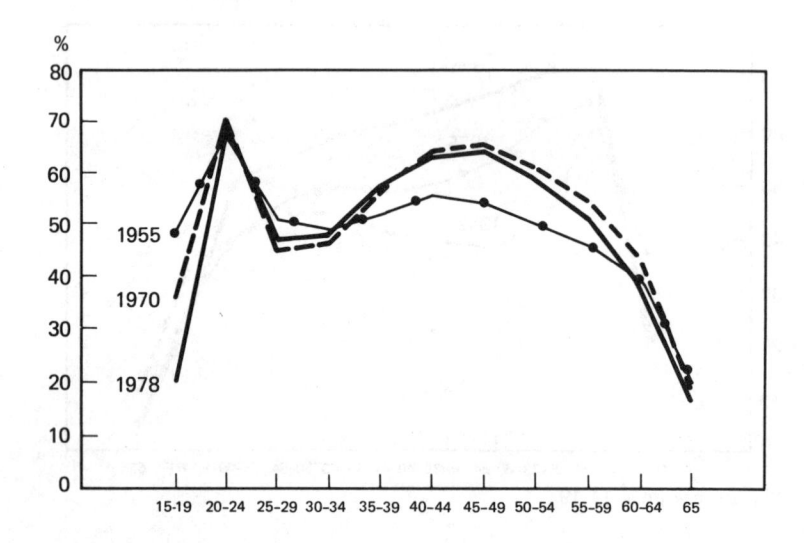

FIGURE 8.7 *Japan*

175

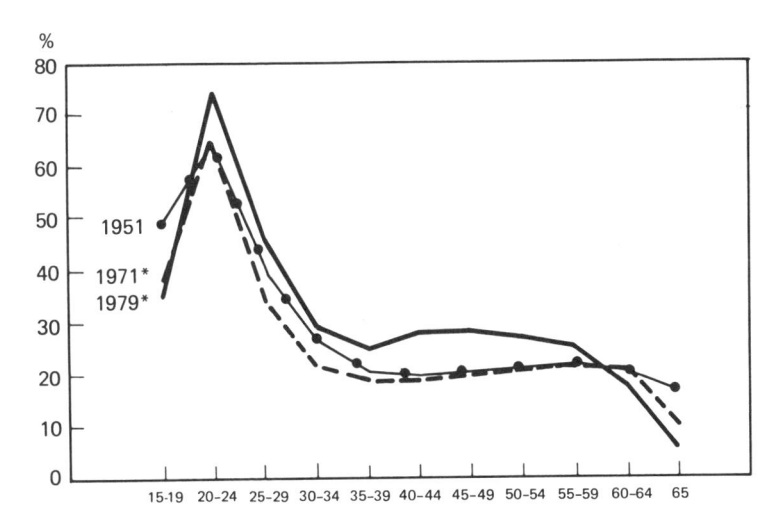

* Lowest age group 14-19

FIGURE 8.8 *Ireland*

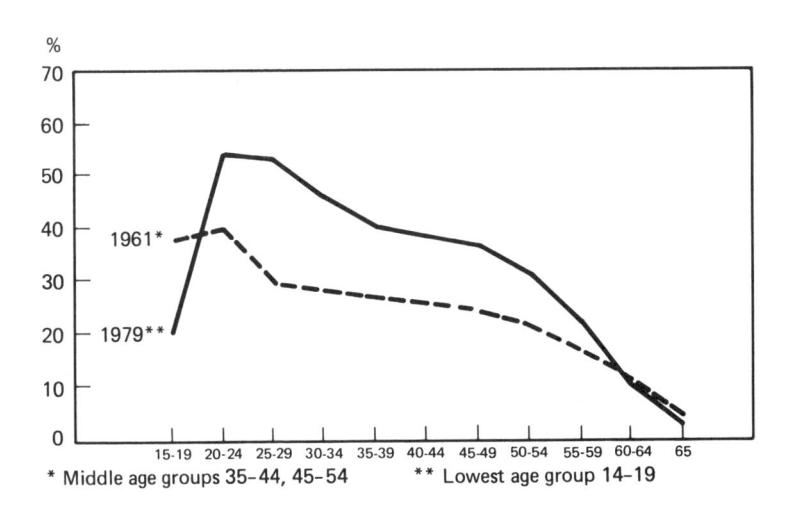

* Middle age groups 35-44, 45-54   ** Lowest age group 14-19

FIGURE 8.9 *Italy*

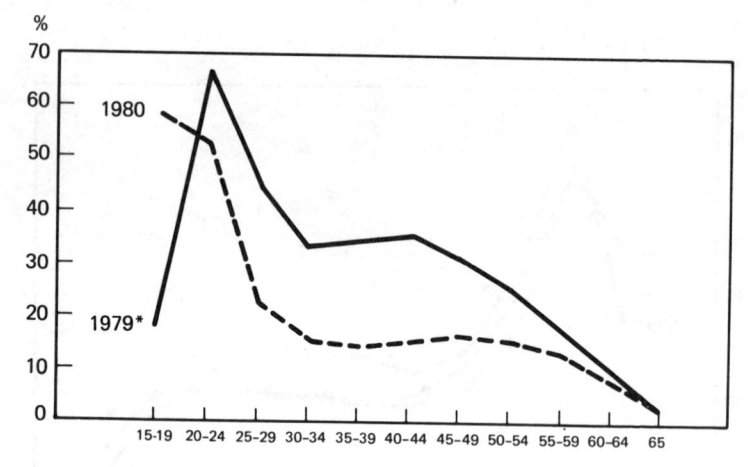

* Lowest age group 14-19

FIGURE 8.10 *Netherlands*

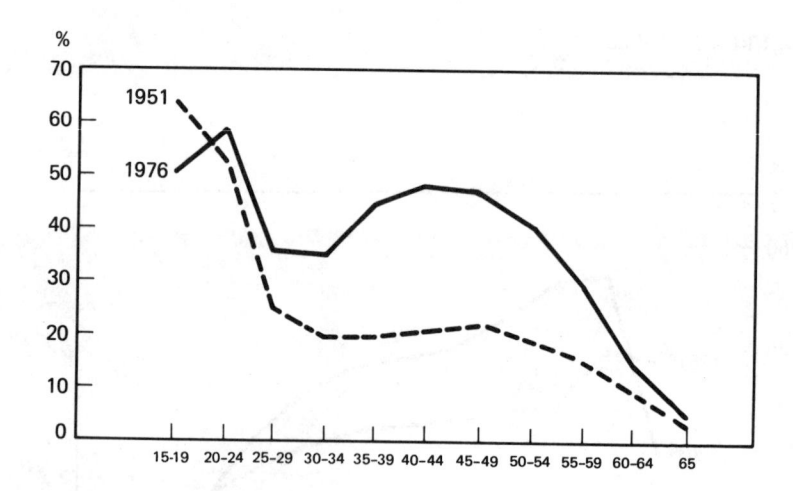

FIGURE 8.11 *New Zealand*

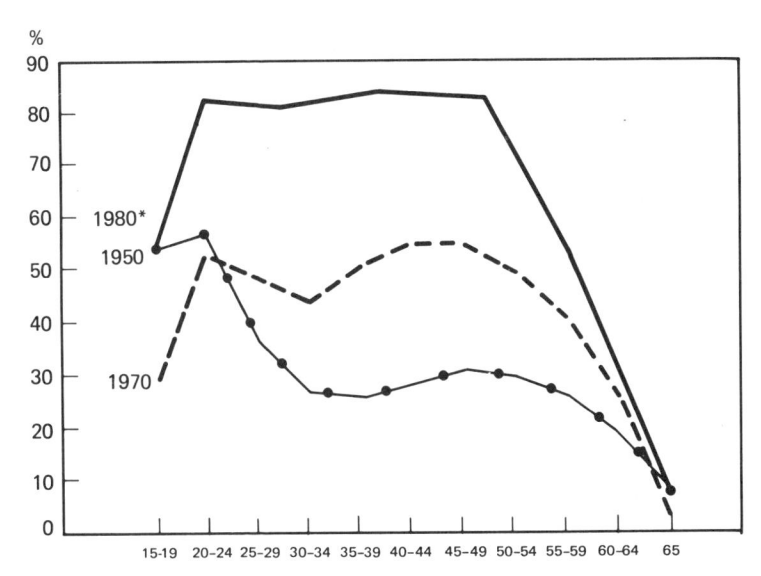

* Age groups   16-19, 20-24, 25-34, 35-44, 45-54, 55-64, 65-74

FIGURE 8.12   *Sweden*

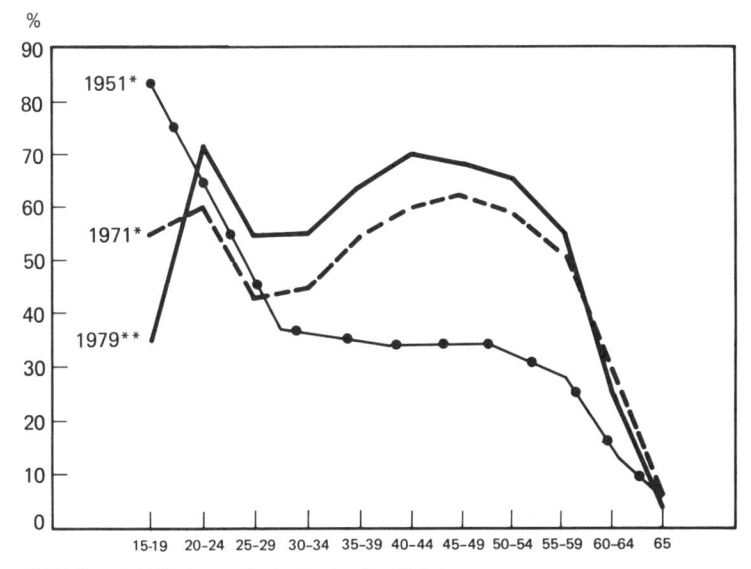

* 1951 and 1971 data refer to England and Wales
** 1979 - lowest age group 14-19

FIGURE 8.13   *United Kingdom*

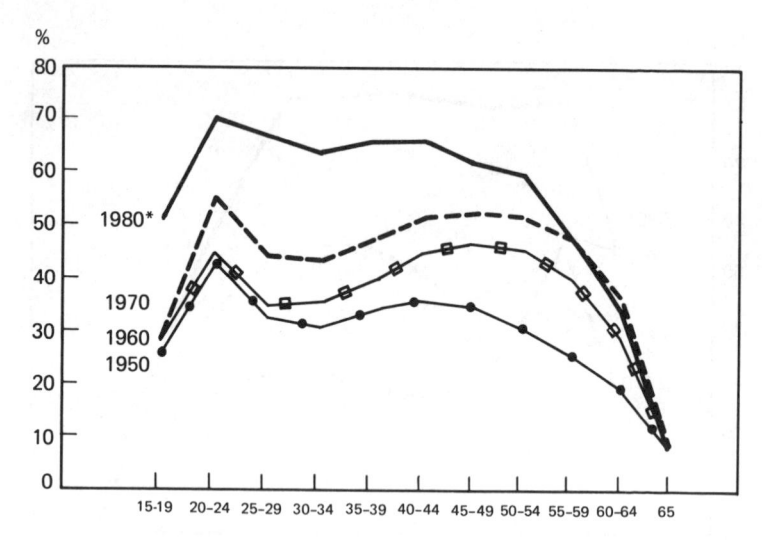

* Lowest age group 16-19

FIGURE 8.14 United States

SOURCE Figures 8.1 to 8.14 are reproduced with OECD permission from Paukert, L., *The Employment and Unemployment of Women in OECD Countries*, OECD, Paris, 1984.

NOTE (Figures 8.1 to 8.14). The participation curves for 1979 and 1980 are based on official estimates or labour force surveys, not on census data, as are the curves for earlier years. They are not, therefore, strictly comparable.

age groups and then steadily declined as age increased. This pattern occurred in Australia, Belgium, Denmark, West Germany, New Zealand, Sweden and Britain. Two important exceptions were the USA and Japan, where the bi-modal pattern, i.e. economic activity being at a peak in the early 20s and in middle age, had already established itself by 1950. The bi-modal pattern then started to establish itself in several other countries as the female economic activity rate rose for the 40-55 age group and the economic activity rate for females under 20 years of age fell. These were mainly English-speaking countries and included Australia, New Zealand, Britain and the Scandinavian countries. Since the 1960s the 'dip' in the middle of the bi-modal pattern has started to flatten out in these economies, and it has almost disappeared in Sweden and the USA. Thus in the first two postwar decades it seems that most of the female labour force growth was due to middle-aged married women entering employment, but since then there has been an increase in the number of economically active women in the age groups most likely to have small children. This flattening out of the age economic activity rate profile to approach the shape of the male age economic activity relationship has not occurred in Japan, though, where the same bi-modal distribution has remained almost unchanged for thirty years.

In continental Europe there are several exceptions to this bi-modal pattern. Nearly everywhere there has been a drop in the economic activity rate of the under 20s. However, instead of a bi-modal pattern there is a tendency in Belgium, Denmark, France, West Germany, Italy and the Netherlands for the female economic activity rate to rise to a peak in the mid-20s age group and then decline continuously to retirement age without a second peak appearing. The female economic activity rate in Denmark, though, remains higher than the figure found in most other countries, for all age groups. In Ireland the age profile of female economic activity rates has hardly altered since 1950, with economic activity peaking around the age of 20 and then falling sharply with age, with no second peak in middle age.

A rising percentage of the married female workers who have entered the labour force in many countries are employed only on a part-time basis. However, as Table 8.6 shows, part-time working by females is not as common in other European countries as it is in Britain, which also has a higher proportion of female part-time workers than the USA (see Chapter 7). The relatively recent legislation regarding equality of opportunity that has come into force in many countries has not yet had a great deal of effect, and females are generally still concentrated in a relatively small number of occupations and industries. Even in the Scandinavian nations, where the greatest efforts have been made by the state to promote equality of opportunity, women are still underrepresented in most of the traditionally 'male' jobs, although the degree of inequality is generally less than in other

TABLE 8.6 *Part-time working in the EEC, 1979*

	% of females in employment working part-time	Female % of all part-time workers
Belgium	16.5	89.0
Denmark	46.3	86.9
Eire	13.1	70.9
France	17.0	82.0
Italy	10.6	61.4
Luxembourg	17.1	88.0
Netherlands	31.7	82.5
United Kingdom	39.0	92.8
West Germany	29.0	91.6
Total EEC	25.9	86.8

SOURCE   *EEC Labour Force Sample Survey.*

Western economies. What is also common is the lack of females in the higher grade jobs, even when they do succeed in entering male-dominated areas of employment. Table 8.8 reveals that although there is generally a sizeable proportion of women in the professional and technical occupation group, which includes occupations such as teaching and nursing, very few women hold administrative and managerial positions. On the other hand, women tend to dominate clerical employment in most countries.

Because of the concentration of women in the lower grades of the less well paid occupations and industries, the earnings differentials shown in Table 8.7 are not surprising. In most industrialised nations there now exists legislation making explicit sex discrimination in payment for work illegal. Details of the progress made in individual countries are given in a survey by the OECD (1979). Differential payments for the same work have not disappeared just because they have officially been made illegal, but even if complete equality in payment for the same work were achieved, the biased occupational structure would still result in women receiving on average less than males.

TABLE 8.7 *Ratio of female to male earnings (annual), selected years*

Under 60% of male earnings	60-65% of male earnings	65-70% of male earnings	70%+ of male earnings
Japan (1975)	Australia (1971)	Czechoslovakia (1970)	Hungary (1972)
USA (1974)	Austria (1953)	France (1970)	Israel (1970)
	Belgium (1964)	Poland (1972)	
	Canada (1960-1)		
	Finland (1960)		
	UK (1975)		

SOURCE Based on J. R. Maroney, 'Do Women Earn less under Capitalism?' *Economic Journal*, September 1979, vol. 89, no. 355, p. 605.

WOMEN IN THE SOVIET UNION

In the USSR women have played a more significant role in the labour force than have women in Britain and the USA. As soon as the first communist government came to power in 1917 the principle of equality between the sexes with regard to economic, political and social rights was established as being necessary if the country was going to operate as a true communist system. The inferior economic status of women under capitalism was,

TABLE 8.8 Female proportion of occupation groups, 1982 (%)

	Professional technical and related	Administrative and managerial	Clerical and related	Sales workers	Service workers	Agriculture, forestry and fishing	Production, transport and labourers	Total** labour force
Australia	44.6	14.1	70.6	52.9	63.0	22.5	12.2	36.7
Canada	50.8	29.1	78.8	39.7	54.3	21.4	13.1	41.2
W. Germany	39.3	17.1	59.6	56.9	56.3	47.2	15.3	38.0
Japan	45.9	5.5	54.4	38.3	54.8	48.6	28.2	39.0
Norway	53.3	18.0	77.3	56.1	77.1	29.6	13.5	42.0
Portugal*	54.0	11.5	46.1	44.9	64.3	52.8	22.7	41.5
Spain*	36.2	2.7	37.0	42.0	58.5	26.4	13.0	28.4
Sweden	54.0	19.4	80.7	46.6	75.1	24.7	17.5	46.1
USA	45.1	28.0	80.7	45.4	61.9	17.5	18.7	43.5

*Figures for 1981.
**Including unemployed persons and members of the armed forces.
SOURCES International Labour Office, Year Book of Labour Statistics, 1982, 42nd issue, pp. 94–5; 1983, 43rd issue, pp. 98–9, 104–5, 114–21, Copyright 1982 and 1983, International Labour Organisation, Geneva.

Marx had argued, a result of the way that the capitalist system operated (see Chapter 9). Ideas differed about the role that the family should play in a communist system. Some saw the family as a means of prolonging the exploitation of women by men, and wanted it dismantled and replaced by a system of totally socialised child care and state provision of the services previously provided through the domestic labour of women. In practice, though, it was recognised that the family fulfilled certain social and economic needs, and instead of abolishing it measures were introduced to make it easier for women to participate fully in the economy while still living in a family unit, e.g. day-care nurseries were provided. Lenin argued that it was not enough just to grant women equal access to employment opportunities without also making it possible for them to take up these opportunities, by alleviating the disproportionately heavy burden of household responsibilities that they shouldered. These principles were incorporated in the 1936 Constitution of the USSR, Article 122. This established that women should be offered the same rights as men with respect to work, payment, social insurance and education and also offered assistance to allow them to take up these opportunities, in the form of maternity leave from work, child-care facilities, etc. Subsequent legislation and provision of facilities have reinforced these rights. Biryukova (1980) provides a summary of current protective and equal opportunity legislation for women in the Soviet Union.

TABLE 8.9 *Economic activity in the USSR*

1970 age groups	Males economically active Number (000's)	%	Females economically active Number (000's)	%	Female % economically active
under 20	4 694	10.0	4 043	9.0	46.3
20-29	13 853	89.7	13 323	86.3	49.0
30-39	18 103	97.6	17 791	92.7	49.6
40-49	12 956	96.0	16 085	90.6	55.4
50-54	3 086	90.0	4 365	77.3	58.6
55-59	3 417	80.0	2 046	26.4	37.4
60+	1 846	20.0	1 358	7.0	42.4
(unknown)	(35)	(26.5)	(27)	(19.3)	(43.6)
1970 all ages	57 990	52.1	59 037	45.3	50.4
1979 all ages	67 919	55.7	67 505	48.1	49.8

SOURCES International Labour Office, *Year Book of Labour Statistics*, 1977, 37th issue, p. 51; 1983, 43rd issue, p. 37. Copyright 1977 and 1983, International Labour Organisation, Geneva.

On the face of it the figures in Table 8.9 suggest that Soviet policy on equality has been successful. By 1979 women made up almost exactly half of the USSR's total labour force. In 1970 the female economic activity rates in each age group were close to the male figures and much higher than the female economic activity rates found in most Western economies, with the exception of the 55-59 age group. This is because in the USSR the official retirement age is 55 for females and 60 for males. There is no dropping back in the female economic activity rate in the prime child-bearing age groups, as in Britain and the USA, although the age groups that statistics are available for are not narrow enough to rule out this possibility completely. It would have been interesting to compare the female economic activity rate for the 20-24 age group with that for the 25-29 age group, for instance.

These aggregate figures, however, do not tell the whole story. Although official policy has played an important role in altering the pattern of female employment since the 1917 revolution, other factors have also contributed, particularly demographic changes. Also, while the total female employment figures suggest that equality in employment has been achieved, a closer examination of employment patterns reveals that the industrial and occupational distribution of males and females differ substantially.

Historical changes

One of the paradoxes of the Soviet situation is that despite the moves to promote equality of opportunity after the revolution, the female economic activity rate declined slightly in the following few decades according to some estimates. Dodge (1966) estimated that the proportion of the total female population (including children) in the labour force fell from 51 per cent in 1926 to 47 per cent in 1959. However, it is difficult to get even reasonably accurate employment figures for the early years of the USSR. Estimates of the peasant workforce are particularly likely to be inaccurate. For this reason some researchers only use official statistics for the numbers known to be in state employment for these early years, which give a much lower figure for female labour force participation. From 1959 to 1970 McAuley (1981) estimated that for all age groups between 20 and 55 the female economic activity rate rose. The economic activity rate fell for females aged 15 to 20, due to the growth in the number prolonging their education, and for those above 55, as more women became eligible for a pension. The proportion of all females in the labour force was estimated to have fallen from 47 per cent in 1959 to 45 per cent in 1970. However, as Table 8.9 shows, it rose again to 48.1 per cent by 1979.

These overall changes in the female labour force hide two distinct trends. The Soviet Union at the time of the revolution was primarily an agricultural economy and most women worked on the land. Dodge (1966) estimated that over 90 per cent of the female labour force in 1926 was employed in agriculture, using figures from Eason (1963). At that time 87 per cent of women in peasant households worked, compared with only 40 per cent of urban women, according to Buckley (1981). As the Soviet Union industrialised, employment in agriculture fell both in terms of absolute numbers and relative to employment in other sectors. The absolute drop in the number of females employed in agriculture was small compared with the drop in the number of males, but the total female workforce grew substantially, so that by the 1970 census only 20 per cent of employed women worked in agriculture.

Counterbalancing this fall in the female agricultural workforce there was a rise in female economic activity in urban areas. Dodge (1966) estimated that the economic activity rate for urban women in the 16-59 age group rose from 40.1 per cent to 67.0 per cent between 1926 and 1959. This was partly the result of the growth of manufacturing industry, and then the service sector, coupled with equality of employment opportunity policy. This move from rural to urban employment was not uniform throughout the Soviet Union. European Russia industrialised quite early, but in parts of Central Asia development has been slower, as Lubin (1981) explains.

However, perhaps the most important factor influencing female employment was the imbalance in the population due to the losses of large numbers of males at different times in the country's history. At the start of the century the number of males in the population was almost exactly equal to the number of females. Both grew, but the First World War, and internal strife subsequent to the revolution, claimed a large number of lives, mainly male, so that by 1939 the male population was only 92 per cent of the female population. This imbalance was greatly increased by the tremendous loss of lives that the Soviet Union suffered in the Second World War, again mostly male. By 1946 there were only 74 males for every 100 females, an imbalance of 20 million. Time and the growth of a new generation have now partially eroded this imbalance, but only partially, and by 1979 there were still only 87 males per 100 females.

Thus although according to some estimates there was a slight fall in the female economic activity rate in the first few decades after the revolution, the female labour force grew both in terms of absolute numbers and relatively to the male labour force. The figure for the actual ratio of female to male employment depends on the way in which the employment figures are estimated. If one uses estimates of total employment, like Dodge (1966), then the figure for the proportion of females in the labour force in the 1920s is around 46 per cent, but if one uses official statistics for the numbers engaged in state employment, like Buckley (1981), then the figure is about 25 per cent. Post-war employment estimates are more consistent. McAuley (1981) and Buckley (1981) agree that the female proportion of the labour force rose above 50 per cent in the war and the years immediately following, fell back to just under 50 per cent in the 1950s, and then rose again above 50 per cent in the 1960s. By the time of the 1979 census the number of females in the workforce was almost exactly equal to the number of males, at 67.5 million.

Structure of the female labour force in the USSR

Although recent figures show approximately equal numbers of males and females in the total labour force, there is not such an even split throughout all the different sectors of the labour force. There are no comprehensive Soviet statistics on earnings, but from fragmentary evidence McAuley (1981) was able to conclude that on average women earn less than men. As in the West, this earnings differential is not due to direct discrimination in wage levels but is a result of the different distributions of males and females over industries and occupations (horizontal segregation), the male dominance of the more senior grades of employment within industries and occupations (vertical segregation), and the lower number of hours that women work.

The Soviet education system has for some time put a great emphasis on the training of women for occupations that in the West are usually male-dominated, e.g. engineering. According to Lapidus (1976) females make up 44 per cent of the total number of engineers and technicians. However, although the Soviet record on equality of employment opportunity may be better than that in most other countries, there still remain some substantial inequalities in the sex distribution of employment. In 1974 females made up only 24 per cent of the total number of workers in the transportation industry and only 29 per cent of the construction industry workforce. These figures contrast with the sectors of banking and state insurance, and public health, physical culture and social culture, where females made up over 80 per cent of the workforce. Buckley (1981) reports that 99 per cent of typists and 96 per cent of telephone operators are women. She also explains that most women industrial workers are employed in light industry, as opposed to the better paid heavy industries, with the garment and textile industries being the main source of light industry employment for women. There is also a biased distribution within individual industries. For example, in 1974 in the mechanical engineering industry 44 per cent of industrial workers and 42 per cent of engineering and technical workers were women compared with 88 per cent of office and professional workers. A general observation seems to suggest that women have made some inroads into what are often thought of as 'male' occupations, but not many men have entered the 'female' occupations, such as nursing, secretarial work or primary school teaching.

Although examples such as those above give some insight into the sex distribution of the Soviet workforce, they do not provide a complete picture or allow comparisons over time to see how patterns of inequality have changed. To try to overcome these problems McAuley (1981) constructed some indexes to measure the degree of horizontal occupational segregation throughout all industries. He found that the proportion of all non-agricultural manual female employees who were employed in occupations where the workforce was more than 75 per cent female grew from under 20 per cent in 1939 to over 50 per cent in 1970, while the proportion of non-agricultural manual male employees in occupations that were more than 75 per cent male grew from just over 40 per cent to over 60 per cent. Thus for manual workers segregation increased. McAuley considered that this increased segregation was not just the result of the growth of the service sector, female-employing industries. The growth in female employment was spread over all industries and the increase in segregation was unambiguous.

The situation with respect to non-manual female employees was found to be rather different. The proportion of all non-manual women employed in occupations that were more than 75 per cent female grew from just under 30 per cent to just over 50 per cent. However, the proportion of non-manual male employees in occupations that were more than 75 per cent male fell from three-quarters to one-fifth. In contrast to manual occupations, where the proportion of both males and females working in those occupations that had a more equal sex distribution fell, there was an increase in the non-manual occupations. By 1970 about half of male white-collar employment was in job categories that were 25–50 per cent female. Thus overall most of the growth in female employment has taken place in occupations that are predominantly female-employing, but there has been some evening out of the sex distribution in those occupations that were male-dominated.

There is also a substantial degree of vertical segregation within the Soviet labour force, with women usually being concentrated in the lower echelons of the seniority hierarchy. Female manual workers are concentrated in unskilled and semi-skilled occupations that require less training and involve much repetitive work, such as assembling and packaging. Consistent statistics on occupational status are not available for the whole of the USSR, but McAuley (1981) provides some figures for the RSFSR (Russian Soviet Socialist Republic), which is the largest of the Soviet republics, containing half of the country's total population and three-fifths of its industry. Industrial workers in the RSFSR for 1970-2 are classified into six skill grades. In engineering, 1.1 per cent of females were employed in the highest two skill grades, but 67.7 per cent worked in the lowest two grades, compared with figures of 25.8 per cent and 23.8 per cent respectively for males. In textiles more women worked in the intermediate skill grades, but only 5 per cent in the top two grades. In baking as many as 37.5 per cent of women were employed in the highest two skill grades, but even here 53.0 per cent of men also worked in these grades and relatively few males worked in the lower grades.

Throughout the USSR in agriculture women mainly do manual jobs, and work involving the use of mechanical equipment and administration is usually done by men. According to Buckley (1981), two-thirds of women employed on state farms are field workers. Lapidus (1976) reported that females made up over 90 per cent of milking personnel, swineherd and poultry workers, 80 per cent of vegetable growers and less than 10 per cent of workers in the mechanised sector of agriculture. This situation is rapidly changing, though, and according to Buckley (1981) rural women workers are now predominantly middle-aged and elderly, and among state farm employees aged under 29 males outnumber females by about 28 per cent.

In the non-manual occupations women have made some advances into the professions, but men usually fill the top positions, especially where decision-making and administration are involved. For example, Lapidus (1976) reports that over 70 per cent of physicians are female but over 50 per cent of chief physicians are male. According to McAuley (1981) over 70 per cent of schoolteachers are female but only 32 per cent of school principals. In industry and business there is even greater vertical segregation, with many women being relegated to routine clerical work or the non-administrative grades of professions and occupations. In 1973 women made up only 9 per cent of enterprise directors and 10 per cent of chief engineers but 49 per cent of engineers (excluding chief engineers). In 1976 in state agriculture women made up only 1.6 per cent of directors and 11.7 per cent of chief specialists but 37.6 per cent of veterinarians and 45.6 per cent of zoo technicians.

In this picture of vertical segregation in the Soviet Union there are some echoes of the situation in Britain and the USA, which perhaps give some indication of what the future state of employment equality will be in the West. The main advances of females into male-dominated occupations, in both the USSR and the West, appear to be in those professions where a large proportion of the required training is provided through the education system before employment commences, e.g. medicine, science and, more so in the USSR, engineering. However, although the government can try to ensure equality of opportunity within the education system, once women leave and enter the world of work the biases and prejudices, both at work and within the home, that cause discrimination in employment patterns begin to operate. In Western Europe, in a report to the EEC, Riffault (1980) has pointed out that, after the provision of equal opportunity in education and entry into employment, the next area that needs to be tackled is the inequality of internal training and promotion by employers. This also appears to be a necessity in the USSR if women are to be employed in areas of control and administration instead of just working in the professions in which they have been formally trained.

The inequalities in the Soviet labour force are not just due to biases in employment. Within the home women still take on the greatest share of domestic responsibilities and consequently have less time and energy to devote to paid employment, or the study and extra work that is often required for advancement in their occupation. In a study of the time spent each day on different tasks Szalai (1972) found that in a sample of families in one Soviet city women spent on average over five times as much time doing housework, and only half as much time in study and participation, as males. Similar ratios were found when a comparable sample was examined for a US city. Moskoff (1982) has produced evidence which suggests that a large number of women would prefer to work part-time because, although about 30 per cent of males now co-operate in doing housework, and 50 per cent in looking after children, women still do some 15-20 per cent more than men in the home. Although these reasons for wanting to work part-time are similar to those given by women in the West, there is a certain amount of reticence on the part of employers to allow part-time working because of the labour shortage that exists in the USSR, and the fear that women might be enticed out of full-time work. Moskoff (1982) found that 90 per cent of those who wanted to work part-time were women, and up to 22 per cent of women not working or at school, and 10 per cent of employed women, would like to work part-time. Out of a sample of women working part-time who were asked what they would do if they could no longer work part-time, 17 per cent said they would work full-time, 46 per cent would leave the labour force, 29 per cent would take home work, and 8 per cent would try to arrange a more convenient work schedule. Thus there is some limited potential for increasing the workforce by allowing part-time working for those who would otherwise not work at all, although managers in the USSR are often reluctant to take on part-time workers because they can make productivity figures appear lower.

As in Britain and the USA, in the USSR the decision of females, especially married women, to enter the workforce is influenced by other considerations in addition to opportunities available and domestic responsibilities. Three articles, published together, have attempted to explain the labour force participation decision of Soviet families in terms of the neoclassical theory of the allocation of time explained in Chapter 4. Berliner (1983) and Kuniansky (1983) used aggregate census data, while Ofer and Vinokur (1983) obtained data from a sample of emigrants from the USSR to Israel, which admittedly was not a representative sample. In general these studies found that this type of model incorporating a standard set of influencing factors gave a reasonable explanation of labour force participation, although the nature of the relationship was rather different to that found in Britain and the USA. In particular, the labour supply curve was found to be 'backward bending', i.e. above a certain wage, labour supply decreases.

In concluding this survey of women in the Soviet economy some comparisons with the West need to be made. Although the occupational and industrial distributions of men and women are not entirely the same this should not detract from the fact that sex equality in employment is much closer in the USSR than in most capitalist economies. Some areas may still be heavily segregated, but across the board the degree of segregation is less than in the West and, as stated at the start of this section, the aggregate degree of female labour force participation is much higher.

9 A Marxian Perspective

An alternative approach to the analysis of the role of women in the economy, which is often ignored by many of the mainstream economists whose work is referred to in other chapters, is the Marxian paradigm. Marx and Engels considered the question of the role of women in the economy, and over the years, particularly in the last few decades, other writers have added to or suggested alterations to those strands of Marxian analysis concerned with this question. This compares with those economists who belonged to the neoclassical school of economic thought where, as Pujol (1984) explains, the position of women in the economy was not properly considered; only in the post-war period has neoclassical economic analysis been applied in depth to this topic. One cannot really understand a Marxian analysis of the role of women in the economy without first knowing something about the main ideas of Marxian theory. However, it is not possible to explain properly, in a page or so, a set of ideas that encompasses such a wide range of economic, political and social concepts, and the reader unfamiliar with this subject may wish to refer to an introductory text on Marxian economics, e.g. Hunt and Sherman (1981), to gain a better understanding of the ideas involved.

There are several broad themes in the Marxian literature on the role of women in the economy. An area of recent interest has been the question of whether or not the post-war growth of female employment can be interpreted as an example of the use of women as part of the reserve army of unemployed. A more fundamental question that has been asked is whether the relatively inferior economic position of women can be explained with Marxian theory. Why are many women secondary workers who are only drawn into the labour force at certain times and who take on most of a family's domestic responsibilities?

Some radical feminists point to the unequal position of women that persists in state planned economies and argue that while Marxian analysis can explain the exploitation of workers in general by capitalists, the

A Marxian Perspective

relatively inferior economic position of women is due to another set of factors, i.e. there is a theory of patriarchy, elements of which can operate in a non-capitalist system, which explains how males in general exploit females regardless of the economic system they live in. This is sometimes referred to as the 'dual systems' approach, there being two separate sets of reasons that explain the economic position of women. Others, however, believe that the Marxian paradigm does explain why it is the capitalist system itself that causes the inferior economic position of women.

References to the position of women in society do not form a central theme in the various works of Marx and Engels. The most widely referred to original work in this context is Engels's (1968) *The Origins of the Family, Private Property and the State*. Essentially Engels argued that the institution of the family, and hence the role of women, is based on the historical development of social and economic factors dating back to pre-capitalist times, i.e. women's relatively inferior economic position is not a direct result of capitalism. Taking the form of the institution of the family as given, Engles then develops an explanation concerning the way in which the family is connected to the process of production under capitalism. Engels predicted that women would become emancipated through participation in the labour force and he put forward some arguments against the retention of the traditional family institution because of the way it exploited women. Both Marx and Engels, however, believed that true equality for women would not be achieved just through their being brought into the labour force under a capitalist system. This would leave them exploited by both employers at work and men in the home. They saw women being fully emancipated only under socialism when the disappearance of exploitation by capitalist employers would in turn mean that exploitation within the traditional family institution would disappear. What many modern writers have criticised is the fact that Engels did not properly explain how the role of women both in providing domestic labour and raising children, fitted into a Marxian framework. Basically Engels suggested that it was first a question of getting rid of capitalist exploitation; then under socialism, as they fully participated in the economic system, women would find emancipation. Beechey (1977) and other radical feminist writers have argued that letting women enter employment will not by itself bring about equality, and that it is necessary also to provide the means to allow women to work on equal terms with men by the provision of facilities such as socialised child care.

The most common reference by Marx to the role of women in the economy is a section in *Capital* concerned with attempts by capitalists to maintain their profit. Marx (1970, Vol. 1, p. 395) suggested that if an employer was currently paying a male worker enough for the subsistence of his whole family, it would be worth his while also to bring the worker's wife and children into the labour force. The subsistence wage could then be shared among them. For the same total wage payment an employer would get the labour of all the members of the family able to work instead of just one member, which would temporarily allow profits to be maintained or increased. The introduction of technological advances in the mechanisation of production reduced the amount of physical strength needed in many jobs, which made it easier to bring women and children into the factories. This form of exploitative employment was not the emancipation of women that Marx suggested would come about through the entry of women into the labour force. He stressed that political change was needed and also that the participation of women in the political process was required if socialism was to come about and provide the means for achieving true equality.

However, some contemporary feminists in Western economies do not agree that this need necessarily be the order of events. They would like to see a movement towards equality within the capitalist system, given that the system itself cannot be easily changed, that would involve more than just the exploitative employment of women in furtherance of profits. Matthaei (1982) in fact suggests that the breakdown of sexual division of labour can itself help change the way that an economic and social system operates. As women enter male employment domains and men take a more active part in domestic work, Matthaei suggests that this will diminish the effect that the male's aggressively competitive nature has on the way in which the economy works. Others, however, consider that the achievement of socialism is a first priority and that, while they are not unwelcome, moves to bring about equality within a capitalist system can only achieve a limited degree of success because of the way in which the system itself operates.

It was not just the way that capitalism affected the lives of workers' families that Marx discussed. Marx saw the role of the family for the capitalist class as a means of maintaining a concentration of wealth in the hands of a small group of individuals and passing it from one generation to the next. The elimination of private property under socialism would eliminate this reason for the continuation of the institution of the family.

Although some radical writers on the topic of women and the economy have concentrated on a limited number of passages from Marx and Engels, centring on the two themes above, others have undertaken a more comprehensive survey of the literature. Vogel (1983), after a thorough search through the available works of Marx and Engels, including some unpublished manuscripts, concludes that Marx, but not Engels, does provide an explanation of why it is capitalism itself that causes the inferior economic position of women. Interpretations and modifications of Marxian theory by modern radical feminist writers are expanded more fully in the two sections below. There are two central issues that these works concentrate on, namely the role of domestic labour and the question of how women fit into the theory of the reserve army of labour.

THE ROLE OF DOMESTIC LABOUR

A central question is whether the domestic labour that women provide in the home in some way assists the capitalist production process. Benston (1969) suggested that women's labour in the home creates use value, i.e. it provides goods or services that satisfy needs, but the allocation of labour to domestic work and the allocation of goods and services that it produces are not decided via a capitalist production mode. Dalla Costa (1973) argued that housework creates use values and provides some of the means of subsistence that a family needs to live on. Thus if women work in the home a capitalist has to pay workers less than he would have to if all the commodities needed for subsistence had to be bought out of wages. Hence some of the labour of housewives is expropriated by the capitalist because he can reduce the wage paid to workers according to the amount of work done in the home by women to provide the means of subsistence. Harrison (1973) considered that although household labour produces a surplus, it does not create value because it is a different production mode to that which produces commodities sold on the market.

In one sense the argument about the role of domestic labour has now been settled. Most radical feminist writers accept the conclusion of Himmelweit and Mohun (1977) that non-wage labour does not create labour value that is expropriated by capitalists in the same way that wage labour is. However, although there may be a general agreement on what domestic labour is not, the question of what it actually *is* still remains unanswered.

Other writers have concentrated on the role of reproduction in explaining the economic position of women. Folbre (1982) sees the family as a capitalist production mode in itself, with unequal production and exchange within it. Over time the expansion of capitalism has led to the industrial concentration of production in large firms and the need for an educated workforce. In the past women invested a large proportion of their time in rearing children, parents expecting some return from them in their old age. However, nowadays, Folbre suggests, each child requires a greater investment in education but, for various reasons, fewer children now look after their parents in old age. Thus from a family's viewpoint it appears preferable for a wife to invest more of her time in working for a wage than investing her time in rearing a large family. This, Folbre suggests, can help explain the drop in fertility rates in the developed world.

Vogel (1983) considers that Marx's theory of social reproduction can, with some further developments, provide an explanation of the economic position of women. In order to cope with periods of expansion capitalism needs a supply of new workers or a pool of unemployed to draw on. The sex of the workers is immaterial when mechanisation eliminates the heaviest physical tasks, and the new workers could come from a shrinking agricultural sector, immigration, or through natural population growth. If women are to bear children then somehow they must receive means of subsistence while they are unable to engage in paid work, and this is usually managed through the family. For the capitalist this causes a contradiction. He must pay to a woman's family, usually via her husband's wage, enough to ensure her enough to live on when she stops work to have her children, and thus he loses the surplus that he can extract from her labour in paid employment. On the other hand, he needs new workers, and if no other source is available he has to allow a new generation to be raised. Vogel suggests that capitalists will balance these two considerations in their decision on the amount of wages paid to workers and will try to minimise the wage paid over the long term, taking into account the constraint of the need for new workers. Because men were paid enough to support their wives when they could not work because they were bearing children this differential persisted at other times, as it is difficult to pay different wages to workers doing the same job according to whether or not their wives can work. It was easy, though, to pay a lower wage to all female workers as none were expected to support their husbands since men did not have to stop work to have children.

It must also be remembered that in the last century, when Marx was writing, the time in a married woman's life when she was not bearing or looking after children was much shorter than it is today. Families were often very large and there were no schools or nurseries for most working-class women to send their children to. Both male workers and employers had something to gain from this male-female wage differential and it became established as a permanent feature of the labour market, giving males a degree of economic superiority over females. The actual size of the wage differential can vary over time depending on whether employers see a greater need for women workers or for a generation of new workers. For example, in the early nineteenth century, and in the last few decades, there was a need for women to enter the workforce and so wage inequalities were allowed to diminish, although some differential had to be maintained to win the co-operation of male workers with the system. Vogel sees the way to women's emancipation as being through the granting of unequal treatment at times. Instead of a woman having to rely on her husband's wage when bearing children, which perpetuates the wage inequalities of the labour market, a woman should receive support from elsewhere, e.g. the state. Other writers have also emphasised the need for this sort of action, although not always in the context of the analysis of the role of reproduction as an explanation of the position of women under capitalism. This idea is, of course, embodied in the famous quote from Marx (1969, p. 160): 'From each according to her/his ability, to each according to her/his needs' (in the original German the possessive pronoun does not distinguish the sex of the possessor).

WOMEN AND THE RESERVE ARMY OF LABOUR

In analyses of the post-war rise in the female labour force a number of researchers have asked whether or not this can be interpreted as the use of women as part of the part of the reserve army of labour. Beechey (1977) sets out the advantages to the capitalist of employing married women. The employer gets more labour from a family for the same aggregate subsistence wage; married female workers can be more easily dismissed; they help keep wages down; and they have a lower labour value because they are usually relatively unskilled and untrained. This creates a problem for single women who must either depend on their parents' family or live in poverty if female wages in general reflect the assumption of support from a husband's wage. There is also a contradiction for the capitalist in that if women do less work in the home in order to work in paid employment then wages must be increased to compensate for the loss of those commodities that were previously produced by the domestic labour of women.

Anthias (1980) argues that Beechey has not fully explained why women are secondary workers in the first place. Although Marx said that the value of labour can vary according to the level of skill and effort involved, there is no reason why women's labour by definition should have less value than male labour. Just because women are paid less than men, which is a reflection of labour market conditions, including discrimination, this does not mean that their labour has less value in the Marxian sense. This point has been brought home by a recent ruling by an industrial tribunal, reflecting changes in British equal pay legislation that became operative at the start of 1984. The new amendments give an employee the right to claim equal pay at an industrial tribunal for work which he or she considers to be of equal value to that done by a member of the opposite sex, employed by the same or an associated employer. In the first test case (see *The Times*, 31 October 1984) a female cook in a shipyard had her wage increased to a level comparable with that received by painters and other male workers who were judged to have been doing work of equal value.

The debate as to why women are usually secondary workers has already been examined and so now the different arguments as to why they have been brought into the labour force can be considered. Marx divided the reserve army of labour into different categories. The floating reserve consists of those unemployed workers who have some experience of work but who are now unemployed, perhaps temporarily, because of a drop in demand, technical change, or the availability of cheaper workers. The latent reserve refers to potential workers who have not yet entered the capitalists' workforce. Originally this latent reserve was the agricultural workforce, but it can also be interpreted to include women who are not currently in the labour force. The stagnant reserve is a residual of the poorest groups in society with the worst employment prospects, where again women are disproportionately highly represented. Even if they do find work these workers are usually employed in low-paid insecure jobs without any prospects. However, Marx himself did not allocate women to any one specific section of the reserve army and it is, perhaps, a fruitless task to try to determine which of these parts of the reserve army of labour women belong to if, in fact, they can be represented in each one.

Empirical research centres on the question of whether more females have been employed in the last few decades because they are fulfilling a temporary need for extra labour in cyclical peaks of economic activity, and can be easily replaced, or because they are cheaper than male workers and they are being substituted for males on a long-term basis. Milkman (1976) has argued that sex divisions in the occupational structure of the labour force prevent substitution and that this occupational segregation in fact prevented female workers in the USA from feeling the full force of the 1930s depression. According to Lewenhak (1977), the male fear of having their wages undercut by female workers led to early legislation in Britain which kept women out of many industries and forced them to take up employment in domestic service and other occupations where they were not a serious threat to male workers. Hartmann (1979) has also suggested that in the USA men have been on the offensive against female intrusion into male employment preserves because they have wanted to maintain some form of employment segregation, in their own interests. Walby (1983) argues that men will strive to keep women out of the labour force not only because of the threat to their own wage levels, but also because greater female economic activity would threaten the position of males in the household which in the past involved relatively little contribution to domestic labour, although the balance will change over time.

The cyclical labour demand case is opposed by Gardiner (1976), who believes that women have been employed as substitutes for male workers. She points out that it is against the interests of capitalists to dispose of female employees if they are so cheap. However, one could argue that if it is a question of getting rid of cheaper female workers or getting rid of more expensive male workers, an employer may wish to cut back on his male labour force, but he will still cut back on his female labour force if this is the only option open. Female workers are not just more disposable because they can usually be fired more easily but because an employer can more easily run down a female labour force by not employing new workers to replace those who leave work to have children. Legislation guaranteeing re-employment after maternity leave has only cut down the scale on which this can be practised, but not eliminated it, because not all women return to work when their maternity leave has been exhausted.

So far only the growth of female employment in industrialised economies has been analysed in a Marxian context, but large multinational companies can switch production from one country to another, including Third World nations, in search of the least-cost location for their operations. Nash and Fernandez-Kelly (1983) explain how this can reinforce inequalities between male and female workers, particularly in the electronics and textile industries. For example, young single females in South East Asia are employed on a short-term basis in electronic assembly work. Because they usually leave when they have families the companies employing them do not have to pay for child-care facilities or pay male workers a wage sufficient to support a family, as Green (1983) explains. One could argue that this period of employment does at least provide a means of temporary escape for these women from the pressures of a society where women, in or out of work, are subject to the rules of a traditional patriarchal system. Lim (1983) points out that the main reason for them having this source of employment in the first place is that they live in a society where women are exploited and female wages are low. A movement away from a patriarchal system to one of greater wage equality may drive away these internationally mobile employers and remove one avenue of at least partial escape from patriarchal exploitation. However, Lim argues, employment by an international capitalist can never provide proper emancipation in the long run and both the economic system and the social system need to be changed to achieve this. The problem is how not to advance so fast towards one objective that progress towards the other objective recedes.

Recent evidence suggests that female employment may have expanded both because of the relative cheapness of female workers and because of their disposability. It depends on where they work. Bruegel (1979) pointed out that in Britain in the 1974-5 recession the female labour force in aggregate was more cushioned from the effects of the recession than the male labour force, but individual women were more likely to lose their jobs than males. In an econometric analysis using British data, Rubery and Tarling (1982) found evidence which supported the cyclical employment theory in manufacturing industries but not elsewhere. As most women work in the service sector the substitution effect on the aggregate labour force was not so apparent. Another statistical test using US data, by Humphries (1983), provides evidence to support the substitution theory at an industrial level. She found that in the last few decades females had been entering male-dominated industries faster than the growth of numbers in the 'female' industries, and where this had happened male unemployment had risen. Humphries also makes the point, though, that the rise in female employment cannot all be classed as all substitution or all temporary cyclical employment growth. In Canada Connolly (1978) considers women as part of a reserve army temporarily pulled into the labour force, and cites as evidence the fact that women employees are last in and first out as far as many employers are concerned. Yanz and Smith (1983), however, argue that much of the growth in the Canadian labour force has been of a more permanent structural nature, and in some occupations, e.g. clerical work, women are not mainly temporary workers just called in to meet a temporary peak in demand.

Evidence suggests, then, that women can be employed both as substitutes for more expensive male workers and as temporary workers employed in cyclical upswings in the economy. The growth of part-time employment, particularly in Britain, is an example of the use of workers who are relatively cheap and easy to get rid of. However, the reason for using them will vary from one industry to another, and it is a matter of how much of each rather than one reason or the other applying. The extent to which females are employed because they are cheaper than males and the extent to which they are employed because they are more easily disposable depends on the nature of the industry concerned.

CONCLUSION

Marx and Engels explained the role of women in a market economy by analysing the relationship between the family and the capitalist production process. They suggested that in a socialist society women would be emancipated through economic equality. This would entail the provision of means to relieve them of their disproportionately high burden of domestic responsibilities, as well as offering them the opportunity of employment, so enabling them to work on a more equal basis with men. There are two main areas of current debate on how the Marxian paradigm can be interpreted to explain the position of women in the economy today.

On the question of why women are in a relatively inferior economic position to men, and are saddled with an unfair share of domestic work, some feminists believe that the Marxian model alone cannot explain this situation. They hold the 'dual systems' view that a theory of patriarchy is needed to explain the exploitation of women by men in addition to the general Marxian theory which explains the exploitation of all workers by capitalists. Others, however, suggest that although Engels did not properly explain the reasons for the institution of the family in a capitalist society, Marx's analysis of the role of reproduction can provide an explanation. Because capitalists require new workers women must stop work, temporarily at least, to bear children. They receive means of subsistence while they are not working via the family, with males receiving a wage above that received by female workers in order to be able to support a wife who has stopped work to bear children. This sex differential in wages has become established even in situations where males are not supporting a non-working wife. Thus, it is argued, only when the state provides support for women who stop work to bear children will the reason for this sex differential in wages be removed.

The second major area of debate is whether women have been brought into the labour force in recent decades because they are part of a reserve army brought in during peaks of economic activity, and who can be easily disposed of when employers no longer need their labour, or whether they are being employed as substitutes for male workers because, for various reasons, their wage costs are lower. Evidence exists to support both viewpoints, and as Marx did not allocate specific groups of the population to the different parts of the reserve army of workers, some writers now consider that it is not really possible to analyse all female employment in the same manner. Some female workers may be employed because they are easy to dismiss when the need arises, while others may be taken on because of their relative cheapness.

References and Selected Bibliography

Andrews, H. F. (1978) 'Journey to Work Considerations in the Labour Force Participation of Married women', *Regional Studies*, vol. 12, pp. 11-20.

Anthias, F. (1980) 'Women and the Reserve Army of Labour; A Critique of Veronica Beechey', *Capital and Class*, no. 10, Spring, pp. 50-63.

Arnold, E., Huggett, C., Senker, P., Swords-Isherman, N., Shannon, C. Z. (1982) *Microelectronics and Women's Employment in Britain*, SPRU Occasional Paper Series no. 17, Science Policy Research Unit, University of Sussex.

Ballard, B. (1984) 'Women Part-time Workers: Evidence from the 1980 Women and Work Survey', *Department of Employment Gazette*, vol. 92, no. 9, pp. 409-16.

Beacham, R. (1984) 'Economic Activity: Britain's Workforce 1971-1981', *Population Trends*, no. 37, Autumn, pp. 6-14.

Becker, G. S. (1965) 'A Theory of the Allocation of Time', *Economic Journal*, vol. 75, September, pp. 493-517.

Becker, G. S. (1971) *The Economics of Discrimination*, University of Chicago Press, Chicago.

Becker, G. S. (1975) *Human Capital*, University of Chicago Press, Chicago.

Beechey, V. (1977) 'Some Notes on Female Wage Labour in Capitalist Production', *Capital and Class*, no. 3, pp. 45-66.

Ben-Porath, Y. (1973) 'Labor-Force Participation Rates and the Supply of Labor', *Journal of Political Economy*, vol. 81, pp. 697-704.

Benston, M. (1969) 'The Political Economy of Women's Liberation', *Monthly Review*, vol. 21, no. 4, pp. 13-27.

Berliner, J. S. (1983) 'Education, Labor-Force Participation, and Fertility in the Soviet Union', *Journal of Comparative Economics*, vol. 7, pp. 131-57.

Bird, E. (1980) *Information Technology in the Office: the Impact on Women's Jobs*, Equal Opportunities Commission, Manchester.

Biryukova, A. P. (1980) 'Special Protective Legislation and Equality of Opportunity for Women Workers in the USSR', *International Labour Review*, vol. 119, no. 1, January-February, pp. 51-65.

Bisset, L. and Huws, U. (1984) *Sweated Labour: Homeworking in Britain Today*, Low Pay Unit, London.
Blackaby, F. (1979) *Deindustrialization*, Heinemann, London.
Blandy, A. (1984) 'New Technology and Flexible Patterns of Working Time', *Department of Employment Gazette*, vol. 92, October, pp. 439-43.
Blau, D. M. (1984) 'Family Earnings and Wage Inequality Early in the Life Cycle', *Review of Economics and Statistics*, vol. 66, pp. 200-7.
Bosworth, D. and Dawkins, P. (1982) 'Women and Part-time Work', *Journal of Industrial Relations*, Autumn, pp. 32-9.
Bosworth, D. L. and Wilson, R. A. (1980) 'The Labour Market', in Maunder, P. (ed.) *The British Economy in the 1970s*, Heinemann, London.
Bowen, W. G. and Finnegan, T. A. (1969) *The Economics of Labor Force Participation*, Princeton University Press, New Jersey.
British Community Relations Commission (1975) *Who Minds: A Study of Working Mothers and Child Minding in Ethnic Minority Communities*, Community Relations Commission, London.
Brown, I. (1976) *Economics and Demography*, Allen & Unwin, London.
Bruegel, I. (1979) 'Women as a Reserve Army of Labour: A Note on Recent British Experience', *Feminist Review*, vol. 3, pp. 12-23.
Buckley, M. (1981) 'Women in the Soviet Union', *Feminist Review*, Summer, pp. 79-106.
Butz, W. P. and Ward, M. P. (1979) 'The Emergence of Countercyclical US Fertility', *American Economic Review*, vol. 69, no. 3, June, pp. 318-29.
Cain, G. (1966) *Married Women in the Labour Force*, University of Chicago Press, Chicago.
Cairnes, J. E. (1874) *Political Economy*, Harper, New York.
Carliner, G., Robinson, C. and Tomes, N. (1980) 'Female Labour Supply and Fertility in Canada', *Canadian Journal of Economics*, vol. 8, no. 1, February, pp. 46-64.
Chiplin, B. and Sloane, P. J. (1976) *Sex Discrimination in the Labour Market*, Macmillan, London.
Claydon, S. (1980) 'Counting our Skills: The National Training Survey', *Department of Employment Gazette*, vol. 8, no. 11, pp. 1150-4.
Clutterbuck, D. (1979) 'Why a Job Shared is Not a Job Halved', *International Management*, vol. 34, no. 10, October, pp. 45-7.
Cogan, J. (1980) 'Married Women's Labor Supply: A Comparison of Alternative Estimation Procedures', in Smith, P. (1980) *op. cit.*
Cohen, C. F. (1983) 'The Impact on Women of Proposed Changes in the Private Pension Scheme', *Industrial and Labor Relations Review*, vol. 36, no. 2, January, pp. 258-70.
Connolly, P. (1978) *Last Hired, First Fired - Women and the Canadian Work Force*, Women's Educational Press, Toronto.
Corcoran, M. E. (1979) 'Work Experience, Labor Force Withdrawals and Women's Wages: Empirical Results Using the 1976 Panel of Income Dynamics', in Lloyd, C. B., Andrews, E. S, and Gilroy, C. L. (eds) *Women in the Labor Market*, Columbia University Press, New York.

Corry, B. A. and Roberts, J. A. (1970) 'Activity Rates and Unemployment. The Experience of the UK 1951-1966', *Applied Economics*, vol. 2, pp. 179-201.

Corry, B. A. and Roberts, J. A. (1974) 'Activity Rates and Unemployment. The UK Experience: Some Further Results', *Applied Economics*, vol. 6, pp. 1-21.

Cragg, A. and Dawson, T. (1984) *Unemployed Women: A Study of Attitudes and Experiences*, Research Paper no. 47, Department of Employment, London.

Cramer, J. C. (1980) 'Fertility and Female Employment: Problems of Causal Direction', *American Sociological Review*, vol. 45, pp. 397-432.

CSE (1980) *Microelectronics, Capitalist Technology and the Working Class*, CSE (Conference of Socialist Economists) Books, London.

Dalla Costa, M. (1973) 'Women and the Subversion of the Community', in *The Power of Women and the Subversion of the Community*, Falling Wall Press, Bristol.

Department of Employment (1973a) *Equal Pay - a Guide to the Equal Pay Act 1970* (revised), HMSO, London.

Department of Employment (1973b) 'Part-time Women Workers 1950-1972', *Department of Employment Gazette*, vol. 81, November, pp. 1088-92.

Department of Employment (1976) 'The Unregistered Unemployed in Great Britain', *Department of Employment Gazette*, vol. 84, December, pp. 1331-6.

Department of Employment (1982) 'Changes in the Basis of the Unemployment Statistics', *Department of Employment Gazette*, vol. 90, p. 20.

Deutermann, W. V. and Brown, S. C. (1978) 'Voluntary Part-time Workers: a Growing Part of the Labor Force', *Monthly Labor Review*, vol. 101, no. 6, June, pp. 3-10.

Disney, R. and Szyszczak, E. M. (1984) 'Protective Legislation and Part-time Employment in Britain', *British Journal of Industrial Relations*, vol. 22, part 1, May, pp. 78-100.

Dodge, N. T. (1966) *Women in the Soviet Economy*, John Hopkins Press, Baltimore.

Doeringer, P. B. and Poire, M. J. (1971) *Internal Labor Markets and Manpower Analysis*, Lexington Books, Lexington.

Dunlop, J. T. and Galenson, W. (1978) *Labor in the Twentieth Century*, Academic Press, New York.

EEC Commission (1982) *Proposal for a Council Directive on Voluntary Part-time Work*, 4053/82, COM(81)775 Final, European Economic Community, Brussels.

Eason, W. W. (1963) 'Labor Force', in Bergson, A. and Kuznets, S. (eds) *Economic Trends in the Soviet Union*, Cambridge, Mass.

Elias, P. and Main, B. (1982) *Women's Working Lives: Evidence from the National Training Survey*, University of Warwick, Institute for Employment Research, Coventry.

Elliott, R. F. (1977) 'Growth of White Collar Employment in Britain', *British Journal of Industrial Relations*, vol. 15, no. 1, pp. 39-44.

Engels, F. (1968) *The Origin of the Family, Private Property and the State*, in *Marx and Engels Selected Works*, Laurence & Wishart, London (originally published in 1884 in German).

Equal Opportunities Commission (1982) *The Fact about Women is . . .*, Statistics Unit, EOC, Manchester.

ETUI (1980) *The Impact of Microelectronics on Employment in Western Europe in the 1980s*, The European Trade Union Institute, Brussels.

Fair, R. C. (1971) 'Labor Force Participation, Wage Rates, and Money Illusion', *Review of Economics and Statistics*, vol. 53, pp. 164-8.

Fearn, R. M. (1981) *Labor Economics*, Winthrop, Cambridge, Mass.

Fields, J. M. (1976) 'A Comparison of the Intercity Differences in the Labor Force Participation Rates of Married Women in 1970 with 1940, 1950, and 1960', *Journal of Human Resources*, vol. 11, no. 4, April, pp. 568-77.

First Division Association (1982) *Who Flies Highest*, Equal Opportunities Sub-Committee, First Division Association, London.

Fleisher, B. M. and Knieser, T. J. (1980) *Labor Economics: Theory, Evidence and Policy*, 2nd edn, Prentice Hall, New Jersey.

Fleisher, B. M. and Rhodes, G. (1976) 'Unemployment and the Labor Force Participation of Married Men and Women', *Review of Economics and Statistics*, vol. 58, pp. 398-406.

Folbre, N. (1982) 'Exploitation Comes Home: a Critique of the Marxian Theory of Family Labour', *Cambridge Journal of Economics*, vol. 6, pp. 317-29.

Frank, R. H. (1978) 'Why Women Earn Less, the Theory and Estimation of Differential over Qualification', *American Economic Review*, vol. 68, no. 3, pp. 360-73.

Frank, R. H. (1978) 'Family Location Constraints and the Geographic Distribution of Female Professionals', *Journal of Political Economy*, vol. 86, no. 11, pp. 117-30.

Friedman, M. (1957) *A Theory of the Consumption Function*, NBER, Princeton University Press, New Jersey.

Fuller, D. (1979) 'To Work or Not to Work – the Case of Women', *Journal of Industrial Relations*, September, pp. 316-30.

Galenson, W. and Smith, R. J. (1978) 'The United States', in Dunlop, J. T. and Galenson, W. (eds) *Labor in the Twentieth Century*, Academic Press, New York.

Gales, K. E. and Marks, P. H. (1974) 'Twentieth Century Trends in the Work of Women in England and Wales', *Journal of the Royal Statistical Society, Series A*, vol. 137, part 1, pp. 60-74.

Gardiner, J. (1976) 'Women and Unemployment', *Red Rag*, No. 10.

Gitlow, A. L. (1963) *Labor and Industrial Society*, Irwin, Homewood.

Graham, J. W. and Green, C. A. (1984) 'Estimating the Parameters of a Household Production Function with Joint Products', *Review of Economics and Statistics*, vol. 66, pp. 277-82.

Green, S. S. (1983) 'Silicon Valley's Women Workers: A Theoretical Analysis of Sex Segregation in the Electronics Industry Labor Market', in Nash, N. and Ferandez-Kelly, P. (1983) *op. cit.*

Greenhalgh, C. A. (1977) 'A Labour Supply Function for Married Women

in Great Britain', *Economica*, vol. 44, August, pp. 249-65.
Greenhalgh, C. A. (1979) 'Male Labour Force Participation in Britain', *Scottish Journal of Political Economy*, vol. 26, no. 3, pp. 275-86.
Greenhalgh, C. A. (1980) 'Participation and Hours of Work for Married Women in Great Britain', *Oxford Economic Papers*, vol. 32, no. 2, July, pp. 296-318.
Gronau, R. (1973) 'The Intrafamily Allocation of Time: the value of the Housewives' Time', *American Economic Review*, vol. 68, September, pp. 634-54.
Gronau, R. (1977) 'Leisure, Home Production, and Work – the Theory of the Allocation of Time Revisited', *Journal of Political Economy*, vol. 85, no. 6, pp. 1099-123.
Gross, E. (1968) 'Plus ça Change . . .? The Sexual Structure of Occupations Over Time', *Social Problems*, vol. 16, Fall, pp. 198-208.
Gunderson, M. (1977) 'Logit Estimates of Labour Force Participation Based on Census Cross-tabulations', *Canadian Journal of Economics*, vol. 10, no. 3, August, pp. 453-62.
Hacker, A. (1983) *A Statistical Portrait of the American People*, Penguin, New York.
Haig, B. D. and Wood, M. P. (1976) 'A Simulation Study of Married Women in the Australian Workforce', *Australian Economic Papers*, vol. 15, pp. 171-85.
Hakim, C. (1979) *Occupational Segregation*, Research Paper No. 9, Department of Employment, London.
Hamermesh, D. S. and Rees, A. (1984) *The Economics of Work and Pay*, Harper & Row, New York.
Hanoch, G. (1980) 'Hours and Weeks in the Theory of Labor Supply', in Smith, J. P. (ed.) *Female Labor Supply: Theory and Estimation*, Princeton University Press, New Jersey.
Harrison, J. (1973) 'The Political Economy of Housework', *Bulletin of the Conference of Socialist Economists*, no. 7, Winter.
Hartmann, H. (1979) 'Capitalism, Patriarchy and Job Segregation by Sex', in Einstein, Z. R. (ed.), *Capitalist Patriarchy*, Monthly Review Press, New York.
Hazledine, T. (1981) 'Employment Functions and the Demand for Labour in the Short Run', in Hornstein, Z., Grice, J. and Webb, A., *The Economics of the Labour Market*, HMSO, London.
Heckman, J. J. (1978) 'A Partial Survey of Recent Research on the Labor Supply of Women', *American Economic Review*, vol. 68, no. 2, pp. 200-7.
Heckman, J. J. and MaCurdy, T. (1980) 'A Life Cycle Model of Female Labour Supply', *Review of Economic Studies*, vol. 47, pp. 47-74.
Heckman, J. J. and MaCurdy, T. (1982) 'Corrigendum on A Life Cycle Model of Female Labour Supply', *Review of Economic Studies*, vol. 49, pp. 659-60.
Heckman, J. J. and Willis, R. J. (1977) 'A Beta-logistic Model for the Analysis of Sequential Labor Force Participation by Married Women', *Journal of Political Economy*, vol. 85, no. 1, pp. 27-58.
Heer, D. M. (1968) *Society and Population*, Prentice Hall, New Jersey.

References and Selected Bibliography

Henry, S. G. B. and Tarling, R. L. (1981) 'Forecasting Employment and Unemployment', in Hornstein, Z. *et al., op cit.*

Hill, M. A. (1983) 'Female Labor Force Participation in Developing and Developed Countries – Consideration of the Informal Sector', *Review of Economics and Statistics*, vol. 65, pp. 459-68.

Himmelweit, S. and Mohun, S. (1977) 'Domestic Labour and Capital', *Cambridge Journal of Economics*, vol. 1, no. 1, pp. 15-31.

Hoffman, E. P. (1982) 'Comparative Labor Supply of Black and White Women', *Review of Black Political Economy*, vol. 11, part 4, pp. 429-39.

Home Office (1975) *Sex Discrimination, A Guide to the Sex Discrimination Act 1975*, HMSO, London.

House of Lords, Select Committee on the European Communities (1982), *Voluntary Part-time Work*, Session 1981-82, 19th Report (216), HMSO, London.

Hughes, J. J. and Perlman, R. (1984) *The Economics of Unemployment: A Comparative Analysis of Britain and the United States*, Harvester Press, Brighton.

Humphries, J. (1983) 'The "Emancipation" of Women in the 1970s and 1980s: from the Latent to the Floating', *Capital and Class*, no. 18, pp. 6-28.

Hunt, E. K. and Sherman, H. J. (1981) *Economics: An Introduction to Traditional and Radical Views*, 4th edn, Harper & Row, London.

Hunter, L. C. and Mulvey, C. (1981) *Economics of Wages and Labour*, 2nd edn, Macmillan, London.

Huws, U. (1984) 'New Technology Homeworkers', *Department of Employment Gazette*, vol. 92, no. 2, January, pp. 13-17.

Institute of Manpower Studies (1984) *New Technology and Employment in Insurance, Banking and Building Societies: Recent Experience and Future Impact*, Gower Publishing, Aldershot.

James, E. (1962) 'Women at Work in Twentieth Century Britain', *The Manchester School*, vol. 20, pp. 283-99.

Johnson, J. L. (1983) 'Sex Differentials in Unemployment Rates: A Case for No Concern', *Journal of Political Economy*, vol. 91, no. 2, pp. 293-303.

Keller, J. F. (1983) 'The Division of Labor in Electronics', in Nash, N. and Fernandez-Kelly, P. (1983) *op. cit.*

Kerr, C. (1954) 'The Balkanization of Labor Markets', in Wight Bakke, E. (1954) *op. cit.*

Knieser, T. J. (1976) 'An Indirect Test of Complentarity in a Family Labor Supply Model', *Econometrica*, vol. 44, no. 4, July, pp. 651-69.

Knudsen, D. R. (1970) *Employment of Women*, Regional Trade Union Seminar, OECD, Paris.

Kraft, A. (1973) 'Preference Orderings as Determinants of the Labor Force Behaviour of Married Women', *Western Economic Journal*, vol. 11, September, pp. 270-84.

Kuch, P. J. and Sharir, S. (1978) 'Added- and Discouraged-Worker Effects in Canada, 1953-74', *Canadian Journal of Economics*, vol. 11, no. 1, February, pp. 112-20.

Kuhn, A. (1956) *Labor - Institutions and Economics*, Harcourt, Brace & World Inc., New York.

Kuniansky, A. (1983) 'Soviet Fertility, Labor-Force Participation, and Marital Instability', *Journal of Comparative Economics*, vol. 7, pp. 114-30.

Laidler, D. (1981) *Introduction to Microeconomics*, 2nd edn, Philip Allan, Oxford.

Lapidus, G. W. (1976) 'Occupational Segregation and Public Policy: a Comparative Analysis of American and Soviet Patterns', in Blaxall, M. and Reagan, B. (eds) *Women and the Workplace: The Implications of Occupational Segregation*, University of Chicago Press, Chicago.

Layard, R., Barton, M. and Zabalza, A. (1980) 'Married Women's Participation and Hours', *Economica*, vol. 47, January, pp. 51-72.

Le Louarn J. and DeCotiis, T. A. (1983) 'The Effect of Working Couple Status on the Decision to Offer Geographic Transfer', *Human Relations*, vol. 36, no. 11, pp. 1031-44.

Leon, C. and Bednarzik, R. W. (1978) 'A Profile of Women on Part-time Schedules', *Monthly Labor Review*, vol. 101, no. 10, October, pp. 3-12.

Leuthold, J. H. (1978) 'The Effect of Taxation on the Hours Worked by Married Women', *Industrial and Labor Relations Review*, vol. 31, no. 4, July, pp. 520-6.

Lewenhak, S. (1977) *Women and Trade Unions*, Ernest Benn, London.

Lewenhak, S. (1980) *Women and Work*, Fontana, London.

Lightman, E. S. and O'Cleireacain, C. C. (1978) 'Activity Rates of Married Women in England and Wales - 1971', *Applied Economics*, vol. 10, pp. 271-7.

Lim, L. Y. C. (1983) 'Capitalism, Imperialism and Patriarchy: the Dilemma of Third-World Women Workers in Multinational Factories', in Nash, N. and Fernandez-Kelly, P. (1983) *op. cit.*

Lipsey, R. G. (1983) *An Introduction to Positive Economics*, 6th edn, Weidenfeld & Nicolson, London.

Lloyd, C. B., Andrews, E. S. and Gilroy, C. L. (1979) *Women in the Labor Market*, Columbia University Press, New York.

Lloyd, C. B. and Niemi, B. (1978) 'Sex Differences in Labor Supply Elasticity: The Implications of Sectoral Shifts in Demand', *American Economic Review*, vol. 68, pp. 78-83.

Long, J. E. and Jones, E. B. (1981) 'Married Women in Part-time Employment', *Industrial and Labor Relations Review*, vol. 34, no. 3, pp. 413-25.

Lord, S. J. (1979) *Women's Work, the Industrial Distribution of Female Employees*, Department of Economics Discussion Paper, University of Keele.

Lubin, N. (1981) 'Women in Soviet Central Asia: Progress and Contradictions', *Soviet Studies*, vol. 33, no. 2, April, pp. 182-203.

McAuley, A. (1981) *Women's Work and Wages in the Soviet Union*, Allen & Unwin, London.

McNabb, R. (1977) 'The Labour Force Participation of Married Women', *The Manchester School*, vol. 45, pp. 221-35.

Mallier, A. T. and Rosser, M. J. (1979) 'The Changing Role of Women in the British Economy', *National Westminster Bank Quarterly Review*, November, pp. 54-65.
Mallier, A. T. and Rosser, M. J. (1980a) 'Female Employment and Unemployment in a Local Labour Market', *Journal of Industrial Affairs*, vol. 8, no. 1, 1980, pp. 13-22.
Mallier, A. T. and Rosser, M. J. (1980b) 'Part-time Workers and the Economy', *International Journal of Manpower*, vol. 1, no. 2, pp. 2-7.
Mallier, A. T. and Rosser, M. J. (1980c) 'Part-time Workers and the Firm', *International Journal of Manpower*, vol. 1, no. 3, pp. 25-8.
Mallier, A. T. and Rosser, M. J. (1981) 'Part-timers also Need Training', *The Training Officer*, vol. 17, no. 6, June, pp. 158-60.
Mallier, A. T. and Rosser, M. J. (1982) 'Training for Tomorrow: Implication of Part-time Employment', *Journal of European Industrial Training*, vol. 6, no. 2 (monograph issue).
Mallier, A. T. and Rosser, M. J. (1983) 'Part-time Working: Employment Conditions, Legislation and the Trade Union Response', *Employee Relations*, vol. 5, no. 2, pp. 6-11.
Martin, J. and Roberts, C. (1984) *Women and Employment: A Lifetime Perspective*, Department of Employment/Office of Population Censuses and Surveys, HMSO, London.
Marx, K. (1969) 'Critique of the Gotha Programme', in *Marx and Engels: Basic Writings on Politics and Philosophy* (ed. L. S. Feur), Fontana, London (written in 1875, but not originally published until 1891, in German).
Marx, K. (1970) *Capital*, vol. 1, International Publishers, London (originally published in German in 1867; first English translation in 1886).
Matthaei, J. A. (1982) *An Economic History of Women in America: Women's Work, the Sexual Division of Labor, and the Development of Capitalism*, Harvester Press, Brighton/Schocken Books, New York.
Metcalf, R. and Richardson, R. (1982) 'Labour', Ch. 5 in Prest, A. R. and Coppock, D. J. (eds) *The UK Economy: A Manual of Applied Economics*, Wiedenfeld & Nicolson, London.
Meyer, P. J. and Maes, P. L. (1983) 'The Reproduction of Occupational Segregation Among Young Women', *Industrial Relations*, vol. 22, no. 1, pp. 115-24.
Milkman, L. (1976) 'Women's Work and the Economic Crisis', *Review of Radical Political Economy*, vol. 8, no. 1.
Miller, P. W. and Volker, P. A. (1983) 'A Cross-Section Analysis of the Labour Force Participation of Married Women In Austrialia', *Economic Record*, vol. 59, part 164, pp. 28-42.
Mincer, J. (1962a) 'Labor Force Participation of Married Women' in Gregg Lewis, H. (ed.), *Aspects of Labor Economics*, A Report of the National Bureau of Economic Research, University of Princeton Press, Princeton.
Mincer, J. (1962b) 'On the Job Training: Costs, Returns and Some Implications', *Journal of Political Economy*, vol. 70, supplement, pp. 50-79.
Mincer, J. and Polachek, S. (1974) 'Family Investments in Human Capital: Earnings of Women', *Journal of Political Economy*, vol. 82, pp. S. 76-S. 108.

Moffitt, R. (1984) 'Profiles of Fertility, Labour Supply and Wages of Married Women: A Complete Life-Cycle Model', *Review of Economic Studies*, vol. 51, no. 2, pp. 263-78.

Molho, I. I. (1983) 'A Regional Analysis of the Distribution of Married Women's Labour Force Participation Rates in the UK', *Regional Studies*, vol. 17, no. 2, pp. 125-34.

Molho, I. I. and Elias, P. (1984) 'A Study of the Regional Trends in the Labour Force Participation of Married Women in the UK, 1968-1977', *Applied Economics*, vol. 16, pp. 163-73.

Monck, E. and Lomas, C. B. G. (1975) *The Employment and Socio-economic Conditions of the Coloured Population*, Centre for Environmental Studies, CEC RP 21, London.

Morgan, C. A. (1966) *Labor Economics*, Dorsey Press, Homewood.

Moskoff, W. (1982) 'Part-time Employment in the Soviet Union', *Soviet Studies*, vol. 34, no. 2, April, pp. 270-85.

Nakamura, A. and Nakamura, M. (1983) 'Part-time and Full-time Work Behaviour of Married Women: A Model with a Doubly Truncated Dependent Variable', *Canadian Journal of Economics*, vol. 16, no. 2, pp. 229-57.

Nakamura, M., Nakamura, A. and Cullen, D. (1979) 'Job Opportunities, the Offered Wage, and the Labor Supply of Married Women', *American Economic Review*, vol. 69, no. 5, pp. 787-805.

Nash, N. and Fernandez-Kelly, P. (eds) (1983) *Women, Men, and the International Division of Labour*, State University of New York Press, Albany.

Oaxaca, R. (1973) 'Male-Female Wage Differentials in Urban Labor Markets', *International Economic Review*, vol. 14, October, pp. 693-709.

OECD (1979) *Equal Opportunities for Women*, OECD, Paris.

Ofer, G. and Vinokur, A. (1983) 'The Labor-Force Participation of Married Women in the Soviet Union: A Household Cross-Section Analysis', *Journal of Comparative Economics*, vol. 7, pp. 158-76.

Office of Manpower Economics (1972) *Equal Pay, First Report on the Implementation of the Equal Pay Act 1970*, HMSO, London.

Oppenheimer, V. K. (1976) *The Female Labor Force in the United States: Demographic and Economic Factors Governing its Growth and Change*, Greenwood Press, Westport.

Owen, J. D. (1978) 'Why Part-time Workers Tend to be in Low-wage Jobs', *Monthly Labor Review*, June, pp. 11-14.

Paterson, P. and Armstrong, M. (1972) *An Employer's Guide to Equal Pay*, Kogan Page, London.

Paukert, L. (1984) *The Employment and Unemployment of Women in OECD Countries*, OECD, Paris.

Phelps-Brown, E. H. (1951) *A Course in Applied Economics*, Pitman & Sons, London.

Pollard, S. (1979) *Development of the British Economy 1914-1967*, Edward Arnold, London.

Pujol, M. (1984) 'Gender and Class in Marshall's Principles of Economics', *Cambridge Journal of Economics*, vol. 8, no. 3, pp. 217-34.

Riche, R. W., Hecker, D. E. and Burgan, J. U. (1983) 'High Technology Today and Tomorrow: A Small Slice of the Employment Pie', *Monthly Labor Review*, vol. 106, no. 11, November, pp. 50-8.
Riffault, H. (1980) *European Women in Paid Employment: their Perception of Discrimination at Work*, supplement no. 5 to *Women of Europe*, EEC, Brussels.
Robertson, R. M. and Walton, G. M. (1979) *History of the American Economy*, Harcourt, Brace, Janovich, New York.
Robinson, C. and Tomes, N. (1982) 'Family Labour Supply and Fertility: a Two-Regime Model', *Canadian Journal of Economics*, vol. 15, no. 4, pp. 706-34.
Robinson, O. (1979) 'Part-time Employment in the European Community', *International Labour Review*, vol. 118, no. 3, May-June, pp. 299-314.
Robinson, O. and Wallace, J. (1977) 'National Wage Rates and Earnings Composition. A Note on Potential Sources of Sex Discrimination in Pay', *British Journal of Industrial Relations*, vol. 15, no. 1, March, pp. 101-7.
Robinson, O. and Wallace, J. (1981) 'Relative Pay and Part-time Employment in Britain', *Oxford Bulletin of Economics and Statistics*, vol. 43, pp. 149-71.
Robinson, O. and Wallace, J. (1984) 'Growth and Utilisation of Part-time Labour in Britain', *Department of Employment Gazette*, vol. 92, September, pp. 391-7.
Routh, G. (1980) *Occupation and Pay in Great Britain 1906-1979*, Macmillan, London.
Rubery, J. and Tarling, R. (1982) 'Women in the Recession', pp. 46-108 in *Socialist Economic Review*, Merlin Press, London.
Rytina, N. F. and Bianchi, S. M. (1984) 'Occupational Reclassification and Changes in Distribution by Gender', *Monthly Labor Review*, March, pp. 11-17.
Sample, C. J. (1974) *Patterns of Regional Economic Change*, Ballinger, Cambridge, Mass.
Sandell, S. H. (1980) 'Is the Unemployment Rate of Women Too Low? A Direct Test of the Economic Theory of Job Search', *Review of Economics and Statistics*, vol. 62, pp. 634-8.
Schultz, T. P. (1978) 'Influence of Fertility on Labor Supply of Married Women', in Ehrenberg, R. G. (ed.) *Research in Labor Economics*, vol. 2, Jai Press, Greenwich.
Shapiro, D. and Shaw, L. B. (1983) 'Growth in the Labor Force Attachment of Married Women: Accounting for Changes in the 1970s', *Southern Economic Journal*, vol. 50, no. 2, October, pp. 461-73.
Simpson, W. (1982) 'Job Search and the Effect of Urban Structure on Unemployment and Married Female Participation Rates', *Applied Economics*, vol. 14, pp. 153-65.
Smith, A. (1970) *The Wealth of Nations*, Dent, London (originally published 1776).
Smith, J. P. (1977) 'Family Labor Supply over the Life Cycle', *Explorations in Economic Research*, vol. 4, no. 2, pp. 205-76.

Smith, P. (ed.) (1980) *Female Labor Supply: Theory and Estimation*, Princeton University Press, New Jersey.
Smith, R. E. (1977) 'A Simulation Model of the Demographic Composition of Employment, Unemployment and Labor Force Participation', in Ehrenberg, R. G. (ed.) *Research in Labor Economics*, vol. 1, Jai Press, Greenwich.
Snell, M. W., Glucklich, P. and Povall, M. (1981) *Equal Pay and Opportunities*, Research Paper no. 20, Department of Employment, London.
Snow, R. T. (1983) 'The New International Division of Labor and the US Workforce: the Case of the Electronics Industry', in Nash, N. and Fernandez-Kelly, P. (1983) *op. cit.*
Spencer, B. (1973) 'Determinants of the Labour Force Participation of Married Women: a Micro Study of Toronto Households', *Canadian Journal of Economics*, vol. 6, pp. 222-38.
Standing, G. (1976) 'Education and Female Participation in the Labour Force', *International Labour Review*, vol. 114, no. 3, November-December, pp. 281-97.
Stewart, C. M. (1961) 'Future Trends in the Employment of Married Women', *British Journal of Sociology*, vol. 12, pp. 1-11.
Stewart, M. B. and Greenhalgh, C. (1984) 'Work History Patterns and the Occupational Attainment of Women', *Economic Journal*, vol. 94, September, pp. 493-519.
Stolzenberg, R. M. and Waite, L. J. (1984) 'Local Labor Markets, Children and Labor Force Participation of Wives', *Demography*, vol. 21, no. 2, pp. 157-69.
Sweezy, A. (1971) 'The Economic Explanation of Fertility Changes in the United States', *Population Studies*, vol. 25, pp. 255-67.
Szalai, A. (1972) *The Use of Time*, Mouton, The Hague.
Tavernier, G. (1979) 'New Deal for Part-time Workers', *International Management*, vol. 34, no. 10, October, pp. 40-5.
Thatcher, A. R. (1979) 'Labour Supply and Employment Trends', in Blackaby, F. (ed.) *Deindustrialization*, Heinemann, London.
Theeuwes, J. (1981) 'Family Labour Force Participation: Multinomial Logit Estimates', *Applied Economics*, vol. 13, pp. 481-98.
Theil, H. (1971) *Principles of Econometrics*, John Wiley & Sons, New York.
Tobin, J. (1958) 'Estimation of Relationships for Limited Dependent Variables', *Econometrica*, vol. 26, pp. 24-36.
Urquhart, M. (1984) 'The Employment Shift to Services: Where Did It Come From?', *Monthly Labor Review*, April, pp. 15-22.
Vickery, C. and Bergmann, B. R. (1978) 'Unemployment Rate Targets and Anti-inflation Policy as More Women Enter the Workforce', *American Economic Review*, vol. 68, no. 2, pp. 90-4.
Vogel, L. (1983) *Marxism and the Oppression of Women: Towards a Unitary Theory*, Rutgers University Press, New Jersey, and Pluto Press, London.
Wabe, J. S. (1969) 'Labour Force Participation Rates in the London Metropolitan Region', *Journal of the Royal Statistical Society*, vol. 132, part 2, pp. 245-64.

Wachter, M. L. (1972) 'A Labor Supply Model for Secondary Workers', *Review of Economics and Statistics*, vol. 54, no. 2, pp. 141-50.
Wachter, M. L. (1974) 'A New Approach to the Equilibrium Labour Force', *Economica*, vol. 41, pp. 35-51.
Walby, S. (1983) 'Women's Unemployment, Patriarchy and Capitalism', *Socialist Economic Review*, Merlin Press, London.
Waldman, E. and McEaddy, B. J. (1974) 'Where Women Work', *Monthly Labor Review*, May, pp. 3-12.
Werneke, D. (1978) 'The Economic Slowdown and Women's Employment Opportunities', *International Labour Review*, vol. 117, no. 1, January-February, pp. 37-51.
Werther, W. B. Jr (1975) 'Part-timers: Overlooked and Undervalued', *Business Horizons*, February, pp. 13-20.
Wight Bakke, E. (ed.) (1954) *Labor Mobility and Economic Opportunity*, John Wiley & Sons, New York.
Williams, C. G. (1970) *Labor Economics*, Wiley, New York.
Williams, G. (1976) 'Trends in Occupational Differentiation by Sex', *Sociology of Work and Organizations*, vol. 3, no. 1, pp. 38-62.
Williams, G. (1979) 'The Changing US Labor Force and Occupational Differentiation by Sex', *Demography*, vol. 16, no. 1, pp. 73-87.
Williams, R. M. (1978) *British Population*, Heinemann, London.
Williams, V. (1984) 'Employment Implications of New Technology', *Department of Employment Gazette*, vol. 92, no. 5, pp. 210-5.
Winegarden, C. R. (1984) 'Women's Fertility, Market Work and Marital Status: a Test of the New Household Economics with International Data', *Economica*, vol. 51, pp. 447-56.
Woytinsky, E. S. (1967) *Profile of the US Economy*, Praeger, New York.
Wright, J. F. (1979) *Britain in the Age of Economic Management*, Oxford University Press, Oxford.
Yanz, L. and Smith, E. (1983) 'Women As a Reserve Army of Labor: a Critique', *Review of Radical Political Economy*, vol. 15, part 1, pp. 92-106.
Zabalza, A. (1983) 'The CES Utility Function, Non-Linear Budget Constraints and Labour Supply. Results on Female Participation and Hours', *Economic Journal*, vol. 93, June, pp. 312-30.

Author Index

Andrews, E. S. 65
Andrews, H. F. 77
Anthias, F. 195
Armstrong, M. 118
Arnold, E. 158, 161

Ballard, B. 140
Barton, M. 69, 82
Beacham, R. 52
Becker, G. S. 66, 126, 128
Bednarzik, R. W. 134, 140
Beechey, V. 191, 195
Ben-Porath, Y. 67
Benston, M. 193
Berliner, J. S. 189
Bianchi, S. M. 58, 91
Bird, E. 163
Biryukova, A. P. 182
Bisset, L. 165
Blandy, A. 158
Blau, D. M. 73
Bosworth, D. L. 112, 143
Bowen, W. G. 70, 82
British Community Relations Commission 77
Brown, I. 9
Brown, S. C. 137, 138, 142
Bruegel, I. 198
Buckley, M. 184, 185, 187
Burgan, J. U. 162
Butz, W. P. 10

Cain, G. 70, 81
Cairnes, J. E. 93
Carliner, G. 70
Chiplin, B. 120, 122, 125

Claydon, S. 129
Clutterbuck, D. 143
Cogan, J. 70
Connolly, P. 198
Corcoran, M. E. 68
Corry, B. A. 79, 82
Cragg, A. 150
Cramer, J. C. 74
Cullen, D. 70, 72

Dalla Costa, M. 193
Dawkins, P. 143
Dawson, T. 150
DeCotiis, T. A. 79
Department of Employment 131, 135, 149
Deutermann, W. V. 137, 138, 142
Disney, R. 142
Dodge, N. T. 183, 184
Doeringer, P. B. 93, 112, 127

EEC Commission 144
Eason, W. W. 184
Elias, P. 76, 79, 81, 82, 140
Elliott, R. F. 109
Engels, F. 191
Equal Opportunities Commission 121, 129
ETUI 157

Fair, R. C. 83
Fearn, R. M. 111, 123
Fernandez-Kelly, P. 197
Fields, J. M. 82, 83
Finnegan, T. A. 70, 82
First Division Association 120

Author Index

Fleisher, B. M. 80, 82
Folbre, N. 193
Frank, R. H. 79, 124
Friedman, M. 67
Fuller, D. 70

Gales, K. E. 11
Galenson, W. 11
Gardiner, J. 197
Gilroy, C. L. 65
Gitlow, A. L. 92
Glucklich, P. 132
Graham, J. W. 67
Green, C. A. 67
Green, S. S. 197
Greenhalgh, C. A. 67, 68, 69, 70, 72, 74, 79, 85
Gronau, R. 67
Gross, E. 50, 56, 120
Gunderson, M. 70

Hacker, A. 118
Haig, B. D. 80
Hakim, C. 55, 89
Hamermesh, D. S. 29
Hanoch, G. 68
Harrison, J. 193
Hartmann, H. 196
Hazledine, T. 89
Hecker, D. E. 162
Heckman, J. J. 65, 67, 69, 80
Heer, D. M. 15
Henry, S. G. B. 89
Hill, M. A. 70
Himmelweit, S. 193
Hoffman, E. P. 77
Home Office 132
House of Lords, Select Committee on the European Communities 144
Hughes, J. J. 150, 153
Humphries, J. 198
Hunt, E. K. 190
Hunter, L. C. 31
Huws, U. 165

Institute of Manpower Studies 194

James, E. 10
Johnson, J. L. 183
Jones, E. B. 141

Keller, J. F. 161
Kerr, C. 92
Knieser, T. J. 67, 81
Knusden, D. R. 112
Kraft, A. 75
Kuch, P. J. 80
Kuhn, A. 112
Kuniansky, A. 189

Laidler, D. 66
Lapidus, G. W. 185, 187
Layard, R. 69, 70, 82
Le Louarn, J. 79
Leon, C. 134, 140
Leuthold, J. H. 85
Lewenhak, S. 113, 196
Lightman, E. S. 70
Lim, L. Y. C. 197
Lipsey, R. G. 90
Lloyd, C. B. 65, 85, 154
Lomas, C. B. G. 77
Long, J. E. 141
Lord, S. J. 122
Lubin, N. 184

McAuley, A. 183, 185, 186, 187
MaCurdy, T. 67, 69, 80
McEaddy, B. J. 54, 109, 115
McNabb, R. 70, 72
Maes, P. L. 58
Main, B. 76, 140
Mallier, A. T. 64, 130, 134, 141, 142, 143
Marks, P. H. 11
Martin, J. 86, 156
Marx, K. 191, 195
Matthaei, J. A. 192
Metcalf, R. 109, 113
Meyer, P. J. 58
Milkman, L. 196
Miller, P. W. 70
Mincer, J. 67, 70, 128
Moffitt, R. 67, 73
Mohun, S. 193
Molho, I. I. 79, 81, 82

Author Index

Monck, E. 77
Morgan, C. A. 108
Moskoff, W. 188
Mulvey, C. 31

Nakamura, A. 70, 71, 72
Nakamura, M. 70, 71, 72
Nash, N. 197
Niemi, B. 85, 154

Oaxaca, R. 125
O'Cleireacain, C. C. 70
OECD 118, 125, 180
Ofer, G. 189
Office of Manpower Economics 115
Oppenheimer, V. K. 55, 85, 89, 94, 112
Owen, J. D. 140

Paterson, P. 118
Paukert, L. 148
Perlman, R. 150, 153
Phelps-Brown, E. H. 124
Polachek, S. 68
Poire, M. J. 93, 112, 127
Pollard, S. 108
Povall, M. 132
Pujol, M. 190

Rees, A. 29
Richardson, R. 109, 113
Riche, R. W. 162
Riffault, H. 188
Rhodes, G. 80
Roberts, C. 86, 156
Roberts, J. A. 79, 82
Robertson, R. M. 91
Robinson, C. 70, 75
Robinson, O. 115, 140, 142, 144
Rosser, M. J. 64, 130, 134, 141, 142, 143
Routh, G. 46, 51
Rubery, J. 198
Rytina, N. F. 58, 91

Sample, C. J. 108
Sandell, S. H. 155
Schultz, T. P. 15, 70

Shapiro, D. 82, 87
Sharir, S. 80
Shaw, L. B. 82, 87
Sherman, H. J. 190
Simpson, W. 77
Sloane, P. J. 120, 122, 125
Smith, A. 9
Smith, E. 198
Smith, J. P. 67, 76
Smith, P. 65
Smith, R. E. 103
Smith, R. J. 11
Snell, M. W. 132
Snow, R. T. 162
Spencer, B. 69, 70, 76
Standing, G. 76
Stewart, C. M. 19
Stewart, M. B. 68
Stolzenberg, R. M. 74
Sweezy, A. 10
Szalai, A. 188
Szyszczak, E. M. 142

Tarling, R. 89, 198
Tavernier, G. 143
Thatcher, A. R. 101
Theeuwes, J. 67
Theil, H. 68
Tobin, J. 69
Tomes, N. 70, 75

Urquhart, M. 35, 110

Vickery, C. 154
Vinokur, A. 189
Vogel, L. 192, 194
Volker, P. A. 70

Wabe, J. S. 65, 70, 83
Wachter, M. L. 79
Wallace, J. 115, 140, 142
Waite, L. J. 74
Walby, S. 197
Waldman, E. 54, 109, 115
Walton, G. M. 91
Ward, M. P. 10
Werneke, D. 151
Werther, W. B., Jr 143
Williams, G. 58

Williams, R. M. 19
Williams, V. 159
Wilson, R. A. 112
Winegarden, C. R. 71, 168
Wood, M. P. 80
Woytinsky, E. S. 102, 109

Wright, J. F. 92, 107

Yanz, L. 198

Zabalza, A. 69, 70, 72, 82, 85

Subject Index

added worker hypothesis 75, 79–80, 88
administration and management 49–52, 58, 119, 180, 187
age
    and economic activity 22–7, 76, 171–9
    female population 13–16
    of first marriage 3, 18–19
    part-timer workers 137–40
    unemployed 155–6
agriculture 30, 32–3, 35, 40, 51, 168–170, 109, 184, 187, 194
anti-social hours 142
apparel and kindred trades *see* clothing and footwear
apprenticeships 129–30
assembling and packaging 159–61, 187
attitudes, changes in 5, 65, 82, 87–8
Australia 70, 80, 178
automation 121, 157, 159

backward-bending labour supply curve 66, 72–3
baking 86, 187
banking 33, 40, 164, 185
Belgium 168, 178–9
bi-modal distribution 24, 178–9
birth rate 83, 151
black women 77
building societies 77

Canada 70–2, 75, 80, 145, 168, 198

capitalism 166, 180, 182, 189–99
catering 51, 86, 115, 140, 164
cause and effect, problems of establishing 4, 9–10, 74–5, 78, 80
Census of Population, Great Britain 10–11, 22, 46, 59, 70, 134, 138
Census of Population, US 10–11, 46, 140
Census of Employment 111, 135
child-care facilities 16, 74, 182, 191
children 4, 15–16, 73–5, 83, 139, 178, 192–4
civilian labour force 84–106
Civil Rights Act 58, 132
Civil Service 120
cleaners 51, 111, 140, 163
clerical work 7, 49–50, 52–4, 56, 110, 115, 120, 124, 157, 163–5, 180, 185
clothing and footwear industry 38, 43, 45, 50–1, 86, 122, 162
communism 180, 182, 190–1
computers *see* new technology
consumer demand 31, 89–90
craft and kindred trades *see* skilled manual work
cross-section studies
    female activity rate 4, 64, 70–1, 80, 82
    part-time working 141
Current Population Survey 58, 135, 150
cyclical fluctuations

Subject Index

economic activity 79-80, 84, 151
  reserve army 196-8
  unemployment 145, 150, 153

data sources 10-2, 70-1, 81, 133-4
demand for female labour 5, 31-2, 89-113
  effect on economic activity 78, 84-5
demographic factors 9-10, 15-6, 29
Denmark 178-9
deskilling 50
discouraged worker hypothesis 75, 79-80, 84, 150
discrimination 5-6, 140, 180
  and promotion 119-20, 123, 130, 132
  economic explanations 120-5
  pre-entry 114
  post-entry 114
  theories of 125-30
distribution *see* retailing and wholesale trade
divorced women 60-1, 140
doctors *see* physicians
domestic labour, value of 182, 193, 197
domestic responsibilities 40, 66-7, 87, 111, 144, 157, 182, 188, 190
domestic service 3, 41-3, 45, 51-3, 86, 135
dual career families 79
dual labour market 127-8
dual systems theory 199
dummy variables, use of 69

earnings *see* pay *and* wages
economic activity rate 3, 11, 21-9, 60-3, 122-3
  factors affecting 64-89
  international comparisons 166-8, 170-9, 183
  and part-time working 141
  potential 10
economic change 9-10
economic development 31, 43, 52, 168

education 97, 100, 102, 113, 138, 140, 165, 182
  effect on economic activity 22, 29, 72, 75-6, 84
  new technology 165
  international comparisons 170, 182
elasticity, of female labour supply with respect to wages 71-2, 82, 85
electronics industry 33, 161-3
emancipation 191, 195
employers 19, 89-92, 123-7
employment protection legislation 91, 121, 142, 182
employment trends 19-21, 30-58, 142
encouraged worker hypothesis *see* added worker hypothesis
engineering 38, 128, 185-8
  electronic 7, 161
equality 2, 5-6, 114-32, 144-5, 153, 185, 187-8, 195
equal opportunity 55, 114-32, 182, 188
Equal Pay Act 55, 131-2, 142, 153, 195-6
ethnic origin 77-8
European Economic Community (EEC) 144
exploitation 182, 191-2

Fair Labor Standards Act 58, 131
family
  labour supply 67
  Marxian theory of 182, 191-4
  size 10, 73-5, 194
farming 4, 187
  and economic activity 15, 78
  see also agriculture
fertility 3, 10, 15, 75 (*see also* birth rate)
financial sector 11, 164
Finland 168
First World War 5, 13, 20, 30, 40, 50, 184
food preparation and manufacturing 40, 122, 164
foremen and supervisors 49, 119

Subject Index

France 130, 179
free market 90, 158, 166
full-time employment 121-2, 133-4, 139, 141, 151

General Household Survey 70
geographical mobility 79, 86
Germany (West) 130, 168, 170, 178-9
Greece 168-9

hairdressing 163
heavy industry 168, 185
hidden unemployment 6, 149-50, 156
higher education 80, 128-9, 138
home working 165
hotels 51, 111
hours of work 87, 111, 113, 121-2, 125, 134, 141-2, 144, 157-8
  factors affecting 4, 66-7, 71, 82
housework see domestic responsibilities
human capital 128-30
husband's income, effect on MFAR 4, 66-7, 73, 76, 81, 85, 194

ill-health 79, 139
immigration 13, 97, 102, 107, 194
income tax 85, 143
industrial segregation 185-7
industrial structure of female employment 31-3, 43-5, 106-112
inflation 29, 80
insurance 33, 40, 164, 185
international comparisons
  female labour force 166-89
  factors affecting economic activity 70-1
investment
  in education see human capital
  new technology 158, 163
involuntary short-time working 134-5
Ireland 11, 168, 179
Italy 168-9, 179

Japan 70-1, 168-9, 178

labourers see unskilled manual work
labour force 3, 19-21, 29, 60-1, 64, 154-5
  attachment 122-3
  definitions 11
labour market 15, 27, 58, 72, 91-3
labour-saving devices 86
labour supply 59-88, 94-7, 100-3, 106
labour value 193, 195-6
legal profession 55-6
leisure-income preference 66-7
leisure facilities 16
life-cycle theory of labour supply 67-9, 73-4, 76
local labour markets 64, 69, 92-3
long-term trends 3, 19-21, 64, 73, 80-8

males
  labour force changes 96-7, 100-3
  economic activity 11, 19, 67, 122-3
  part-time employment 138, 140-1, 144
  unemployment 148-50
managers see administration
manual work 49-52, 140, 157, 159-63, 170-1, 178, 186-7
manufacturing industry 4, 30, 79, 142, 149, 151, 153, 159-63, 168-70
marital status 16-19 (see also married women)
married women 10-11, 16-19, 111, 133
  economic activity 22-9, 40, 60-1
  factors affecting economic activity rate 22-8, 64-89
Marxian analysis 8, 190-99
maternity leave 83, 182, 197
mathematics 123
mechanisation 194
medical care 16, 113, 140

Subject Index

methodology of economic theory 2, 64-5
microelectronics industry 157, 162
microprocessors 133, 157
migration 13, 79
military service 97
mining 30, 33
miscellaneous services 40-3, 45, 140
multinationals 197-8

National Insurance contributions 85, 87, 143, 148-50
National Longitudinal Survey 70
National Training Survey 129, 140
neoclassical economic theory 66, 71, 189-90
new technology 7, 30-2, 43, 133, 157-65
non-manual work 121, 163, 186-7
non-married women
  economic activity 60-1
  part-time employment 140
  (*see also* single women)
non-monetary benefits from employment 114, 143
New Zealand 178
Northern Ireland 11
Norway 168
nursing 40, 46, 53-4, 180

occupational choice 123-4
occupational distribution of females 30, 32, 45-52, 55-8
occupational segregation 4, 55-8, 91-3, 110-11, 112-3
  and unemployment 154
  international comparisons 180, 185-6
  Marxian analysis of 196-7
occupational structure 30-3, 52-5, 118
office staff 186 (*see also* clerical work)
operatives *see* semi-skilled manual work
overtime working 85, 121-2, 142

participation rate 22 (*see also* economic activity rate)
part-time employment 6, 111, 116, 133-45, 149, 151, 153
  characteristics of part-time workers 138-41
  definitions 134-6
  explaining growth of 141-3
  industrial distribution 134, 140, 142-3
  international comparisons 179, 188
  trends in GB 135, 151
  trends in USA 137-8
  voluntary and involuntary 135
patriarchy 8, 191, 197, 199
pay 116-8, 121-2, 125, 128, 131-2, 140, 180, 185 (*see also* wages)
peasants 169, 183-4
pensions 139, 143, 148-9, 183
permanent income hypothesis 67, 79
personal services 115, 140
physicians 187
population
  changes in female by marital status 16-19, 60-1
  growth 3, 12-13, 153, 194
Portugal 168
potential labour force 13, 156
primary markets 76, 93, 113, 127-8
printing industry 162-3
probit analysis 69
productive sector 30, 33-40, 43, 45, 107-113
professional and scientific services 40, 140, 180
professional classes 46, 52-4, 58, 187
profits 90, 128, 143, 192
promotion 119-20, 123, 130, 132, 140-1, 144, 188
public utilities 33

qualifications 72, 76 (*see also* education, skills)
questionnaire surveys 65, 68, 145, 146

recession 151, 153, 198
redundancies 142, 197-8
re-entry to labour force 4, 130, 155
regional variations in economic activity 78-9, 82
regression analysis 69, 81
reliability 143
repetitive work 7, 159-60, 187
reproduction, and capitalism 194-5, 199
reservation wage 70, 72, 155
reserve army of labour 190, 195-9
restaurants 51, 86, 111, 164
retailing and wholesale trade 40, 52, 87, 111, 115, 140
retirement age 139, 183
rural areas, and economic activity 77, 184

sales workers *see* retailing and wholesale trade
Scandinavia 144, 178-9
schooling 22, 123, 128-30 (*see also* education)
school-leaving age 22, 61, 68, 170
science 123, 162, 188
search costs 155
secondary markets 76, 93, 112, 127-8, 155
secondary workers 190, 196
Second World War 5, 13, 15, 32, 40, 50, 112, 132
self-employed 135
semi-skilled manual work 50-1, 53-4
service sector 3-4, 30, 33-5, 40-5, 52, 107-14, 151, 153
  international comparisons 168-70
  part-time employment 141-2
Sex Discrimination Act 132, 153
shipbuilding 33
single career families 79
single-period decision model of labour supply 66-8
single women
  economic activity 28-9, 60-1, 123, 170-1
  Marxian analysis 195

unemployment 148-9
  see also non-married women
skilled manual work 50-1, 160
skills 7, 76, 140, 151, 159-60, 165, 187
social insurance 182 (*see also* National Insurance)
social services 16
socio-economic status 78
Spain 168
spinsters 18-19 (*see also* single women)
state planning *see* communism
statistical testing: econometric methods 2, 65, 68-9, 80-3
students 84, 138-9 (*see also* higher education)
subsistence wage 192-4
supplementary benefit 149
supply of female labour 4-5, 59-89, 94-106
  definition 59
  and demand 80, 85
  and unemployment 150-1
surplus value 193
Sweden 131, 178-9

teaching 40, 46, 53-4, 119-20, 129, 180, 187
technological change 4, 15-16, 30-1, 50, 86, 91, 121, 133 (*see also* new technology)
telephone operators 164, 185
temporary workers 198
testing theories *see* statistical testing
textile industry 33, 38, 43, 45, 50-1, 162, 168, 186-7
theory, of labour supply 59, 65-8
time trends 64, 82-3
trade unions 121-3, 131, 158, 163
training 87, 125, 128-30, 132, 140-1, 151, 153, 188
transport and communications industries 33
travel to work time 77, 86
typing/typists 52, 91-2, 151, 164, 185

unemployment 6, 59, 94–106, 145–56
 benefit 6, 148–9
 definition 149, 155–7
 effect on economic activity 4–5, 75, 80, 84
 hidden/unregistered 5, 149–50, 150, 156
 influences on 150–3
 length of 155
 measurement 145, 148–50
 reserve army of 196
unpaid family workers 169
unskilled manual work 51, 54, 140, 187
urban areas 184
USSR 7, 180–9

vacancies 59, 148
value of labour 193, 195
vehicle industry 33
voluntary part-time working 135, 137–8

wages 110
 female, effect on economic activity 66–7, 71–3, 81–2, 84–6, 194–5
 male, effect on female economic activity 73, 81–2, 194–5
 and unemployment 150, 153
widows 60–1, 140
word processors 91, 163
work history patterns 68

youths/young workers
 part-time employment 138–9, 149, 151
 unemployment 6, 133, 155–6